iOS Game Programming Cookbook

Over 45 interesting game recipes that will help you create your next enthralling game

Bhanu Birani

Chhavi Vaishnav

BIRMINGHAM - MUMBAI

iOS Game Programming Cookbook

First published: March 2015

Production reference: 1200315

Published by Packt Publishing Ltd.
Livery Place
35 Livery Street
Birmingham B3 2PB, UK.

ISBN 978-1-78439-825-5

www.packtpub.com

Credits

About the Authors

Bhanu Birani has 5 years of experience in the software industry and a lifetime association with the technical industry. After years of programming experience in different programming languages, he started developing applications for iOS devices. He started software development along with his graduation and was really interested in learning the new technologies in the market. He then joined a software company and started developing games for them, focusing on artificial intelligence development in games.

He has also authored *Application Development with Parse using iOS SDK* and *Getting Started with Flurry Analytics*, both published by Packt Publishing.

I would like to dedicate this book to my family, which gave me the courage and confidence to write this book and supported me throughout the entire process. I would also like to give special thanks to my mom and dad for their relentless efforts to assist me in every way imaginable as well as for helping me keep my life together. Finally, I would like to thank all my friends for sharing my happiness when I started this project, which was followed with encouragement when it seemed too difficult to be completed.

Chhavi Vaishnav has more than 4 years of experience in the software industry. After her master's, she started working with IBM as a test engineer and then with extraordinary talent, she was promoted to the role of release manager in the organization. Despite being in the management profile, she has a relentless inclination towards iOS and mobility. She has contributed and worked on several projects directly and indirectly by strategizing and managing the technology in depth. She is a complete package for the organization with a *get it done* mindset.

I would like to dedicate this book to my mother (Mrs. RP Massey), who has given her relentless support to me in every phase of life.

About the Reviewers

Rahul Borawar is a computer science graduate from Jodhpur Institute of Engineering and Technology in Rajasthan, India. He is a passionate software craftsman and loves designing software for mobile. From the start, he has been a mobile application developer creating applications for iOS and Android platforms. He has been working since 2011 on mobile development and has published many apps on the App Store, such as *Catch the Aliens* (a 2D level-based game) and *Draw Your Stories* (a kid's app to create fables with drawing stuffs). He is currently working as a software development engineer in the mobile team for a real estate product-based company (CommonFloor).

You can follow him on Twitter (`https://twitter.com/RahulBorawar`) and on GitHub (`https://github.com/Rahul2389`). You can also check out his website `http://rahulborawar.branded.me`.

> First of all, I would like to thank Packt Publishing for giving me the opportunity to review this technology-rich cookbook and enlighten my game development skills. Secondly, thanks to my family for supporting me in my career as a technical guy. Last but most important Praveen Kansara and Robin Kansara, who have guided me for a very long period, helping me enrich my skills. A huge thanks to both of them.

Andrew Kenady is a game developer from Bowling Green, KY, with a strong passion for both playing and creating compelling video games. Starting in his youth, Andrew graduated from the Gatton Academy of Mathematics and Science at WKU at the age of 17 in May 2011, and continued his educational path at Western Kentucky University. He received his bachelor's degree in computer science at the age of 19 and continued to work as the lead game developer for the Kentucky-based software company `Hitcents.com` after spending time working as a computer science tutor for local colleges. Now, Andrew works with a team of developers to design and produce exciting and engaging new titles for mobile, PC, and console platforms while satisfying his creative itch by developing his own indie prototypes and games at home. Titles to which Andrew is credited include *Draw a Stickman: EPIC* and *Battlepillars*.

Chinab Shah is an entrepreneur who owns a company called Nextsavy Technologies, which is based in Ahmedabad. They provide services in mobile application designing and development. He is also an iOS developer and a technology evangelist. He believes in creativity and thinks that everyone and everything in this world can be creative.

www.PacktPub.com

Support files, eBooks, discount offers, and more

For support files and downloads related to your book, please visit www.PacktPub.com.

Did you know that Packt offers eBook versions of every book published, with PDF and ePub files available? You can upgrade to the eBook version at www.PacktPub.com and as a print book customer, you are entitled to a discount on the eBook copy. Get in touch with us at service@packtpub.com for more details.

At www.PacktPub.com, you can also read a collection of free technical articles, sign up for a range of free newsletters and receive exclusive discounts and offers on Packt books and eBooks.

https://www2.packtpub.com/books/subscription/packtlib

Do you need instant solutions to your IT questions? PacktLib is Packt's online digital book library. Here, you can search, access, and read Packt's entire library of books.

Why Subscribe?

- ▶ Fully searchable across every book published by Packt
- ▶ Copy and paste, print, and bookmark content
- ▶ On demand and accessible via a web browser

Free Access for Packt account holders

If you have an account with Packt at www.PacktPub.com, you can use this to access PacktLib today and view 9 entirely free books. Simply use your login credentials for immediate access.

Table of Contents

Preface

Since the iOS devices are breathing in the market, the games have been started ruling this segment as well. iOS devices provide us with a really powerful gaming platform, which enables all the game developers to develop amazing games for this segment.

This book provides you with simple, direct solutions to all your common problems faced during game programming in iOS devices. This book covers a wide range of topics with detail and practical explanations. This book serves starts with simple game animations and an introduction to SpriteKit and then will grow the horizon towards working with the physics engine, 3D game programming, Artificial Intelligence for games and finally we will end up learning multiplayer game programming.

The book contains more than 45 interesting game recipes, which you need to learn and implement in your next game. This book serves as an all-in-one package for beginners, intermediates, and experts. You have complete control of each step of the game development. We also provide the solution kit at the end of each chapter once the recipe is finished.

What this book covers

Chapter 1, iOS Game Development, gets you started with the game development techniques with an understanding of the default game template and developing a mini game.

Chapter 2, SpriteKit, explains the basic structure of SpriteKit with the anatomy of game projects. Then later in the chapter we will take a deeper look into scenes, sprites and nodes. By end of the chapter we will be able to build a mini game with infinite scrolling.

Chapter 3, Animations and Texture, helps us to explore the depth of animations, which can be accomplished in iOS games. We will learn to create a texture atlas and create animations on them. We will also explore character animations and parallax backgrounds in this chapter.

Chapter 4, Particle System and Game Performance, makes us learn and understand the anatomy of particle effects and emitter system in games. In addition to that we will be exploring the evaluation of game performance in this chapter.

Chapter 5, Adding Music to iOS Games and an Introduction to iCloud, teaches us the numerous ways to add the music in the games. We will explore the various events to add music to the games such as background music and various other sounds effects on specific events. At end of the chapter, we will learn about iCloud integration in our games.

Chapter 6, Physics Simulation, gets us started on working with the physics engine in games in order to add more reality to the games. In this chapter, we will learn some exciting real-world simulations by creating a small game.

Chapter 7, Adding Reality to Games, broadens your scope in physics simulation by explaining the nitty gritty of physics joints, contact detection, and collision. In this chapter, we will explore the depth of physics and its impact on the overall game development process.

Chapter 8, Introduction to Game Math and Physics, brushes up your basic mathematics skills in the initial half of the chapter and then going forward explains their usage in the games. This chapter explains various aspects and properties of math and physics that are used in games.

Chapter 9, Autonomous Moving Agents, reveals the most interesting part of the games that is, artificial intelligence. In this chapter, we will practically implement various artificial intelligent behaviors in our game. We will explore, seek, flee, wander, arrive, pursuit, evade behaviors. Other than this, we will also learn group behaviors such as alignment cohesion and separation.

Chapter 10, 3D Game Programming with OpenGL, helps you in exploring 3D game programming. In this chapter we will learn the basics of OpenGL and then going forward in the chapter we will learn create a working 3D game model.

Chapter 11, Getting Started with Multiplayer Games, starts from the basics of the multiplayer game including the anatomy of multiplayer games. You will learn to set up a connection between two iOS devices and then will also learn to send and receive data from one device to another.

Chapter 12, Implementing Multiplayer Games, creates a multiplayer game using which two players can play simultaneously. In this chapter, we will use all the methodologies that we have learned in the introduction chapter.

What you need for this book

You'll need the following setup to get started with iOS game programming using SpriteKit:

- An Intel-based Macintosh running Snow Leopard (OS X 10.6.8 or later)
- Xcode
- You must be enrolled as an iPhone developer in order to test the example projects on your device
- iOS device with 7.0 or later

Who this book is for

If you are willing to learn game programming to develop your own games, then this book is for you. In this book, you will learn about various verticals of game development. This book will teach you a step-by-step way to write your own game.

This book uses Objective-C as its main language, so some basic knowledge of Objective-C is a must. This book assumes that you understand the fundamentals of object-oriented programming and programming in general.

This book is designed to get you started using game programming instantly, so you should be familiar with the iPhone/iPad itself. The iPhone is a great platform for programming. It looks nice and feels nice. This book teaches you about various easy-to-use approaches to get started with game programming.

Sections

In this book, you will find several headings that appear frequently (Getting ready, How to do it, How it works, There's more, and See also).

To give clear instructions on how to complete a recipe, we use these sections as follows:

Getting ready

This section tells you what to expect in the recipe, and describes how to set up any software or any preliminary settings required for the recipe.

How to do it...

This section contains the steps required to follow the recipe.

How it works...

This section usually consists of a detailed explanation of what happened in the previous section.

There's more...

This section consists of additional information about the recipe in order to make the reader more knowledgeable about the recipe.

See also

This section provides helpful links to other useful information for the recipe.

Conventions

In this book, you will find a number of styles of text that distinguish between different kinds of information. Here are some examples of these styles, and an explanation of their meaning.

Code words in text are shown as follows: "In `AppDelegate.h` file, find the `application:didFinishLaunchingWithOptions:` method and where we are registering for push notifications."

A block is set of code will be shown as follows:

```
SKAction *sequence = [SKAction sequence:@
    [[SKAction rotateByAngle:degreeToRadian(-3.0f) duration:0.2],
    [SKAction rotateByAngle:0.0 duration:0.1],
    [SKAction rotateByAngle:degreeToRadian(3.0f) duration:0.2]]];
[touchedNode runAction:[SKAction repeatActionForever:sequence]];
```

New terms and **important words** are shown in bold. Words that you see on the screen, for example, in menus or dialog boxes, appear in the text like this: "Select a location on the drive to save the project and click on **Create**."

Warnings or important notes appear in a box like this.

Tips and tricks appear like this.

Reader feedback

Feedback from our readers is always welcome. Let us know what you think about this book—what you liked or disliked. Reader feedback is important for us as it helps us develop titles that you will really get the most out of.

To send us general feedback, simply e-mail `feedback@packtpub.com`, and mention the book's title in the subject of your message.

If there is a topic that you have expertise in and you are interested in either writing or contributing to a book, see our author guide at www.packtpub.com/authors.

Customer support

Now that you are the proud owner of a Packt book, we have a number of things to help you to get the most from your purchase.

Downloading the example code

You can download the example code files from your account at http://www.packtpub.com for all the Packt Publishing books you have purchased. If you purchased this book elsewhere, you can visit http://www.packtpub.com/support and register to have the files e-mailed directly to you.

Downloading the color images of this book

We also provide you with a PDF file that has color images of the screenshots/diagrams used in this book. The color images will help you better understand the changes in the output. You can download this file from: https://www.packtpub.com/sites/default/files/downloads/8255OS_ColorImages.pdf

Errata

Although we have taken every care to ensure the accuracy of our content, mistakes do happen. If you find a mistake in one of our books—maybe a mistake in the text or the code—we would be grateful if you could report this to us. By doing so, you can save other readers from frustration and help us improve subsequent versions of this book. If you find any errata, please report them by visiting http://www.packtpub.com/submit-errata, selecting your book, clicking on the **Errata Submission Form** link, and entering the details of your errata. Once your errata are verified, your submission will be accepted and the errata will be uploaded to our website or added to any list of existing errata under the Errata section of that title.

To view the previously submitted errata, go to https://www.packtpub.com/books/content/support and enter the name of the book in the search field. The required information will appear under the **Errata** section.

Piracy

Piracy of copyrighted material on the Internet is an ongoing problem across all media. At Packt, we take the protection of our copyright and licenses very seriously. If you come across any illegal copies of our works in any form on the Internet, please provide us with the location address or website name immediately so that we can pursue a remedy.

Please contact us at `copyright@packtpub.com` with a link to the suspected pirated material.

We appreciate your help in protecting our authors and our ability to bring you valuable content.

Questions

If you have a problem with any aspect of this book, you can contact us at `questions@packtpub.com`, and we will do our best to address the problem.

1

iOS Game Development

Since the launch of iOS devices, game development has always attracted developers in ever-increasing numbers. There are various game engines available in the market, which allow developers to start developing their games for iOS devices.

In this chapter, we will be focusing on the following topics:

- Getting started with the SpriteKit game framework
- Developing a mini game using SpriteKit

Introduction

Apple has launched its first game engine that allows you to create games for iOS without being dependent on the third-party game libraries. It is a very powerful framework similar to other iOS frameworks and is similar to other frameworks when it comes to its usage. It's also very easy to adopt and learn. It also supports lots of features such as physics simulations, texture atlas, gravity, restitution, animations, particle emitters, game center support, and many more. Moreover, it comes with very rich developer documentation for SpriteKit at the Apple development center. It's very useful and very well written. You might need to understand the anatomy of game development first to get started with game development in SpriteKit. There are two basic and most important terms here; one is scenes and the other is sprites. Scenes can be considered as the layers in the games. Therefore, in any game there are various layers such as the score layer, hud layer, and gameplay layer that can act as different scenes. However, any object in the scene such as a player or an enemy can be considered as a sprite.

Getting started with the SpriteKit game framework

With the release of iOS 7.0, Apple has introduced its own native 2D game framework called SpriteKit. SpriteKit is a great 2D game engine, which has support for sprite, animations, filters, masking, and most important is the physics engine to provide a real-world simulation for the game.

Apple provides a sample game to get started with the SpriteKit called Adventure Game. The download URL for this example project is `http://bit.ly/Rqaeda`.

This sample project provides a glimpse of the capability of this framework. However, the project is complicated to understand and for learning you just want to make something simple. To have a deeper understanding of SpriteKit-based games, we will be building a bunch of mini games in this book. To understand the basics of the SpriteKit game programming, we will build a mini AntKilling game in this chapter.

Getting ready

To get started with iOS game development, you have the following prerequisites for SpriteKit:

- You will need the Xcode 5.x
- The targeted device family should be iOS 7.0+
- You should be running OS X 10.8.X or later

If all the above requisites are fulfilled, then you are ready to go with the iOS game development. So let's start with game development using iOS native game framework. We will be building a mini game in the chapter and will be taking it forward in every chapter to add more and more features and enhancements.

How to do it...

Let's start building the AntKilling game. Perform the following steps to create your new SpriteKit project:

1. Start your Xcode. Navigate to **File | New | Project...**.

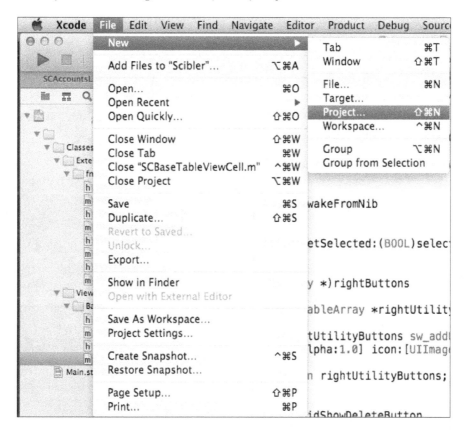

2. Then from the prompt window, navigate to **iOS** | **Application** | **SpriteKit Game** and click on **Next**.

3. Fill all the project details in the prompt window and provide AntKilling as the project name with your **Organization Name**, device as **iPhone**, and **Class Prefix** as AK. Click on **Next**.

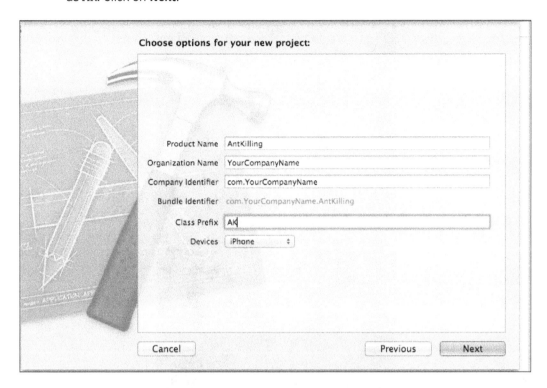

4. Select a location on the drive to save the project and click on **Create**.

5. Then build the sample project to check the output of the sample project. Once you build and run the project with the play button, you should see the following on your device:

How it works...

The following are the observations of the starter project:

1. As you have seen, the sample project of SpriteKit plays a label with a background color.

2. SpriteKit works on the concept of scenes, which can be understood as the layers or the screens of the game. There can be multiple scenes working at the same time; for example, there can be a gameplay scene, hud scene, and the score scene running at the same time in the game.

Now we can look into the project for more detail arrangements of the starter project. The following are the observations:

1. In the main directory, you already have one scene created by default called **AKMyScene**.

2. Now click on AKMyScene.m to explore the code to add the label on the screen. You should see something similar to the following screenshot:

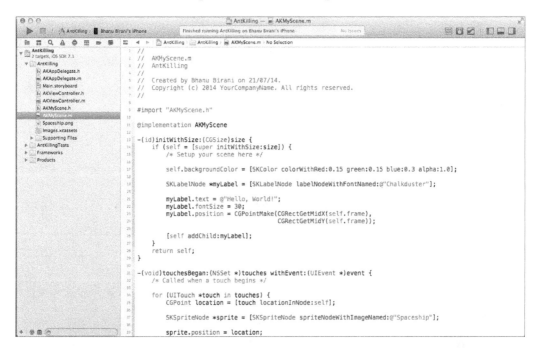

3. Now we will be updating this file with our code to create our AntKilling game in the next sections.

4. We have to fulfill a few prerequisites to get started with the code, such as locking the orientation to landscape as we want a landscape orientation game.

5. To change the orientation of the game, navigate to AntKilling project settings | **TARGETS** | **General**. You should see something similar to the following screenshot:

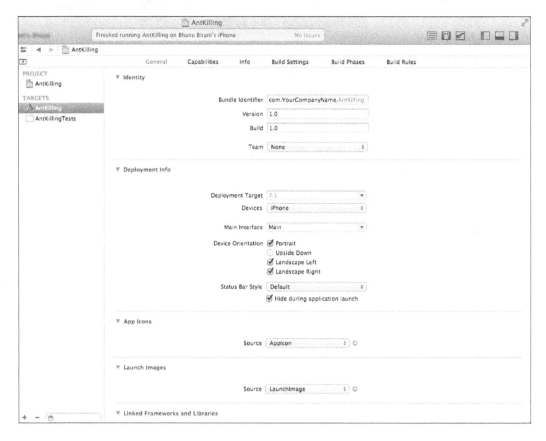

6. Now in the **General** tab, uncheck **Portrait** from the device orientation so that the final settings should look similar to the following screenshot:

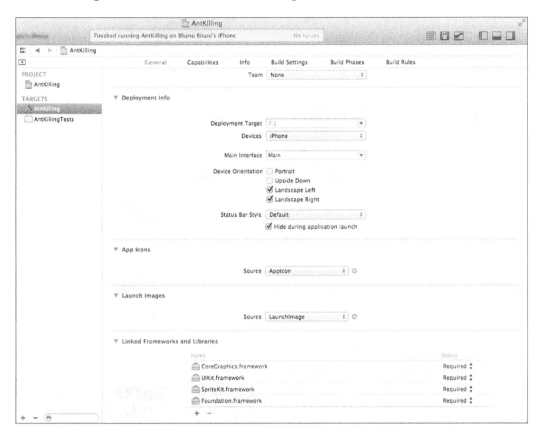

7. Now build and run the project. You should be able to see the app running in landscape orientation.

8. The bottom-right corner of the screen shows the number of nodes with the frame rate.

Developing a mini game using SpriteKit

Now you have learned enough about SpriteKit. To explore this in more depth, let's create a mini game that will help you to understand the concepts in much more detail. We are going to create an AntKilling game. In this game, we will place an ant on the screen; the ant will animate when you click on it.

Getting ready

We will use the project we created in the previous section. To create a mini game, we will have to update the source files we have got with the starter project. Now it's time to update AKMyScene to hold our ant sprites.

Before getting into the steps to update the code, download all the resources for this chapter and check for the `assets` folder, which has all the images used in this project.

How to do it...

Execute the following steps sequentially to create a mini game:

1. Open the `Resources` folder and add them to your Xcode project.

2. While adding the resources to the Xcode, make sure that the selected target is **AntKilling** and **Copy items into destination group's folder (if needed)** is checked.

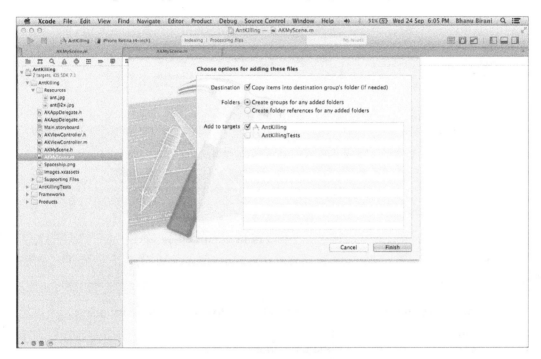

3. Now delete all the existing code from `AKMyScene.m` and make it look similar to the following screenshot:

```
 1  //
 2  //  AKMyScene.m
 3  //  AntKilling
 4  //
 5  //  Created by Bhanu Birani on 21/07/14.
 6  //  Copyright (c) 2014 YourCompanyName. All rights reserved.
 7  //
 8
 9  #import "AKMyScene.h"
10
11  @interface AKMyScene ()
12
13  @property (nonatomic) SKSpriteNode *ant;
14
15  @end
16
17  @implementation AKMyScene
18
19  -(id)initWithSize:(CGSize)size {
20      if (self = [super initWithSize:size]) {
21          /* Setup your scene here */
22
23          NSLog(@"Size: %@", NSStringFromCGSize(size));
24
25          self.backgroundColor = [SKColor colorWithRed:1.0 green:1.0 blue:1.0 alpha:1.0];
26
27          self.ant = [SKSpriteNode spriteNodeWithImageNamed:@"ant.jpg"];
28          self.ant.position = CGPointMake(self.size.width/2, self.size.height/2);
29          [self addChild:self.ant];
30
31      }
32      return self;
33  }
34
35  @end
36
```

4. Now, firstly, we have created a private interface to declare private variables:

```
@interface AKMyScene ()
@property (nonatomic) SKSpriteNode *ant;
@end
```

5. Then, in the `init` method, we have printed a log to print the size of the screen:

```
NSLog(@"Size: %@", NSStringFromCGSize(size));
```

6. Now we will change the screen background color to white using the following line of code:

```
self.backgroundColor = [SKColor colorWithRed:1.0
  green:1.0 blue:1.0 alpha:1.0];
```

7. Then we will change the screen background color to white using the `backgroundColor` property in the following line of code.

```
self.backgroundColor = [SKColor colorWithRed:1.0
   green:1.0 blue:1.0 alpha:1.0];
```

8. In the following line of code, we are creating a sprite object using the `spriteNodeWithImageNamed` method and passing the image name to the same. Then we have positioned it to `100, 100` of the screen, which is in the bottom-left corner of the screen. Then finally we have added it as a child.

```
self.ant = [SKSpriteNode spriteNodeWithImageNamed:@"ant.jpg"];
self.ant.position = CGPointMake(100, 100);
[self addChild:self.ant];
```

Downloading the example code

You can download the example code files from your account at `http://www.packtpub.com` for all the Packt Publishing books you have purchased. If you purchased this book elsewhere, you can visit `http://www.packtpub.com/support` and register to have the files e-mailed directly to you.

In games, we have to keep two sets of images, one for the normal display and the second for the retina display. In the preceding block of code, we have provided the name of the sprite as `ant.jpg`, which is going to autoreference to `ant@2x.jpg` for the retina devices.

Now build and run your application; you should see something similar to the following screenshot:

Now as you can see, the screen color has changed to white but there is no ant on the screen. This means something has gone wrong in the code. So, now let's check our logs, which should be printing the following:

```
2014-07-22 19:13:27.019 AntKilling[1437:60b] Size: {320, 568}
```

So the scene size is wrong. The scene should print 568 as the width and 320 as the height but it's printing the opposite. To debug this, navigate to your `AKViewController.m` `viewDidLoad` method. You can find the complete code for this function at `AntKilling/AntKilling/AKViewController.m`.

So, from this method, we can see that our scene is absorbing the size from the bounds of the view and this `viewDidLoad` method is invoked even before the view has been added to the view hierarchy. So it has not responded to the layout changes. Thus, because of the inconsistent view bounds our scene is getting started with wrong bounds.

To solve this issue, we have to move the scene startup code in the `viewWillLayoutSubviews` method. After removing the code from the `viewDidLoad` method and pasting it to `viewWillLayoutSubviews`, you can find the complete code for this function at `AntKilling/AntKilling/AKViewController.m`.

Now, once again build and run the app; you should see the following output:

How it works...

So, congrats! You have fixed the issue. Your ant has now appeared on the screen at the given location. If you observe closely, you can see that the status bar is at the top of the game, which does not look great. To remove the status bar from the screen, open your `AntKilling-Info.plist` file and add an `UIViewControllerBasedStatusBarAppearance` attribute with value `NO`. Your `.plist` file should look like the following screenshot:

Key	Type	Value
▼ Information Property List	Dictionary	(16 items)
Localization native development r...	String	en
Bundle display name	String	${PRODUCT_NAME}
Executable file	String	${EXECUTABLE_NAME}
Bundle identifier	String	com.YourCompanyName.${PRODUCT_NAME:rfc1034identifier}
InfoDictionary version	String	6.0
Bundle name	String	${PRODUCT_NAME}
Bundle OS Type code	String	APPL
Bundle versions string, short	String	1.0
Bundle creator OS Type code	String	????
Bundle version	String	1.0
Application requires iPhone envir...	Boolean	YES
Main storyboard file base name	String	Main
▶ Required device capabilities	Array	(1 item)
Status bar is initially hidden	Boolean	YES
View controller–based status...	Boolean	NO
▶ Supported interface orientations	Array	(2 items)

Build and run your project again; you should be able to see the game without the status bar now:

1 node 60.0 fps

This looks perfect now; our ant has been residing on the screen as expected. So now our next objective is to animate the ant when we tap on it. To accomplish this, we need to add the following code in the `AKMyScene.m` file, just below your `initWithSize` method:

```
-  (void)touchesBegan:(NSSet *)touches withEvent:(UIEvent *)event
{
  UITouch *touch = [touches anyObject];
  CGPoint positionInScene = [touch locationInNode:self];
  SKSpriteNode *touchedNode = (SKSpriteNode *)
    [self nodeAtPoint:positionInScene];
  if (touchedNode == self.ant) {
    SKAction *sequence = [SKAction sequence:@
      [[SKAction rotateByAngle:degreeToRadian
        (-3.0f) duration:0.2],
      [SKAction rotateByAngle:0.0 duration:0.1],
      [SKAction rotateByAngle:degreeToRadian(3.0f) duration:0.2]]];
      [touchedNode runAction:
        [SKAction repeatActionForever:sequence]];
  }
}


float degreeToRadian(float degree) {
  return degree / 180.0f * M_PI;
}
```

You can find the complete code for this function at `AntKilling/AntKilling/AKMyScene.m`.

So, now let's go line-by-line to understand what we have done so far. To begin with, we have added the `- (void)touchesBegan:(NSSet *)touches withEvent:(UIEvent *) event` method to the grab all the touches on the scene.

Now in the function the first line allowed you to grab touch using `CGPoint positionInScene = [touch locationInNode:self];`.

In the next line, we grabbed the touch and converting it to the `CGPoint positionInScene = [touch locationInNode:self];` location.

In the following line, we fetched the sprite, which has been touched:

```
SKSpriteNode *touchedNode = (SKSpriteNode *)
  [self nodeAtPoint:positionInScene];
```

Now, once you have the sprite object, compare and check whether the select object is the ant bug. If it's the ant bug, then animate the object by adding the following line of code:

```
SKAction *sequence = [SKAction sequence:@
  [[SKAction rotateByAngle:degreeToRadian(-3.0f) duration:0.2],
  [SKAction rotateByAngle:0.0 duration:0.1],
  [SKAction rotateByAngle:degreeToRadian(3.0f) duration:0.2]]];
[touchedNode runAction:[SKAction repeatActionForever:sequence]];
```

Using the `SKAction` class, you can execute various sequence of animations such as `rotation`, `moveBy`, `moveTo`, and so on. Also all the rotate methods accept the angle in radians. So to achieve the rotation, we must convert the degree to radians before passing to any `rotate` function.

Now, this code will animate the selected sprite. Build and run the project and you will see the ant animating on tap.

You will soon notice that on tapping the ant, it starts animating, but there is no way to stop this. So now let's add a way to stop this animation once you click anywhere on the scene. Navigate to the `- (void)touchesBegan:(NSSet *)touches withEvent:(UIEvent *)` event method, and update it to the following code:

```
- (void)touchesBegan:(NSSet *)touches withEvent:(UIEvent *)event
{
  UITouch *touch = [touches anyObject];
  CGPoint positionInScene = [touch locationInNode:self];
  SKSpriteNode *touchedNode = (SKSpriteNode *)
    [self nodeAtPoint:positionInScene];
  if (touchedNode == self.ant) {
    SKAction *sequence = [SKAction sequence:@
      [[SKAction rotateByAngle:degreeToRadian(-3.0f)
        duration:0.2],
      [SKAction rotateByAngle:0.0 duration:0.1],
      [SKAction rotateByAngle:degreeToRadian(3.0f) duration:0.2]]];
      [touchedNode runAction:
        [SKAction repeatActionForever:sequence]];
  } else {
  [self.ant removeAllActions];
  }
}
```

Now if you observe closely, you can see that we have added an `if-else` condition to check whether the touch is made on the ant, which allows it to animate; when the touch is made anywhere outside the screen, stop all the actions. To stop all the actions on the sprite, we can use the `removeAllActions` method on the sprite.

2
SpriteKit

In this chapter, we will cover the following recipes:

- ► Learning the basics of SpriteKit – The FlyingSpaceship tutorial
- ► Understanding scenes, nodes, and sprites
- ► Anatomy of game projects
- ► Applying actions on Sprites
- ► Adding infinite scrolling
- ► Moving characters

This chapter explains SpriteKit in detail. We'll start from a discussion on the basics of SpriteKit, and then we will be learning about the anatomy of the game project. Moving ahead, we will learn about scenes, sprites, and nodes. This will provide us a deeper understanding about the basic structure model of the SpriteKit. Then we will be exploring the depth of SpriteKit by adding some actions to the sprites. Moving ahead, we will be adding infinite scrolling to the game that will be created during the chapter.

Introduction

SpriteKit is a graphics rendering and animation framework with features for animating arbitrary textured images called Sprites. It has a rendering loop that renders the contents of the frame. As a process, the content of each frame (that is, input) is given, processed, and then finally rendered by the rendering loop.

Basically, your game identifies the content of the frame and how the content has to be changed in that frame.

Being a new player in the game industry, SpriteKit is doing really well as it has adopted the basics of cocos2d, which is a heavily used game engine for 2D games. It's really well written, documented, and deeply integrated with iOS. However, if you are new to the game development domain, even then this book will serve you as a starter development guide. Each chapter is baked with a recipe to make sure that you learn all the concepts of game development.

Now here are the two most basic concepts: scenes and sprites. iOS games are made up of scenes and scenes in turn hold sprites.

To get started with the SpriteKit, we will be creating a small game that will guide us to understand all the concepts of the SpriteKit.

Learning the basics of SpriteKit – The FlyingSpaceship tutorial

In this section we will learn and explore basic concepts of SpriteKit. We will also develop a mini game, which will help in understanding the concepts with some robust implementation. The best way to learn SpriteKit is to see it in action.

Getting ready

To build a SpriteKit game, firstly you need to understand the basic structure of a SpriteKit project. You can get started with a starter project having a SKScene and an SKNode placed on it. This would equip you with the setup to build your basic game.

How to do it...

To understand the basic concepts of game programming, let's create a new project with the SpriteKit game template with project name FlyingSpaceship. The project will demonstrate the structure of a SpriteKit project. The end goal of the project is that a Spaceship is visible on the screen and in the upcoming topics we can make it fly.

We will follow some of the same steps we performed in *Chapter 1, iOS Game Development* and finally add the Spaceship to the screen:

1. Start your Xcode and navigate to **File | New | Project**. Then from the prompt window navigate to **iOS | Application | SpriteKit Game** and click on **Next**.

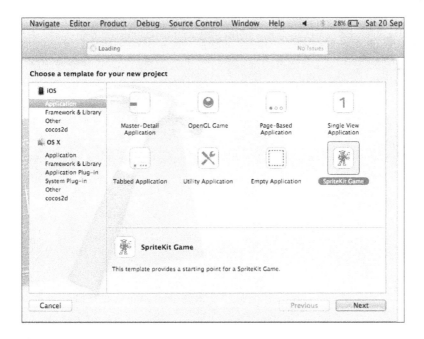

2. Fill all the project details in the prompt window and provide `FlyingSpaceship` as the project name with your **Organization Name**, **Devices** as **iPhone**, and **Class Prefix** as `FS`. Click on **Next** as shown in the following screenshot:

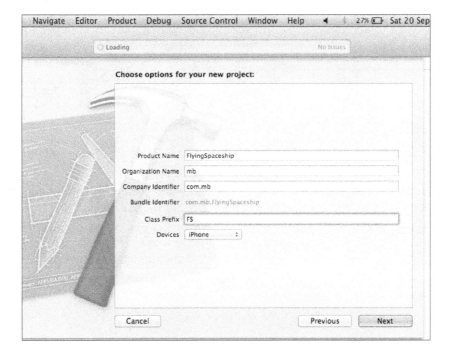

3. Select a location on drive to save the project and click on **Create**.

4. As a result, the FSViewController and FSMyScene files will be created in the project having a Spaceship.png file also. The project directory should look something similar to the following screenshot:

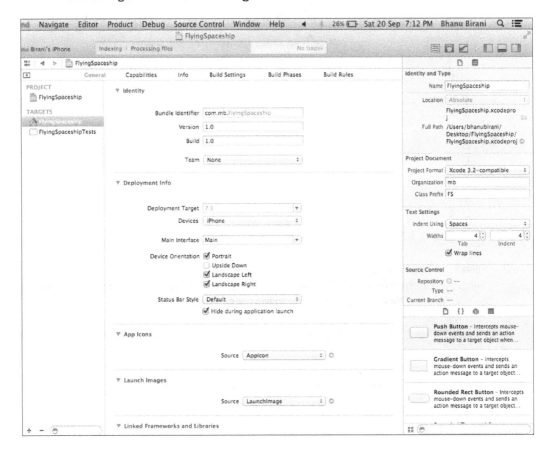

5. Go to the **General** tab, uncheck **Portrait** from the device orientation so that the final orientation is landscape.

6. Cut the code of typecasting UIView to SKView and presenting FSMyScene to SKView from (void) viewDidLoad of FSViewController.

7. Implement - (void) viewWillLayoutSubviews and copy the code from viewDidLoad to viewWillLayoutSubviews.

8. Finally, the code will look like this:

```objc
#import "FSViewController.h"
#import "FSMyScene.h"

@implementation FSViewController

- (void)viewDidLoad
{
    [super viewDidLoad];
}

- (void)viewWillLayoutSubviews
{
    [super viewWillLayoutSubviews];

    // Configure the view.
    SKView * skView = (SKView *)self.view;
    skView.showsFPS = YES;
    skView.showsNodeCount = YES;

    // Create and configure the scene.
    SKScene * scene = [FSMyScene sceneWithSize:skView.bounds.size];
    scene.scaleMode = SKSceneScaleModeAspectFill;

    // Present the scene.
    [skView presentScene:scene];
}
```

9. Now, let's go to `FSMyScene.m`, remove the default code added in the `init` method and also the method for touch detection.

10. Make a property for a `SKSpriteNode` called spaceship in the private interface:

    ```objc
    @interface FSMyScene ()
    @property (nonatomic, strong) SKSpriteNode*     spaceShipSprite;
    @end
    ```

11. Add this `spaceShipSprite` to the `FSMyScene` file in its `init` method:

    ```objc
    self.spaceShipSprite = [SKSpriteNode spriteNodeWithImageNamed:@"Sp
    aceship"];
    self.spaceShipSprite.position = CGPointMake(self.spaceShipSprite.
    size.width, size.height/2);
    [self addChild:self.spaceShipSprite];
    ```

    The default `Spaceship.png` provided is appropriate, so delete and add `Spaceship.png` provided in the `Resources` folder of the Starter kit.

12. Now if you run the app, the spaceship doesn't look good on a black background, so give the sky color background color to `FSMyScene` file in its `init` method.

```
self.backgroundColor = [UIColor colorWithRed:135.0/255.0
green:206.0/255.0 blue:235.0/255.0 alpha:1.0];
```

So finally we have reached the goal and have placed a spaceship in the sky.

The final `FSMyScene` class looks like this:

```objc
#import "FSMyScene.h"

@interface FSMyScene()

@property (nonatomic, strong) SKSpriteNode*      spaceShipSprite;

@end

@implementation FSMyScene

-(id)initWithSize:(CGSize)size {
    if (self = [super initWithSize:size]) {
        /* Setup your scene here */

        self.backgroundColor = [UIColor colorWithRed:135.0/255.0
                                               green:206.0/255.0
                                                blue:235.0/255.0
                                               alpha:1.0];

        self.spaceShipSprite = [SKSpriteNode spriteNodeWithImageNamed:@"Spaceship"];

        self.spaceShipSprite.position = CGPointMake(self.spaceShipSprite.size.width,
                                                    size.height/2);

        [self addChild:self.spaceShipSprite];
    }
    return self;
}

-(void)update:(CFTimeInterval)currentTime {
    /* Called before each frame is rendered */
}

@end
```

In the preceding screenshot, you will observe an `update:` method in the `.m` file. This method is automatically invoked while rendering each frame on the screen. If the frame rate of the game is 60, then this method will be executed 60 times in a second. Any real-time calculations can be performed in this method, so actions such as calculating the player's location in real time can be handled in this method.

And the starter kit game, `FlyingSpaceship`, looks like this:

How it works...

The structure of SpriteKit is fundamentally derived and inherited from the UIKit framework. The operating system offers a smooth transition from UIKit to SpriteKit by just typecasting the UIKit view controller's view to a SpriteKit view called SKView. After this, you are ready to play with the SpriteKit stuff. As shown in the following block diagram, create a scene, add some nodes (that is Sprites as players, background stuff, and so on) to it and you have the game environment built. You can also make the environment more live by applying some actions (rotate, move, scale, and many more) to the nodes added.

Hence, in combination, this scene has different kinds of nodes with some actions applied, that make the basic structure of your SpriteKit and also the game you thought of building.

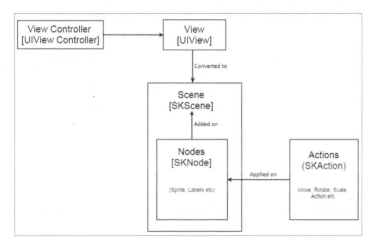

There's more...

SpriteKit can be used for game development on iOS and OS X platforms. The available graphics hardware of the hosting device is used to render composite 2D images at high frame rates. There are several other features of SpriteKit, which support the following kinds of content, including:

- Sprites that can be of any form such as untextured or textured rectangles
- Text
- Arbitrary CGPath-based shapes
- Video

If you are curious to know more, then visit Apple's developer link `https://developer. apple.com/library/ios/documentation/GraphicsAnimation/Conceptual/ SpriteKit_PG/Introduction/Introduction.html`.

You can also play around with the sample you have just created by trying to change the location of the spaceship and applying various colors to its background.

Understanding scenes, nodes, and sprites

The whole game is organized into scenes, which have the content represented by `SKScene` objects.

A scene is an entity that holds all the content, that is, nodes and sprites that are to be rendered. It also implements the setup or anatomy of content processing and updating each frame.

The `SKScene` class is a subclass of SKNode, which is the fundamental building block of SpriteKit. Every entity in SpriteKit is inherited or derived from the node (SKNode). So `SKScene` is the root node for other nodes, which are used to populate the content over a scene.

Similar to UIKit, each node's position is specified according to the coordinate system of its parent. A node also has the basic properties that a content item or entity should have such as moving, rotating, scaling, fading out, and many more. And most important, all node objects are responder objects that respond to the delegates of UIResponder. This is used to detect input touches to the scene for moving objects and some other stuff depending on one's gameplay.

Now, sprites are represented by SKSpriteNode objects. They are nodes with images on them. We can specify content or a textured image to them as we have to make some player or enemies in a game. SKSpriteNode is also inherited from SKNode. Additionally, its content can be changed and animated. The sprites are created and added on scenes with some actions to make the game scene more alive.

Getting ready

To understand these elements of SpriteKit, we need to create a blank project just as we did in the starter project of this chapter. As in this starter kit, a basic `SKScene` and `SKNode` are shown. So we will now go through these terminologies and their sample code snippets.

How to do it...

As we did in the starter kit, follow the same steps to create a `SKScene` and add a `SKSpriteNode` method to it:

1. Create the SpriteKit Game Template from Xcode.

2. A default ViewController and scene will be created for you.

3. Typecast the ViewController view to `SKView` by enabling the `showsFPS` and `showsNodeCount` properties to `YES`.

   ```
   // Configure the view.
   SKView * skView = (SKView *)self.view;
   skView.showsFPS = YES;
   skView.showsNodeCount = YES;
   ```

4. Create a scene using a class method of `SKScene` specifying the size of the scene also, and then present that scene on the `SKView` typecasted before.

   ```
   // Create and configure the scene.
   SKScene * scene = [SKScene sceneWithSize:skView.bounds.size];
   scene.scaleMode = SKSceneScaleModeAspectFill;

   // Present the scene.
   [skView presentScene:scene];
   ```

   All this should be done in the - `(void)viewWillLayoutSubviews` method.

5. Now we have to add some sprite to the scene we created earlier. Create an object of SKSpriteNode by calling a class method and specifying an image of the sprite. Now assign the location where it has to be placed and lastly add it to the scene.

   ```
   SKSpriteNode * spriteNode = [SKSpriteNode spriteNodeWithImageNamed
   :@"Spaceship.png"];
   spriteNode.position = CGPointMake(100,100);
   [self addChild:spriteNode];
   ```

How it works...

As explained in the structural block diagram of the *How it works...* section of the *Learning the basics of SpriteKit – The FlyingSpaceship tutorial* recipe, it's deeply linked with the UIKit framework. For building a game, we should have an environment, which is our scene, and some entities visible over the environment, which are the sprites. So to make it work, or should I say to make something visible on the screen, an environment (that is, scene) is created and on it entities (that is, sprites) are added, as follows:

- When we typecast UIView in to `SKView`, we enter the arena of SpriteKit:

  ```
  SKView * skView = (SKView *)self.view;
  ```

- For debugging purposes, we enable two Boolean parameters to show FPS (Frames per second) and NodesCount (the number of nodes added to the scene):

  ```
  skView.showsFPS = YES;
  skView.showsNodeCount = YES;
  ```

- When creating a scene, we need to specify the size of the scene that is exactly the content size and the scale mode so that the scene fits in `SKView` (that is, scale perspective), here the `SKSceneScaleModeAspectFill` mode is used so that it fits as per the aspect ratio of the `SKView`:

  ```
  SKScene * scene = [SKScene
    sceneWithSize:skView.bounds.size];
  scene.scaleMode = SKSceneScaleModeAspectFill;
  ```

- To make the scene content visible on the view, we present the scene on `SKView`:

  ```
  // Present the scene.
  [skView presentScene:scene];
  ```

- Now about how the sprites work. A sprite object is created by a class method that instantiates a node having an image as its content:

  ```
  SKSpriteNode * spriteNode = [SKSpriteNode
    spriteNodeWithImageNamed:@"Spaceship.png"];
  ```

- The following line of code specifies the position where exactly the sprite needs to be placed:

  ```
  spriteNode.position = CGPointMake(100,100);
  ```

  Lastly, to make the sprite visible, it is added to SKScene as a child:

  ```
  [self addChild:spriteNode];
  ```

Anatomy of game projects

In this section we will see the basics of a game project. This includes understanding the basic architecture and work flow of game projects. Here we will learn about the scene and layers and their importance in games.

Getting ready

Complete game development is dependent on three core components: scenes, nodes, and sprites mentioned earlier. We need to have a command over these components to effectively start on game development.

How to do it...

Internally, the life cycle is executed as per the scenes—nodes are added and actions applied on these nodes. It also includes attaching some physics bodies to the nodes, support for cropping, applying animation and effects to all or a part of the content, detecting forces and collision, drawing in OpenGL, and many more things.

Apart from all this, there is an overridden update method in SKScene, which is called for each frame of the game with the current time interval as a parameter. There you can add your actual game logic specifying what to do at what time and many more things as it is called by every frame that is rendered.

For an example, we can track the difference in time between the current time and the last updated time.

1. As the current time interval is received in the update method, define the properties for difference in time and last updated time.

   ```
   @property (nonatomic, assign) NSTimeInterval
     lastUpdatedTime;
   @property (nonatomic, assign) NSTimeInterval    diffTime;
   ```

2. Now calculate difference in time by subtracting the last updated time from the current time and updating the lastUpdatedTime to the current time.

   ```
   self.diffTime = currentTime - self.lastUpdatedTime;
   self.lastUpdatedTime = currentTime;
   ```

3. At last the update method looks like this:

   ```
   - (void)update:(CFTimeInterval)currentTime
   {
       /* Called before each frame is rendered */
       self.diffTime = currentTime - self.lastUpdatedTime;
       self.lastUpdatedTime = currentTime;
   }
   ```

Now this is the place where we are going add our maximum game logic—all the adding, removing, animating, updating all nodes, sprites, and actions will take place inside this method. We can also take the help of `currentTime` to maintain some timers simply using float variables (updating them by the `diffTime` and firing time events whenever required according to our game design or logic).

How it works...

All that we see running on the screen are just frames added by a time interval, which is driven by a `SKScene` added as a child on the `SKView` that serves as the main scene of the game.

As shown in the following diagram, a frame circle is present, which depicts the execution cycle of the game project for each frame:

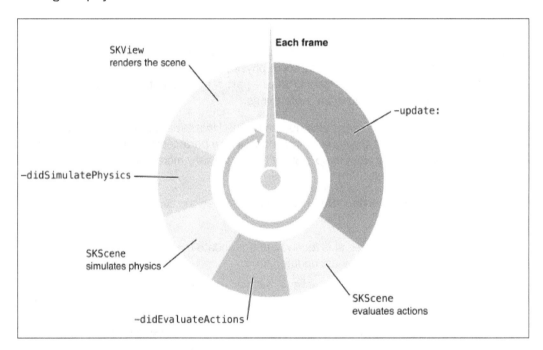

Some of the methods from the preceding diagram are explained as follows:

- An update method of `SKScene` is called where we can add, remove, animate, and update different kinds of nodes and actions.
- `SKScene` evaluates its actions that are running for the current frame following some life cycle calls such as `didEvaluateActions`.
- `SKScene` has its own physics simulation, so if some bodies are added to it, the physics simulation is also evaluated such as collision detection, applying forces, and so on.

▶ All the methods mentioned earlier contribute to the final rendering of SKView, which is displayed as a frame to the user. Hence, regular running of these frames makes the game appear as an environment.

Applying actions on sprites

Sprites are just static images with no life. So actions add that life to the sprites that make your game. Actions help in building the gameplay by moving sprites and animating them differently. An action is an object that makes the scene look alive.

Actions are applied on nodes and sprites, for example, we want to move some object that is a sprite, so we create a move action and run it on that sprite. SpriteKit automatically changes the sprite's position in a form of animation until the action is over.

All actions are implemented using a class called SKAction and different types of actions are instantiated using the class methods of the SKAction class provided for various animation functionality.

Here are the most common actions available in SpriteKit:

▶ Applying transformation (translation, rotation, and scaling)

▶ Changing visibility (fading in and fading out)

▶ Changing the content of the sprite

▶ Changing the colors of sprites

▶ Removing sprites

▶ Calling a block or a selector

▶ Repeating and sequencing actions

Getting ready

To apply different actions on sprites and see them animating, we need to know scenes, sprites, and the overall life cycle of a SpriteKit project. We also need to know about some fundamental actions that are applied on any entity such as move, rotate, scale, and there are many more special effects to explore.

How to do it...

There is a wide variety of actions to be applied on nodes and sprites, some of which are listed next.

To understand this, we will take the spaceship as a sprite to apply different actions.

There are several individual actions provided by the SpriteKit framework. A few of them are explained as follows:

▸ **Move Action**: To move a sprite, call the class method shown below, specifying the location where the sprite has to be moved and in what time. And then call the `runAction` method on the sprite with the move action created.

```
SKAction* moveAction = [SKAction moveTo:CGPointMake(100,100)
duration:1.0];
[self.spaceShipSprite runAction:moveAction];
```

▸ **Rotate Action**: To rotate a sprite, we have to specify an angle in radians, which will make the sprite rotate by or to that angle in a specified time. So specify the angle in degrees, convert to radians, and then feed it to the function thereby applying that action to the sprite.

```
CGFloat angleInDegree = 90.0;
CGFloat angleInRadian = angleInDegree * M_PI/180.0;
SKAction* rotateAction = [SKAction rotateByAngle:angleInRadian
duration:2.0];
[self.spaceShipSprite runAction:rotateAction];
```

▸ **Scale Action**: To scale a sprite, we have to specify a scale factor, which will increase or decrease the size of the sprite, depending on the scale factor given in a time.

```
SKAction* scaleAction = [SKAction scaleBy:2.0 duration:2.0];
[self.spaceShipSprite runAction:scaleAction];
```

▸ **Fade Action**: To make a sprite visible or invisible through animation, there are methods for fading out and fading in a sprite. For now, fading out is shown in the following code, which takes a parameter or the time over which to fadeout.

```
SKAction* fadeOutAction = [SKAction fadeOutWithDuration:1.0];
[self.spaceShipSprite runAction:fadeOutAction];
```

In SpriteKit, there are many more actions for giving delays, changing content, invoking an object or selector, calling blocks, and many special effects.

Similar to the individual actions, there are sequence and repeat actions, which fall under a different category of actions provided by SpriteKit. The sequence action is meant for running actions in a particular sequence we want. As shown in the following code, two actions are created—one for fading out and the other for fading in the sprite. So, both the actions are fed to the sequence action in the order we want and it would run the sequence we asked for:

```
SKAction* fadeOutAction = [SKAction fadeOutWithDuration:1.0];
SKAction* fadeInAction = [SKAction fadeInWithDuration:1.0];
SKAction* sequenceAction = [SKAction sequence:@[fadeOutAction,
fadeInAction]];
[self.spaceShipSprite runAction:sequenceAction];
```

The repeat action allows actions to be repeated for a fixed number of time or to be repeated forever. So using the preceding sequence action, we do both.

- ▸ Animating the sequence for three times regularly:

```
SKAction* repeatThreeTimesAction = [SKAction
repeatAction:sequenceAction count:3];
[self.spaceShipSprite runAction:repeatThreeTimesAction];
```

- ▸ Animating the sequence repeatedly forever:

```
SKAction* repeatForeverAction = [SKAction repeatActionForever:sequ
enceAction];
[self.spaceShipSprite runAction:repeatForeverAction];
```

Another type of action is the group action. Several times in games we may need to repeat a sequence of actions, which means running actions in a particular sequence for any interval of time. As shown previously, two actions were created, one for fading out and second for fading in the sprite. So, both the actions were fed to the sequence action in the order we wanted and it would run the sequence we asked for.

Group actions are used when we have to run many actions at the same point of time. So we can make a group function that moves a sprite by fading out also:

```
SKAction* moveAction = [SKAction moveTo:CGPointMake(100,100)
duration:1.0];
SKAction* fadeOutAction = [SKAction fadeOutWithDuration:1.0];
SKAction *groupAction = [SKAction group:@[moveAction, fadeOutAction]];
[self.spaceShipSprite runAction:groupAction];
```

How it works...

All the actions we have discussed earlier will be working in the same flow. Here is the basic anatomy of all actions, which we apply on sprites:

- ▸ Decide the actions we want to apply, in what sequence they are to be executed, and whether some action needs to be repeated or not.
- ▸ For each action, whatever the type is, specify its respective parameters and the time duration for it.
- ▸ After finalizing the action, just call `runAction` on the sprite to be animated with the action constructed.

Adding infinite scrolling

Now we are all ready with our spaceship. It's time to add some more in the game. So our next target is to add infinite scrolling to the game, so that we can make our spaceship move infinitely in space. In this recipe, we will be learning about the ways to add infinite scrolling to games.

Getting ready

For an infinite scrolling background you need to know about the anatomy of SpriteKit shown earlier. You should be aware of the rendering loop, how in a particular frame the update method functions, and how `SKScene` evaluates the actions and physics simulation thereby rendering all the stuff in the `SKView`. Now using this loop, you implement sky scrolling infinitely giving the feel of a spaceship flying.

How to do it...

Now is the time for action; perform the following steps to add the infinite scrolling background to your game.

1. Import the `SpaceBackground.png` file provided in the `Resources` folder.
2. Add a function in `FSMyScene` for initializing the infinite background.
3. In order to enable scrolling, we have to add two identical background sprite nodes one after the other.
4. In the function, run a `for` loop for two background nodes specifying the position, a name (tag), and then adding to `SKMyScene`.
5. Hence, the `initalizingScrollingBackground` function looks like this:

```
- (void)initalizingScrollingBackground
{
    for (int index = 0; index < 2; index++)
    {
        SKSpriteNode *spaceBGNode =
        [SKSpriteNode spriteNodeWithImageNamed:@"SpaceBackground.
png"];
        {
            spaceBGNode.position =
            CGPointMake(index * spaceBGNode.size.width, 0);
            spaceBGNode.anchorPoint = CGPointZero;
            spaceBGNode.name = @"SpaceBG";

            [self addChild:spaceBGNode];
        }
    }
}
```

6. Add this method into the `init` method and also move the code to add a spaceship into a different method called `addSpaceship`.

 In game programming, the layers of objects are made by the sequence they are added in. So for the preceding example, the Spaceship should be added after `SpaceBackground` giving an appearance that the ship is above the background.

The sequence of the views presented on the screen can be changed by altering their *z* coordinate; the view having highest *z* coordinate will always be on the top. This means we can explicitly define which layer we want to keep on top and which we want to keep at the bottom, which is explained in the following steps:

1. The initial background is added but it's not scrolling. This could be accomplished by the update method discussed in the *Anatomy of game projects* recipe.

2. For this, some math is required to implement this functionality. Build some inline functions and constants to be used for infinitely moving the background. This is the code needed:

```
static const float SPACE_BG_VELOCITY = 100.0;
static inline CGPoint CGPointAdd(const CGPoint a, const CGPoint b)
{
    return CGPointMake(a.x + b.x, a.y + b.y);
}
static inline CGPoint CGPointMultiplyScalar(const CGPoint a, const CGFloat b)
{
    return CGPointMake(a.x * b, a.y * b);
}
```

3. Just add these line of code preceding to the implementation of `FSMyScene`.

4. Now the real way to do it is, in the update method, iterate all nodes added in `FSMyScene`, identify the `SpaceBackground` node by its name assigned in the initialization function, and adjust its position to enable infinite scrolling. Do all of this in a function named `moveSpaceBackground`.

```
- (void)moveSpaceBackground
{
    [self enumerateChildNodesWithName:@"SpaceBG"
                           usingBlock: ^(SKNode *node, BOOL *stop)
        {
            SKSpriteNode * spaceBGNode = (SKSpriteNode *) node;

            CGPoint bgVelocity = CGPointMake(-SPACE_BG_VELOCITY, 0);
```

```
        CGPoint amtToMove = CGPointMultiplyScalar(bgVelocity,se
lf.diffTime);

        spaceBGNode.position = CGPointAdd(spaceBGNode.position,
amtToMove);

        //Checks if Background node is completely scrolled of the
screen, if yes then put it at the end of the other node

        if (spaceBGNode.position.x <= -spaceBGNode.size.width)
        {
            spaceBGNode.position =
            CGPointMake(spaceBGNode.position.x + spaceBGNode.
size.width*2,
                    spaceBGNode.position.y);
        }
    }];
}
```

5. Lastly, call this method every time in the update method of the game scene. After that, you should see the spaceship flying in the sky with some nice white clouds.

How it works...

Implementation of infinite scrolling is divided into three parts. We need to follow the following steps to accomplish infinite scrolling for our game:

▸ Initializing the SpaceBackground: Two space backgrounds are added one after the other so that they are moved at the same time to give a feel of an infinite scrolling background.

▸ SpaceBackground move code: Here, a block method of SKScene is used to iterate all nodes of the scene.

```
[self enumerateChildNodesWithName:@"SpaceBG"
                            usingBlock: ^(SKNode *node, BOOL *stop)
    {

    }];
```

In this iteration, the SpaceBGNode is identified by its name so that its position can be updated.

```
SKSpriteNode * spaceBGNode = (SKSpriteNode *) node;
```

The amount of distance to be moved is calculated using the `CGPointMultiplyScalar` inline function that is fed with the constant value `SPACE_BG_VELOCITY` and the difference of time obtained from the update method in each frame.

```
CGPoint bgVelocity = CGPointMake(-SPACE_BG_VELOCITY, 0);
CGPoint amtToMove =
    CGPointMultiplyScalar(bgVelocity,self.diffTime);
```

After that, the calculated distance is added in the current position of SpaceBGNode.

```
spaceBGNode.position = CGPointAdd(spaceBGNode.position,
    amtToMove);
```

The last but the most important step to enable scrolling, is to set the position of SpaceBGNode to the right edge of the screen whenever it reaches the left edge of the screen.

```
if (spaceBGNode.position.x <= -spaceBGNode.size.width)
{
    spaceBGNode.position =
            CGPointMake(spaceBGNode.position.x + spaceBGNode.size.
width*2,
                    spaceBGNode.position.y);
}
```

The next task is to update each frame to move it infinitely over the scene. Now to make it move regularly, the `moveSpaceBackground` method is called in the update method of `FSMyScene` in each frame.

```
- (void)update:(CFTimeInterval)currentTime
{
    /* Called before each frame is rendered */
    self.diffTime = currentTime - self.lastUpdatedTime;

    self.lastUpdatedTime = currentTime;

    [self moveSpaceBackground];
}
```

The update loop will be executed in every frame. So to move our background in every step, we have called the `moveSpaceBackground` method inside the update loop. Using this approach of infinite scrolling, we can also implement parallax gaming, which is very common nowadays. In parallax scrolling game, there will be background and player in separate layers and they will be moving at the same time at different speeds. This will give the user a perception of some real-time movement of the player against the background.

Moving characters

The most interesting part is making some character live, which we are going to do in this part. We will be detecting a touch on the screen and then applying some cool actions on some nodes, that is, moving the spaceship up and down.

Getting ready

To make the character move, you should know the basic actions (SKAction) that can be applied on nodes (SKNode).

How to do it...

Now, as we have got the spaceship moving in infinite space, it's time to add some more fun in the game. We will now be adding the up-down motion to our spaceship. Perform the following steps to add the up-down motion to the spaceship:

1. Declare some properties for actions, namely up and down actions in FSMyScene.

   ```
   @property (nonatomic, strong) SKAction*         moveUpAction;
   @property (nonatomic, strong) SKAction*         moveDownAction;
   ```

2. Define the distance and over what time the spaceship will move on a screen touch just above the implementation of FSMyScene.

   ```
   static const float SPACE_BG_ONE_TIME_MOVE_DISTANCE = 30.0;
   static const float SPACE_BG_ONE_TIME_MOVE_TIME = 0.2;
   ```

3. Assign up and down actions to their respective properties in the addSpaceShip method as added in the starter kit project.

   ```
   self.moveUpAction = [SKAction moveByX:0
                          y:SPACE_BG_ONE_TIME_MOVE_DISTANCE
                          duration:SPACE_BG_ONE_TIME_MOVE_TIME];
   self.moveDownAction = [SKAction moveByX:0
                           y:-SPACE_BG_ONE_TIME_MOVE_DISTANCE
                           duration:SPACE_BG_ONE_TIME_MOVE_TIME];
   ```

4. Now implement a delegate method of `UIResponder`, which detects touches and UI Events. The method inputs touches as `NSSet` from which any touch is taken and converted into a position with respect to the scene on which the touch event occurred.

```
- (void)touchesBegan:(NSSet *)touches withEvent:(UIEvent *)event
{
    UITouch *touch = [touches anyObject];

    CGPoint touchLocation = [touch locationInNode:self.scene];
}
```

Now, using this `touchLocation` and `SpaceShip` position, the code decides when to apply an up or a down action on the spaceship. It also checks the bounds of the screen so that the spaceship does not move outside the screen.

This is what the code looks like:

```
- (void)touchesBegan:(NSSet *)touches withEvent:(UIEvent *)event
{
    UITouch *touch = [touches anyObject];

    CGPoint touchLocation = [touch locationInNode:self.scene];

    CGPoint spaceShipPosition = self.spaceShipSprite.position;
    CGFloat minYLimitToMove = SPACE_BG_ONE_TIME_MOVE_DISTANCE;
    CGFloat maxYLimitToMove =
    self.frame.size.height - SPACE_BG_ONE_TIME_MOVE_DISTANCE;
    if(touchLocation.y > spaceShipPosition.y)
    {
        if (spaceShipPosition.y < maxYLimitToMove)
        {
            [self.spaceShipSprite runAction:self.moveUpAction];
        }
    }
    else
    {
        if (spaceShipPosition.y > minYLimitToMove)
        {
            [self.spaceShipSprite runAction:self.moveDownAction];
        }
    }
}
```

How it works...

Whenever the user taps on the screen, a delegate method of `UIResponder` is called.

```
- (void)touchesBegan:(NSSet *)touches withEvent:(UIEvent *)event
{
}
```

In this method, the position of the touch is converted into local coordinates of `SKScene`. Based on the location detected, it is compared to the spaceship location and up or down action is applied on it.

Finally, as an outcome of this chapter, you have a small fundamental game with an environment of blue sky with white clouds moving with an infinite scroll and a spaceship flying up and down in a linear motion.

This is what the game looks like now:

There's more...

There can be a lot of other animation that can be used to animate the ship. All the previously discussed animation actions can be used over the ship. A consolidated result of these actions can be used in several places in the games. In the next chapter, we will learn about the animations in more detail and about effects.

See also

The chapter has already given you insights about the animation that can be done on sprites and nodes. You can also visit Apple's developer documentation for more details. You have learned enough in the chapter to get you started with the animation and actions on the sprites.

3
Animations and Texture

In *Chapter 2*, *SpriteKit*, you learned about the basic structure of SpriteKit and its building blocks such as scenes, nodes, sprites, and so on. We got a flying spaceship in the sky by touching the screen, and now in this chapter we will be moving to a fully featured game play for the user.

You will learn about how the content of sprites are changed using animations, how textures (which store sprite data) are used to render the sprites, how to create a large image for all game assets using the texture atlas, some character (spaceship) animations, and last but the most beautiful will be creating a parallax background for the game full of animations.

In this chapter, we will be focusing on the following recipes:

- ▸ Animating your textures
- ▸ Creating a texture atlas
- ▸ Adding animations using a texture atlas
- ▸ Collision detection
- ▸ Parallax background

Introduction

Adding animations into our games using SpriteKit is an easy task, as we did in the previous chapter, where we added some `SKAction` functions to get the spaceship to move. These were the animations related to their movement, orientations, and somewhat related to their transformations. However, now the animation that we are going to talk about is the content change of a sprite. Animations will be animating multiple images (that is, frames) of the same sprite multiple times per second, giving a feel of being alive for the sprite. This is somewhat similar to the way we capture the videos, it's just a sequence of the snapshots per second. These types of animations need a lot of images to be accomplished thereby increasing the memory size for these textures. The texture is represented by a `SKTexture` object created and attached with the sprite. Texture object automatically loads the sprite data (called Texture data) whenever it is visible and is used to render the sprite in the respective scene. And when the sprite is removed or not visible in the scene, it deletes the texture data, and as a result automatic memory management is simplified.

Technically, all of this means that sprites have display frames, which have different textures that change by a fixed delay between each frame. And everything we are going to do in the starter and solution kit will be continued from where we left in the previous chapter.

Animating your textures

In this recipe, we will look at how textures are created and attached to sprites. We will also do some content change (that is, frame changing animations) with the help of textures.

Getting ready

To get started with textures to be animated, we should know about scenes, nodes, and sprites. As sprites are created with an image and are added on scene, which occupies more memory, textures should be a solution to this problem.

How to do it...

As the images are stored in `App Bundle`, the simplest way to create a sprite with texture is to create the texture first and then the sprite using the same texture. At runtime, the images are loaded from the app bundle to become the texture and then the visible entity called sprite.

So in the previous chapter, we created the sprite using its class method:

```
self.spaceShipSprite =
  [SKSpriteNode spriteNodeWithImageNamed:@"Spaceship.png"];
```

Now, we will continue with the final solution kit created in the previous chapter thereby using the SKTexture object to create the sprite in place of the preceding method used to create a sprite:

1. Create the SKTexture object with the same image of the spaceship:

    ```
    SKTexture* spaceShipTexture =
        [SKTexture textureWithImageNamed:@"Spaceship.png"];
    ```

2. Use the preceding texture object to create the SKSpriteNode object:

    ```
    self.spaceShipSprite =
        [SKSpriteNode spriteNodeWithTexture:spaceShipTexture];
    ```

3. Then, follow the same steps to add the sprite to the FSMyScene file making the snippet look like this:

```
SKTexture* spaceShipTexture = [SKTexture textureWithImageNamed:@"Spaceship.png"];

self.spaceShipSprite = [SKSpriteNode spriteNodeWithTexture:spaceShipTexture];

self.spaceShipSprite.position = CGPointMake(self.spaceShipSprite.size.width,
                                            self.frame.size.height/2);

[self addChild:self.spaceShipSprite];
```

Now, as memory management is more optimized with texture, we can start with the animations to change the frames of a sprite by a fixed time. For that, we will be showing a prop in the environment, which is a coin rotating 360 degrees horizontally.

The following are the steps involved to make a coin look like it is rotating 360 degrees horizontally:

1. First of all, copy all the images (that is, frames) of the coin as provided in the Project_Resources folder with the kit. There are total six images of coins, each rotated at an angle horizontally.

2. Add a method to FSMyScene called addCoin in which we create a sprite for the coin with the initial image to be displayed on the sky background using texture (Coin1.png).

    ```
    SKTexture* coinInitialTexture =
        [SKTexture textureWithImageNamed:@"Coin1.png"];
    SKSpriteNode* coinSprite =
        [SKSpriteNode
          spriteNodeWithTexture:coinInitialTexture];
    ```

3. To show the coin on the screen, specify its position; as of now, the position is set to the center of the screen, and then add it to the `FSMyScene`.

```
coinSprite.position = CGPointMake(self.frame.size.width/2,
   self.frame.size.height/2);
[self addChild:coinSprite];
```

4. Similarly, create textures for the remaining frames of the coin to add frame animations.

```
SKTexture* coin2Texture = [SKTexture
   textureWithImageNamed:@"Coin2.png"];
SKTexture* coin3Texture = [SKTexture
   textureWithImageNamed:@"Coin3.png"];
SKTexture* coin4Texture = [SKTexture
   textureWithImageNamed:@"Coin4.png"];
SKTexture* coin5Texture = [SKTexture
   textureWithImageNamed:@"Coin5.png"];
SKTexture* coin6Texture = [SKTexture
   textureWithImageNamed:@"Coin6.png"];
```

Combining all coin textures creates an array of texture.

```
NSArray *coinAnimationTextures =
   @[coinInitialTexture,coin2Texture,coin3Texture,
      coin4Texture,coin5Texture,coin6Texture];
```

5. Create a `SKAction` class for `coinAnimation` using a class method of `SKAction` and run the action on the coin sprite added on `FSMyScene`.

```
SKAction *coinAnimation = [SKAction
   animateWithTextures:
      coinAnimationTexturestimePerFrame:0.2];
[coinSprite runAction:coinAnimation];
```

Adding all these lines of code makes our addCoin method:

```objc
- (void)addCoin
{
    SKTexture* coinInitialTexture = [SKTexture textureWithImageNamed:@"Coin1.png"];

    SKSpriteNode* coinSprite = [SKSpriteNode spriteNodeWithTexture:coinInitialTexture];

    coinSprite.position = CGPointMake(self.frame.size.width/2,
                                      self.frame.size.height/2);

    [self addChild:coinSprite];

    SKTexture* coin2Texture = [SKTexture textureWithImageNamed:@"Coin2.png"];
    SKTexture* coin3Texture = [SKTexture textureWithImageNamed:@"Coin3.png"];
    SKTexture* coin4Texture = [SKTexture textureWithImageNamed:@"Coin4.png"];
    SKTexture* coin5Texture = [SKTexture textureWithImageNamed:@"Coin5.png"];
    SKTexture* coin6Texture = [SKTexture textureWithImageNamed:@"Coin6.png"];

    NSArray *coinAnimationTextures =
    @[coinInitialTexture,coin2Texture,coin3Texture,coin4Texture,
      coin5Texture,coin6Texture,coinInitialTexture];

    SKAction *coinAnimation = [SKAction animateWithTextures:coinAnimationTextures
                                        timePerFrame:0.2];
    [coinSprite runAction:coinAnimation];
}
```

How it works...

When we create a texture object using SKTexture, as we did in the preceding section, the texture stores the image (that is, frame) data into it which is further forwarded to create a sprite. This helps in memory management, because when the sprites are removed, the data associated with them (that is, texture) is also removed thereby releasing the memory.

```objc
SKTexture* spaceShipTexture = [SKTexture
    textureWithImageNamed:@"Spaceship.png"];

self.spaceShipSprite = [SKSpriteNode
    spriteNodeWithTexture:spaceShipTexture];
```

Similarly, the coin is also added using texture in the center of the screen with its initial frame, which looks like this:

Now we will see how animations of frames work using a number of textures. We have just created some textures using some coin images, which are visually designed in increasing order of horizontal rotation angle. So an array in the same order of textures is created.

```
NSArray *coinAnimationTextures =
    @[coinInitialTexture,coin2Texture,coin3Texture,coin4Texture,
        coin5Texture,coin6Texture];
```

Using a class method of SKAction, the coin animation textures array is given as an input with a frame delay of 0.2 seconds.

```
SKAction *coinAnimation = [SKAction
    animateWithTextures:coinAnimationTexturestimePerFrame:0.2];


[coinSprite runAction:coinAnimation];
```

The preceding function takes the textures and shows them with a delay of 0.2 seconds in the order the textures are given.

Hence, the overall addCoin method with the animation code written gives a feel that a coin has rotated horizontally once in the center of the screen, and this is what the scene looks like:

Creating a texture atlas

The texture atlas is a way of combining all the app assets (that is, images) into one or more larger images to improve the performance of the app so that the app can draw multiple images in a single draw call of the scene that is rendered. For example, if we have more than one image file to be loaded in the sprite, SpriteKit will perform one drawing call for each sprite. However, if we combine all the required images in one image file, then SpriteKit can render all the sprites in one draw call that uses very less memory to do so. It is recommended to create an atlas of all the required images for any game project.

Xcode has the capability of building texture atlases for your collection of images to make it a larger image, thereby improving the performance. While creating texture atlases, there should be a balance of too many or very few textures, so that the memory load doesn't increase.

Getting ready

To create a texture atlas, we should be aware of what sprites and textures are, most importantly how the sprite is created using textures. We will take the *Animating your textures* recipe as a reference to start this. In this recipe, we will be learning how to create a texture atlas for a collection of images that are coin images used for animation and the spaceship.

How to do it...

The following are the steps to be performed for creating a texture atlas for a collection of images:

1. Create a system folder where your project is stored in the starter project of `FlyingSpaceship`.

 It should not be an Xcode group folder; it has to be a system folder.

2. In that folder, add all images of coins and the image of the spaceship added previously in the app bundle.

3. Right-click on the `Resources` folder and click on **Add Files to "FlyingSpaceship"**.

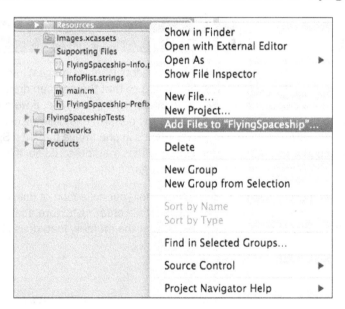

4. A finder view is opened. From there, select `FSGame.atlas` and click on the **Add** button. Whenever we build the project, the compiler looks for folders with a naming convention such as `name.atlas`. Hence, the folders are identified and all the images in that folder are combined to form one or more large images.

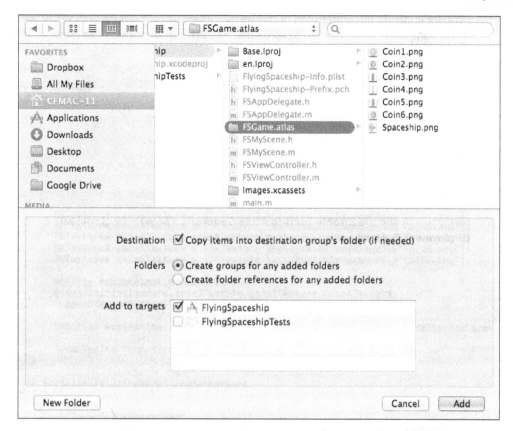

5. After adding the `FSGame.atlas` file to the project, the `Resources` folder looks like this:

6. Now, for enabling the generation of the Texture Atlas, go to the build settings of the project and search for type `Spritekit`; the search results will look like this:

7. Now you can see the **Enable Texture Atlas Generation** field in the **SpriteKit Deployment Options** section. Set that bool to **Yes**.

As a result, whenever we build the project, the compiler generates a property list to access the images of the texture atlas by its name, which we have given to the folder.

How it works...

After the creation of the texture atlas, the most important part is how we will be able to access images from the texture atlas. It's done by enabling the bool **Enable Texture Atlas Generation**. After this, whenever we build the project, the compiler looks for folders with a naming convention such as `name.atlas`. Hence, the folders are identified and all the images in that folder are combined to form one or more large images.

Here, Xcode generates a `.plist` file after setting the bool. After that, the texture atlas name is used to get the texture atlas in the code and from there we can get any image, which is put in that folder that is, texture atlas.

There's more...

Whenever we create a texture atlas, there is always a trade-off between using too many textures or few images. When using few images SpriteKit still needs to make many drawing calls to render each frame. And for many textures, the images in quantity may increase the texture data thereby leading to a load on the memory. So it's up to us how we want to go; we can switch between both the alternatives with relative ease. Hence, different configurations can be tried out to have the best performance.

Adding animations using a texture atlas

We have already learned about animations even before learning how to use textures for loading images from App Bundle. As we have a texture atlas (that is, a larger combined image), we will be loading the images by that texture atlas. All sprites added in the FSMyScene file are loaded by the images from the App Bundle, so now we will be loading all the images by the texture atlas in the sprite. Lastly, some animations will be applied to them using the texture atlas to load the images.

Getting ready

Before starting with the animations using a texture atlas to load images, we should know the process of creating a texture atlas using a combination of images and doing some animations of changing frame after a fixed delay. So here we will be doing the same animation of coin rotation we did earlier, but now using a texture atlas. This recipe will be called *Adding animations using a texture atlas*. After that we will animate a bunch of coins from one end to another (right to left) in the FSMyScene in a random fashion giving a feel that coins are just moving in the sky.

How to do it...

First of all, we will be replacing the creation of textures using the image by the texture atlas images in App Bundle. Perform the following steps:

1. Create an object of SKTextureAtlas by specifying its name that is, FSGame (name of the texture atlas).

   ```
   SKTextureAtlas *textureAtlas =
     [SKTextureAtlas atlasNamed:@"FSGame"];
   ```

    The images previously added to the project bundle should be removed to avoid redundancy.

   ```
   SKTexture* spaceShipTexture =
     [SKTexture textureWithImageNamed:@"Spaceship.png"];
   ```

2. Now create the texture using a texture atlas object by passing the spaceship image that has to be set to the sprite.

```
SKTexture* spaceShipTexture =
    [textureAtlas textureNamed:@"Spaceship.png"];
```

3. In the addCoin method of FSMyScene, use the preceding process to create the textures using the textureAtlas object for all coin textures.

```
SKTextureAtlas *textureAtlas =
    [SKTextureAtlas atlasNamed:@"FSGame"];

SKTexture* coinInitialTexture =
    [textureAtlas textureNamed:@"Coin1.png"];

SKTexture* coin2Texture =
    [textureAtlas textureNamed:@"Coin2.png"];
SKTexture* coin3Texture =
    [textureAtlas textureNamed:@"Coin3.png"];
SKTexture* coin4Texture =
    [textureAtlas textureNamed:@"Coin4.png"];
SKTexture* coin5Texture =
    [textureAtlas textureNamed:@"Coin5.png"];
SKTexture* coin6Texture =
    [textureAtlas textureNamed:@"Coin6.png"];
```

4. Once all the textures are created, use the same code of addCoin to add and animate the coin.

5. Let's make the coin animation more live and natural. Feed the action formed for animating the texture with a fixed delay to another SKAction making it repeat forever giving a feel of continuous rotation of coin (never ending).

```
SKAction *rotateAction =
    [SKAction animateWithTextures:coinAnimationTextures
        timePerFrame:0.2];

SKAction *coinRepeatForeverAnimation =
    [SKAction repeatActionForever:rotateAction];

[coinSprite runAction:coinRepeatForeverAnimation];
```

6. After a little tweaking, remove the last texture from the array so that when the repeatForever action is going to run, the first image will appear after the last image, so there is no need for the last texture.

```
NSArray *coinAnimationTextures =
    @[coinInitialTexture,coin2Texture,coin3Texture,
        coin4Texture,coin5Texture,coin6Texture];
```

Now our forever rotating coin is built and can be used either as a prop or collectables in our game.

These are the steps to make the coins collectables:

1. For making a coin move from the left end to the right end of the screen, we have to calculate the initial and final positions.

    ```
    CGFloat coinInitialPositionX =
        self.frame.size.width + coinSprite.size.width/2;
    CGFloat coinInitialPositionY = arc4random() % 320;
    CGPoint coinInitialPosition =
        CGPointMake(coinInitialPositionX, oinInitialPositionY);

    CGFloat coinFinalPositionX = -coinSprite.size.width/2;
    CGFloat coinFinalPositionY = coinInitialPositionY;
    CGPoint coinFinalPosition =
        CGPointMake(coinFinalPositionX, coinFinalPositionY);
    ```

2. After that, set the initial position as the coin sprite position.

    ```
    coinSprite.position = coinInitialPosition;
    ```

3. The initial position of the coin is set and now we have to animate the coin from the initial position to the final position. This can be done by adding a move SKAction to the coin sprite specifying its final destination.

    ```
    SKAction *coinMoveAnimation =
        [SKAction moveTo:coinFinalPosition duration:5.0];

    [coinSprite runAction:coinMoveAnimation];
    ```

Finally, our addCoin method has been fully prepared for the game. For moving the coins as collectables, perform the following steps:

1. For making these coins move as collectables in the scene, a little bit of refactoring is required in the update method. Update the diffTime and lastUpdatedTime as shown in the following code:

    ```
    if (self.lastUpdatedTime)
    {
        self.diffTime = currentTime - self.lastUpdatedTime;
    }
    else
    {
        self.diffTime = 0;
    }

    self.lastUpdatedTime = currentTime;
    ```

2. Now using `currentTime`, create a timer kind of functionality by declaring a property called `lastCoinAdded` in the private interface of FSMyScene.

    ```
    @property (nonatomic, assign) NSTimeInterval lastCoinAdded;
    ```

3. So this is the timer added in the update method and the diff of `currentTime` and `lastCoinAdded` is checked by 1. Hence, after every 1.0 second, a coin will be added with animation moving from left to right on the screen.

    ```
    if( currentTime - self.lastCoinAdded > 1)
    {
        self.lastCoinAdded = currentTime + 1;

        [self addCoin];
    }
    ```

Finally, our update method is ready to animate multiple coins after a set delay.

How it works...

Before we were creating the sprite using images from `App Bundle`, but now we will be using texture atlas to get the images and passing to the sprites. The preceding texture atlas named `FSGame.atlas` holds multiple images of coins and spaceship in it. The internal code loads the frames and stores them in an array.

▶ SpriteKit first searches for the image file, if not found it searches inside the texture atlases build into the app bundle. If we want to work explicitly with texture atlases, use the `SKTextureAtlas` class. It fetches the texture atlas by specifying its name:

```
SKTextureAtlas *textureAtlas = [SKTextureAtlas
    atlasNamed:@"FSGame"];
```

▶ Then we can use the atlas object to get the required image for creation of sprites.

```
SKTexture* spaceShipTexture = [textureAtlas
    textureNamed:@"Spaceship.png"];
```

Now we will understand how the coins are converted into collectables. For moving the coins, its initial and final positions are to be decided.

▶ The initial position in *x* dimensions, is fixed to the width of the frame plus half of its coin so that it is added outside the screen and *y* dimensions are randomly chosen from 0 to 320 using the `arc4random()` function.

```
CGFloat coinInitialPositionX =
    self.frame.size.width + coinSprite.size.width/2;
CGFloat coinInitialPositionY = arc4random() % 320;
CGPoint coinInitialPosition =
    CGPointMake(coinInitialPositionX,
        coinInitialPositionY);
```

▶ For the final position, the x dimension is set to negative of half of its own width and the y dimension is the same as the initial position x.

```
CGFloat coinFinalPositionX = -coinSprite.size.width/2;
CGFloat coinFinalPositionY = coinInitialPositionY;
CGPoint coinFinalPosition =
    CGPointMake(coinFinalPositionX, coinFinalPositionY);
```

▶ Now the collectable is ready to be added to the scene. But for multiple coins to be added moving left to right on the scene, a timer has to be implemented. The timer looks like this:

```
if( currentTime - self.lastCoinAdded > 1)
{
    self.lastCoinAdded = currentTime + 1;

    [self addCoin];
}
```

After all these implementations, multiple coins are seen moving from left to right as shown in the following screenshot:

Collision detection

We have our game integrated with collectables. Let's see how the spaceship will collect these collectables that is, coins. In character animation, we will be doing the animations on the spaceship and the coins when they collide with each other.

Getting ready

Before moving on to the complex animations to be applied on the entities of the scene, the understanding of actions (that is, SKAction) and update function of scene (SKScene) has to be there. This is so that during updation we can detect the collision between the coin and the spaceship and do some animations on both of them.

How to do it...

The following are the steps involved in detecting the collision and animating both the entities (coin and spaceship):

1. Write an detectSpaceShipCollisionWithCoins method in which we will enumerate the coin objects.

    ```
    - (void)detectSpaceShipCollisionWithCoins
    {
    ```

```
[self enumerateChildNodesWithName:@"Coin"
                            usingBlock: ^(SKNode *node, BOOL *stop)
    {
    }];
}
```

2. In that enumeration, determine that the frame of the spaceship and the frame of any coin intersects with the help of CGRectIntersectsRect().

```
[self enumerateChildNodesWithName:@"Coin"
  usingBlock: ^(SKNode *node,
    BOOL *stop)
    {
        if (CGRectIntersectsRect(self.spaceShipSprite.frame,
  node.frame))
        {

        }
    }];
```

3. When a collision is detected, inform the scene that a coin has collided with the spaceship by a function called spaceShipCollidedWithCoin.

```
[self spaceShipCollidedWithCoin:node];
```

After all this, the detectSpaceShipCollisionWithCoins method looks like this:

```
- (void)detectSpaceShipCollisionWithCoins
{
    [self enumerateChildNodesWithName:@"Coin"
                            usingBlock: ^(SKNode *node, BOOL *stop)
    {
        if (CGRectIntersectsRect(self.spaceShipSprite.frame, node.frame))
        {
            [self spaceShipCollidedWithCoin:node];
        }
    }];

}
```

1. After detecting the collision, the spaceShipCollidedWithCoin function is invoked, which calls two other functions that implement animation methods for the spaceship and coin that have collided. The definition of this method looks like this:

```
- (void)spaceShipCollidedWithCoin: (SKNode*)coinNode
{
    [self runSpaceshipCollectingAnimation];

    [self runCollectedAnimationForCoin:coinNode];
}
```

2. The animation written for the spaceship is as if it is taking the coin into itself. There are two actions created for `scaleUp` and `scaleDown` with a scale factor 1.4 and 1.0 respectively to be played for 0.2 each.

```
- (void) runSpaceshipCollectingAnimation
{
  SKAction* scaleUp = [SKAction scaleTo:1.4
    duration:0.2];

  SKAction* scaleDown = [SKAction scaleTo:1.0
    duration:0.2];
}
```

3. After that, these two animation arrays are formed to be used for creating a sequence action.

```
NSArray* scaleSequenceAnimations =
  [NSArray arrayWithObjects:scaleUp, scaleDown, nil];

SKAction* spaceShipCollectingAnimation = [SKAction
  sequence:scaleSequenceAnimations];
```

Lastly the sequence action formed runs on the spaceship.

```
[self.spaceShipSprite
  runAction:spaceShipCollectingAnimation];
```

4. For the coin, the animation should be as if it is disappearing as it is taken by the spaceship. Thus, two core animations `fadeOut` and `scaleDown` are created with a 0.2 scale factor having a time interval of 0.4 each, forming an array of animations.

```
- (void) runCollectedAnimationForCoin: (SKNode*) coinNode
{
    SKAction* coinFadeOutAnimation =
      [SKAction fadeOutWithDuration:0.4];

    SKAction* scaleDownAnimation =
      [SKAction scaleTo:0.2 duration:0.4];

    NSArray* coinAnimations =
      [NSArray arrayWithObjects:coinFadeOutAnimation,
        scaleDownAnimation, nil];
}
```

5. Using these animations, a group animation is formed.

```
SKAction* coinGroupAnimation = [SKAction
  group:coinAnimations];
```

6. As for the coin, when it collides with the spaceship, it has to be removed from the scene when its animation is over. So create an action using the block to remove the coin after the previously created group animation is completed.

```
SKAction* coinAnimationFinishedCallBack =
  [SKAction customActionWithDuration:0.0
    actionBlock:^(SKNode *node,CGFloat elapsedTime)
  {
    [node removeFromParent];
  }];
```

In the preceding code snippet, we are using the removeFromParent function, which is similar to removeFromSuperview in UIKit.

7. As the animations are ready, create the sequence action for it using an array.

```
NSArray* coinAnimationsSequence =
[NSArray arrayWithObjects:coinGroupAnimation,
coinAnimationFinishedCallBack, nil];

SKAction* coinSequenceAnimation =
[SKAction sequence:coinAnimationsSequence];
```

Hence, the coin looks as if it is disappearing when the preceding complex actions run on the coin.

```
[coinNode runAction:coinSequenceAnimation];
```

8. As all the code of the animation and collision detection is done, call the detechSpaceShipCollisionWithCoins method, so that in each frame the collision is detected and the coin is collected by the character of the game (that is, the spaceship).

```
[self detectSpaceShipCollisionWithCoins];
```

How it works...

The most important part of this section is the collision detection. It is done with the help of the CGRectIntersectsRect method in which the coins are enumerated and checked whether their frames intersect the spaceship frame. If they do, then two different animations are played on the coin and spaceship.

```
[self enumerateChildNodesWithName:@"Coin"
  usingBlock: ^(SKNode *node, BOOL *stop)
  {
    if (CGRectIntersectsRect(self.spaceShipSprite.frame,
      node.frame))
    {

    }
  }];
```

When detection happens, the game looks like this:

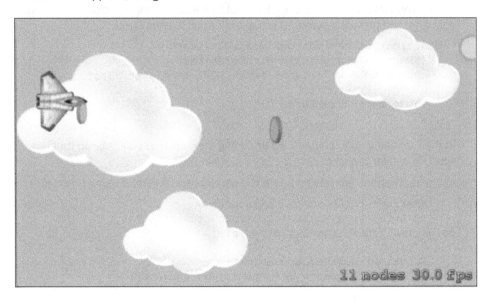

Now we come to animations. The animation of the spaceship is a simple one. Just to give a feel of collecting the coins, `scaleUp` and `scaleDown` animations are used in sequence.

```
SKAction* scaleUp = [SKAction scaleTo:1.4 duration:0.2];

    SKAction* scaleDown = [SKAction scaleTo:1.0 duration:0.2];

NSArray* scaleSequenceAnimations =
    [NSArray arrayWithObjects:scaleUp, scaleDown, nil];

    SKAction* spaceShipCollectingAnimation =
        [SKAction sequence:scaleSequenceAnimations];
```

However, for coins, a complex one with three actions is created, which are as follows:

- ▶ `FadeOutAction` to fade the coin for 0.4 seconds, which appears to be disappearing.

    ```
    SKAction* coinFadeOutAnimation =
        [SKAction fadeOutWithDuration:0.4];
    ```

- ▶ `ScaleDownAction` to scale down the coin to make it shrink into the spaceship in 0.4 seconds.

    ```
    SKAction* scaleDownAnimation =
        [SKAction scaleTo:0.2 duration:0.4];
    ```

▶ A `CallBack` function that is used to remove the coin from the scene when the preceding animations are over.

```
SKAction* coinAnimationFinishedCallBack =
    [SKAction customActionWithDuration:0.0
      actionBlock:^(SKNode *node,CGFloat elapsedTime)
    {
        [node removeFromParent];
    }];
```

After creation of all these actions, a group of `fadeOut` and `scaleDown`, a sequence of animation with a sequence of group animation and callback action is created, which is applied on the coin.

Whenever there is a collision, the spaceship scales up and down with the coin fading out as depicted in the following screenshot:

Parallax background

Now our mini game FlyingSpaceship is about to finish. To give the feel of a game environment we will introduce a parallax scrolling background. A parallax scrolling background is composed of multiple background layers (that is, nodes); animating them simultaneously gives a feel of dynamic background. To add some cool flyers to the game we will add two layers of background: the `SpaceBlueSky` and the `SpaceWhiteMist` in the form of nodes.

Getting ready

To start with this cool feature, we should be aware of the scrolling background created in the previous chapter and have a basic knowledge of sprites, nodes, and math. We are going to cook the *Parallax background* recipe in the FlyingSpaceship game.

How to do it...

To create multiple scrolling backgrounds with varying speeds of scrolling, we will be creating a class for it to accomplish the parallax background. The steps involved in creating a class for parallax background named as `FSParallaxNode` are as follows:

1. Create a new file by right clicking on the **FlyingSpaceship** project.

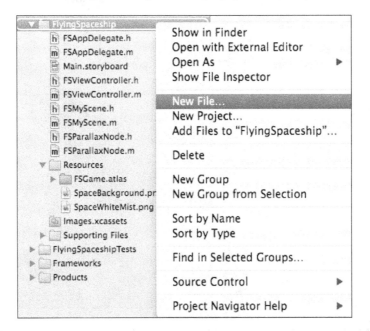

2. Select **Objective-C Class** in the **Cocoa Touch** section.

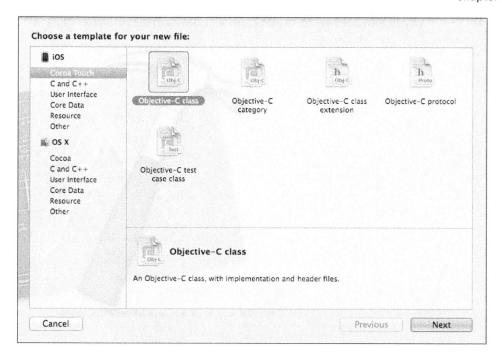

3. Name the class `FSParallaxNode` and click on **Next**.

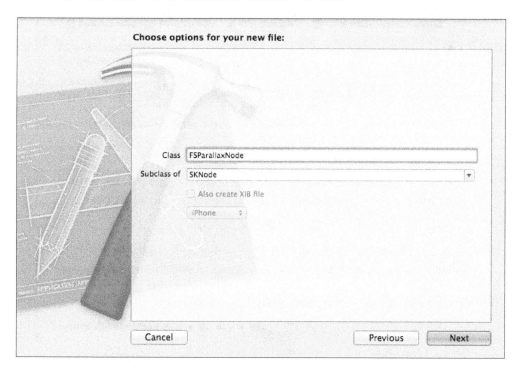

4. Now to create the class, select the `FlyingSpaceship` folder in which it has to be created and click on **Create**.

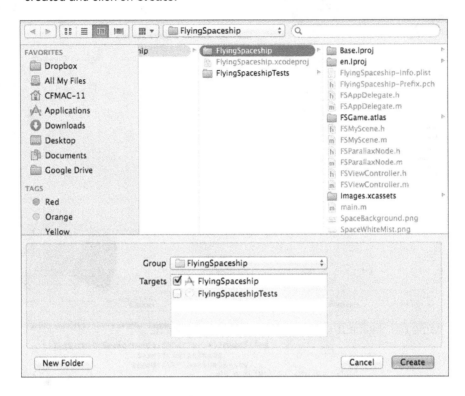

5. Now we need to add two methods in the header of `FSParallaxNode`. Firstly, in the `init` method, we need to specify `imageFiles`, which are the images to be scrolled, the canvas size, and the velocity with which the images will scroll.

    ```
    - (id)initWithBackgrounds:(NSArray *)imageFiles
              size:(CGSize)size
              speed:(CGFloat)velocity;
    ```

    Secondly, an update method called from the update of Scene in which the `FSParallaxNode` method is added so that the scrolling is made infinite.

    ```
    - (void)updateForDeltaTime:(NSTimeInterval)diffTime;
    ```

6. In `FSParallaxNode.m`, declare some properties in its private interface to store all background nodes, counts of backgrounds, and velocity of that parallax node.

    ```
    @property (nonatomic, strong)
      NSMutableArray*  backgrounds;
    @property (nonatomic, assign)
      NSInteger          noOfBackgrounds;
    @property (nonatomic, assign) CGFloat              velocity;
    ```

In definition of the `init` method, first assign all the parameters passed in the function like `velocity`. Now we assign `noOfBackgrounds` using the `imageFiles` count and make an array of backgrounds with a capacity of `noOfBackgrounds`.

```
- (id)initWithBackgrounds:(NSArray *)imageFiles
                size:(CGSize)size
                speed:(CGFloat)velocity
{
    if (self = [super init])
    {
        self.velocity = velocity;
        self.noOfBackgrounds = [imageFiles count];
        self.backgrounds =
        [NSMutableArray
            arrayWithCapacity:self.noOfBackgrounds];

        }];
    }
    return self;
}
```

7. Using the `imageFiles`, enumerate them using the block. In enumeration, add background nodes using the `imageFiles` class, add them to the backgrounds array and on FSParallaxNode.

```
[imageFiles enumerateObjectsUsingBlock:^(id obj,
    NSUInteger idx, BOOL *stop)
{
    SKSpriteNode *backgroundNode =
    [SKSpriteNode spriteNodeWithImageNamed:obj];

    [self.backgrounds addObject:backgroundNode];
    [self addChild:backgroundNode];
}];
```

8. Also, specify the `backgroundNode` size, which is passed in the `init` method, its `anchorPoint` to `CGPointZero`, its position according to the `idx` integer and a name of the node as `background`.

```
backgroundNode.size = size;
backgroundNode.anchorPoint = CGPointZero;
backgroundNode.position = CGPointMake(size.width *
    idx, 0.0);
backgroundNode.name = @"background";
```

After all this, our `init` method is ready as shown in the following screenshot:

```objc
- (id)initWithBackgrounds:(NSArray *)imageFiles
                     size:(CGSize)size
                    speed:(CGFloat)velocity
{
    if (self = [super init])
    {
        self.velocity = velocity;

        self.noOfBackgrounds = [imageFiles count];
        self.backgrounds =
        [NSMutableArray arrayWithCapacity:self.noOfBackgrounds];

        [imageFiles enumerateObjectsUsingBlock:^(id obj, NSUInteger idx, BOOL *stop)
        {
            SKSpriteNode *backgroundNode =
            [SKSpriteNode spriteNodeWithImageNamed:obj];

            backgroundNode.size = size;
            backgroundNode.anchorPoint = CGPointZero;
            backgroundNode.position = CGPointMake(size.width * idx, 0.0);
            backgroundNode.name = @"background";
            [self.backgrounds addObject:backgroundNode];
            [self addChild:backgroundNode];
        }];
    }
    return self;
}
```

Now let's see how these backgrounds added on `FSParallaxNode` are to be scrolled; it will be done by an instance update method.

1. Some `cleanUp` has to be done or in other terms some code movement. Copy the two static methods used in the `FSMyScene` to `FSParallaxNode` class used for some math, remove the initialization of the `SpaceBackground` method and the call of moving background made in the update from `FSMyScene`. Cut the code of the method for moving the background from the `FSMyScene` file and paste in the `updateForDeltaTime` function of `FSParallaxNode`. Now we will be making some tweaks to the method.

2. `SKParallax` node is the parent for all the other nodes of backgrounds added on it. So using the velocity, send in the `init` and `diffTime`, method which will be passed by the `FSMyScene` update methods, we calculate the position of the parent that is, `FSParallax` node.

```objc
- (void)updateForDeltaTime:(NSTimeInterval)diffTime
{
    CGPoint bgVelocity = CGPointMake(self.velocity, 0.0);
    CGPoint amtToMove =
      CGPointMultiplyScalar(bgVelocity,diffTime);
    self.position = CGPointAdd(self.position, amtToMove);
}
```

3. Now enumerate the backgrounds that is, all nodes added to the parent. In this enumeration, find the position of an individual background with respect to the parent node. After this, check whether the position of a background is less than the negative of its width (that is, reached the left end), then change the position of that background to its right end.

```
SKNode *backgroundScreen = self.parent;

[self.backgrounds enumerateObjectsUsingBlock:^(id obj,
    NSUInteger idx, BOOL *stop)
{
    SKSpriteNode *bg = (SKSpriteNode *)obj;

    CGPoint bgScreenPos = [self
        convertPoint:bg.position
                                        toNode:backgroundScreen];

    if (bgScreenPos.x <= -bg.size.width)
    {
        bg.position =
        CGPointMake(bg.position.x + (bg.size.width *
            self.noOfBackgrounds),
                    bg.position.y);
    }
}];
```

4. Finally, our update method is constructed, which provides a functionality of multiple backgrounds scrolling infinitely.

```
- (void)updateForDeltaTime:(NSTimeInterval)diffTime
{
    CGPoint bgVelocity = CGPointMake(self.velocity, 0.0);

    CGPoint amtToMove = CGPointMultiplyScalar(bgVelocity,diffTime);

    self.position = CGPointAdd(self.position, amtToMove);

    SKNode *backgroundScreen = self.parent;

    [self.backgrounds enumerateObjectsUsingBlock:^(id obj, NSUInteger idx, BOOL *stop)
    {
        SKSpriteNode *bg = (SKSpriteNode *)obj;

        CGPoint bgScreenPos = [self convertPoint:bg.position
                                    toNode:backgroundScreen];

        if (bgScreenPos.x <= -bg.size.width)
        {
            bg.position =
            CGPointMake(bg.position.x + (bg.size.width * self.noOfBackgrounds),
                        bg.position.y);
        }
    }];
}
```

As of now, the `FSParallaxNode` class, which provides the functionality of parallax scrolling background is created and it's time to create objects in `FSMyScene` to make a cool environment.

5. We will be adding two background layers BlueSky and WhiteMist, so create two objects for each of them.

```
@property (nonatomic, strong)
  FSParallaxNode*spaceBlueSkyParallaxNode;
@property (nonatomic, strong)
  FSParallaxNode*spaceWhiteMistParallaxNode;
```

Add a method called `addParallaxNodes` and call it in the first line of the `init` method of `FSMyScene`.

```
[self addParallaxNodes];
```

6. For two parallax nodes, we have to add the following two constants for their relative speeds.

```
static const float SPACE_BLUE_SKY_BG_VELOCITY = 20.0;
static const float SPACE_WHITE_MIST_BG_VELOCITY = 100.0;
```

In `addParallaxNodes`, make an array of `blueSkyParallaxBackgroundImages` and create an object of `FSParallax` by passing the size of the scene and velocity at which it is going to scroll.

```
- (void)addParallaxNodes
{
    NSArray *blueSkyParallaxBackgroundNames =
      @[@"SpaceBackground.png", @"SpaceBackground.png",];

    self.spaceBlueSkyParallaxNode =
        [[FSParallaxNode alloc] initWithBackgrounds:blueSkyParallaxB
ackgroundNames
                                              size:self.frame.size
          speed:-SPACE_BLUE_SKY_BG_VELOCITY];
    self.spaceBlueSkyParallaxNode.position =
    CGPointMake(0, 0);

    [self addChild:self.spaceBlueSkyParallaxNode];
}
```

7. Similar to the blue sky background, we have to implement the mist images as well. To add more reality to the game, we will add the `mistParallaxBackgroundImages` function.

```
NSArray *mistParallaxBackgroundNames =
    @[@"SpaceWhiteMist.png", @"SpaceWhiteMist.png",];

self.spaceWhiteMistParallaxNode =
    [[FSParallaxNode alloc] initWithBackgrounds:mistParallaxBack
groundNames
    size:self.frame.size
    speed:-SPACE_WHITE_MIST_BG_VELOCITY];
self.spaceWhiteMistParallaxNode.position =
    CGPointMake(0, 0);

[self addChild:self.spaceWhiteMistParallaxNode];
```

8. Once the nodes have been added to the scene, they need to be updated for scrolling purposes. So call the `updateForDeltaTime` function of `FSMyScene` for both the nodes.

```
if (self.spaceBlueSkyParallaxNode)
{
  [self.spaceBlueSkyParallaxNode
    updateForDeltaTime:self.diffTime];
}

if (self.spaceWhiteMistParallaxNode)
{
  [self.spaceWhiteMistParallaxNode
    updateForDeltaTime:self.diffTime];
}
```

After all these steps, the dynamic environment with a parallax scrolling background is ready for the game.

How it works...

Since we have done the scrolling of background in the previous chapter, it is time we made a separate class for it called `FSParallaxNode`. In this class, multiple backgrounds of the same image are placed and scrolled in each update of the scene. It means that the scrolling is done on the basis of the positions of all background nodes added to `FSParallaxNode`.

Using this `FSParallaxNode`, two objects of it are created: `BlueSkyBackground` and `WhiteMistBackground`. All are added as normal nodes to the scene in the `init` method. For them to scroll, the update method calls the `updateForDeltaTime` function in which the class checks for the position of individual background positions reached at the left end of the screen and changes the position so that it again starts with the right-end side. This whole algorithm makes these individual backgrounds scroll making a full parallax scrolling background. The parallax scrolling background really looks cool as shown in the following screenshot:

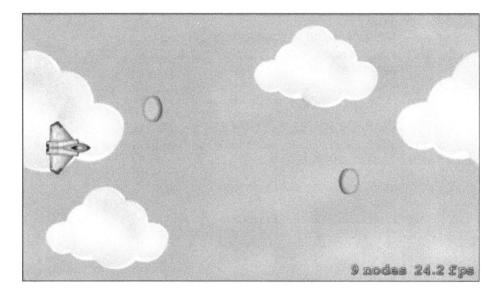

4
Particle System and Game Performance

In this chapter, we will be focusing on the following recipes:

- ▸ Installation of the particle system
- ▸ Using the particle system in games
- ▸ Particle emitter integration
- ▸ Game performance analysis

Introduction

In *Chapter 3*, *Animations and Texture*, we built a full game of collecting coins by a spaceship in a parallax infinite scrolling background. Now we are going to add some flyers to the game by introducing some particle systems, making the effects in the game look more alive and beautiful. Also, we will go through some performance analysis terminologies and tools. In this chapter, a performance-level analysis will be done using some performance and monitoring tools to increase the stability and performance of the game FlyingSpaceship.

Installation of the particle system

A particle system is a collection of separate tiny objects called particles. They are added to scenes and nodes as emitter nodes, which control its position and motion in the scene. These particle systems are used to add some cool effects to the scene, which are highly intense effects such as fire, smoke, explosions, rain, water, and many more.

In this section, we will discuss how the particle system tools are installed and created for specific effect to be added in the game in the upcoming sections.

Getting ready

Before iOS 7, there were open source particle editors used for the creation of particle systems. However, from iOS 7, there is an in-built support to create particle systems using a tool called Particle Editor, which comes integrated with Xcode 5.0. So the prerequisite for this section is having iOS 7 and Xcode 5 to create some cool particle effects.

How to do it

For creation and implementation of particle systems, we will use Particle Editor. This editor doesn't need any installation as it is in-built in the Xcode, which will be used to create particle system files and then can be added as nodes as a part of the implementation.

So we can start with the solution kit of *Chapter 3*, *Animations and Texture*, and continue from there. The following are the steps involved to create a Sprite Kit Particle File:

1. Open Xcode and go to **File | New | File**.

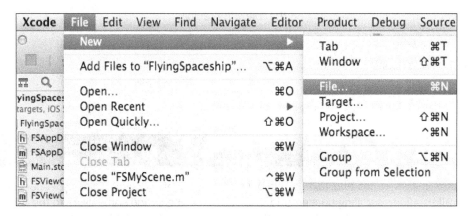

2. Then choose the **Resource** section in **iOS Section**, select **SpriteKit Particle File**, and press **Next**.

3. From a list of particle system templates provided, select the **Fire** particle system template and click on **Next** to create a fire effect, which will be used to depict the thrust of spaceship in the game built so far.

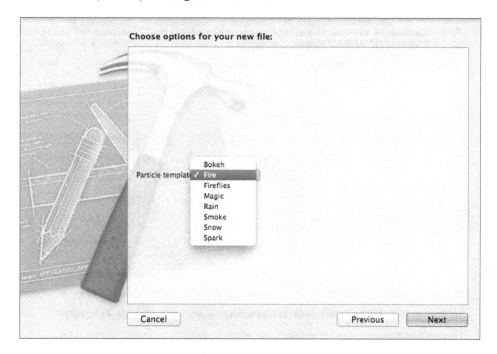

4. Name the file `FireParticle` and click on **Create**.

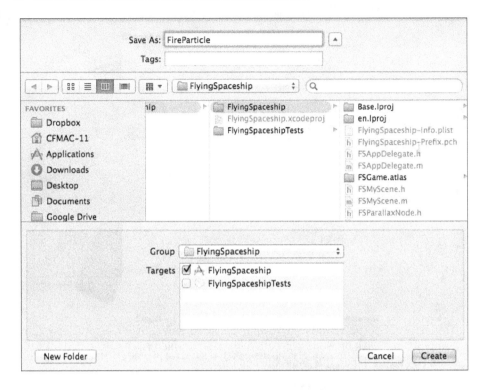

5. As a result, a file named `FireParticle.sks`, which is the particle file, is created and a sample particle image named `spark.png`. `Spark.png` file is autogenerated, which is used as the sks file for the particle system.

6. As shown in the preceding screenshot, when we select the `FireParticle.sks` file, the particle system created in the detail panel with a fire effect looks like this:

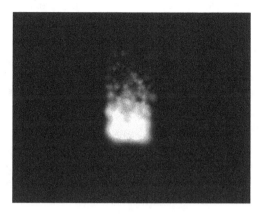

7. Using the right-side inspector panel, we can customize the default particle system as per our need. You can scroll down to explore all the properties in the inspector and hence you can update the settings accordingly.

Now as we have the particle system, we can now directly see the results when some values are changed from this inspector. The implementation also works with a few lines of code without changing any particle system values in the code, just picking the file and adding it to any node or scene.

Let's try out and understand the parameters or the properties of the particle system file.

As we can see from the list in the preceding screenshot, there is a background section that changes the color of the editor background. It is just saved while the game is built, but is not used at runtime.

Below this is a particle texture in which we can choose any image or asset to be used in rendering of the particle system. It should be of lesser dimension and memory as the count of particles will be equal to the count of images used there decreasing the frame rate or performance. Decreasing the frame rate in turn will slow down the game and hence it needs to be used wisely.

Some properties are there to determine the life cycle of the particles such as birthrate, lifetime, and maximum count to be emitted. The particle generation section has **Position Range**, **Angle**, **Speed**, and **Acceleration**.

Apart from all these, it has scale, rotation, and alpha to change the transforms of the particles. Last but not least, the color modifier part in which the blending and color of our particles can be done.

Hence, the project having a `FireParticle` file and explicitly imported image `spark.png` combined called as the particle system is the Starter Kit for this chapter.

How it works

The whole creation of a particle system or a particle file is very easy as discussed earlier. But the effort lies in fine-tuning the properties of the particle emitters, something similar to an anatomy of the particle system we can say. Every particle system has many different properties influencing the look, feel, and behavior of the individual particles and the particle system as one.

So to play with an particle system file the following values are changed accordingly thereby resulting in an effect of particles of the feel we want. The following is a list of properties described with what happens to the particle system if these are changed.

- ▶ **Background**: This is the background of the particle editor. It is just saved at the built time but not reflected during runtime.
- ▶ **Particle Texture**: This is an image or asset texture used as a particle image to render the overall particle system.
- ▶ **ParticleBirthRate**: This is the number of particles generated every second of the system.

- ▶ **Maximum Particles**: This is the number of particles that an emitter has to generate totally; for value zero, infinite stream of particles are generated.

- ▶ **LifeTime**: This is the average lifetime of a particle before it vanishes from the screen; the value is inserted in seconds.

- ▶ **Position Range**: This is the average starting position of a particle.

- ▶ **Emitter Angle**: This is the average initial direction of a particle. It means the angle at which the particle has to be emitted.

- ▶ **Particle Speed and Range**: This is the speed at which the particles should move and there is also a `SpeedRange` parameter; for example, if it is equal to 50 and speed is 100, then the values of speed will vary from 50 (100 - 50) to 150 (100 + 50).

- ▶ **Acceleration**: These are for both *x* (horizontal) and *y* (vertical) accelerations.

- ▶ **Alpha**: This is the initial alpha set for the particles and it also has a range parameter to specify.

- ▶ **Scale**: This is the initial scale factor provided for the particle that is, the size of the particle.

- ▶ **Rotation**: This is the initial rotation of a particle.

- ▶ **Color Blend**: In this whole section, some blend modes are provided by specifying the average initial color of the particle.

There's more

After the tour of the installation and understanding of the particle editor, there are many tweaks to be done with the editor in different particle systems to produce something alive and the cool effect of particles.

In the upcoming section, we will play with the values of the `FireParticle` file to build a thrust of spaceship, which in future will be added at the back of it in the space environment of the game.

See also

For better understanding and to learn more about the particle editor of Xcode and tweaking the values of the particle file, you can visit the following link:

```
https://developer.apple.com/library/ios/documentation/IDEs/
Conceptual/xcode_guide-particle_emitter/Introduction/Introduction.
html
```

Using the particle system in games

Now as a complete tour of particle editor is over, we can have a usage of the particle emitters. We will build some stuff for our game that is, the thrust of spaceship using the same `FireParticle` file and a collision effect when the coin is picked by the spaceship with a default template of smoke.

In this section, editing of the particle file using the particle editor of Xcode will be done to produce a game particle effect such as the thrust of spaceship and a new particle file will be formed named `SmokeParticle` for the collision effect between the coin and spaceship. Also, we will discuss and understand some initial code-level classes.

Getting ready

We should have hands on the particle editor of Xcode with changing values of any particle file and creating some good particle systems that could be used at some places in the game. As the basic elements of particle editor are covered in the previous section, now we will be changing some values of the `FireParticle` file and build some more particle systems.

How to do it

Let's start with the files related to the particle system created and change its property values. There are two files created when building a particle system:

- An sks file, which is the particle file, is used to create an `SKEmitterNode` object to be added on any node or scene.
- A default file called `spark.png` is imported, which is used to specify a particle image in the particle editor for a particular sks file. It can be any image imported externally.

Since the whole process of creating a particle file is clear, we will go further with tweaking some of the properties of the `FireParticle` file to make a thrust of the spaceship.

1. First of all, as the spaceship is headed towards the right side of the screen, we have to make a thrust coming from right to left. In the `FireParticle` file, the default value of the angle is around 89 degrees; change this to 180 to make it look right to left.

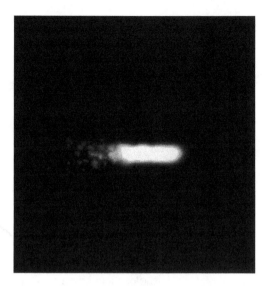

2. As you can see in the preceding snapshot, the particles are more and the birth rate is very high compared to the spaceship. So we need to reduce the particles to 50 and the birth rate to 0.5 giving a smaller particle system with less lifetime, as shown in the following snapshot:

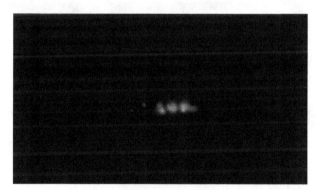

3. Do some more tweaks to make it look like a thrust, set its speed to 50, make the initial alpha to 180, and last and most importantly, set the scale to 0.2 so that it matches the spaceship scale.

4. Now we have our spaceship thrust built, which will look like this:

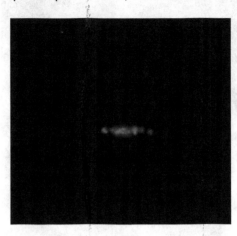

5. The following are the values set in the particle editor of Xcode to create the thrust of the spaceship using the default `FireParticle` file.

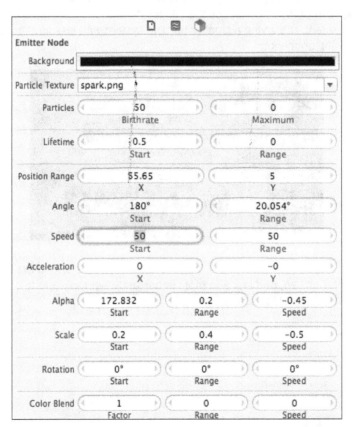

After this, one more particle effect called collision effect is left to be created when a coin is picked by the spaceship. The following are the steps involved to make a `SmokeParticle` file (particle system) for the collision effect of the coin and the spaceship:

1. Open Xcode and go to **File | New | File**.

2. In the **Resource** section of **iOS**, select **SpriteKit Particle File** and click on **Next**.

3. Select the **Smoke** template for the particle system so that an inherited smoke effect is created and click on **Next**.

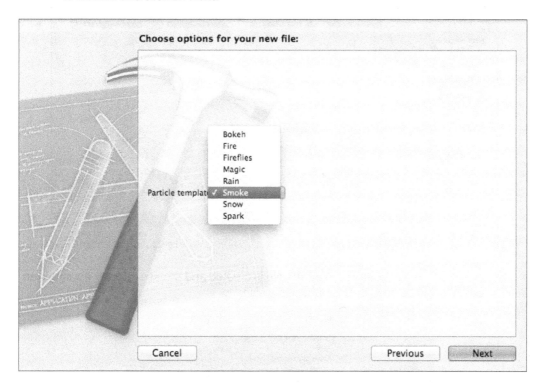

4. Name the file `SmokeParticle` and click on **Create**.

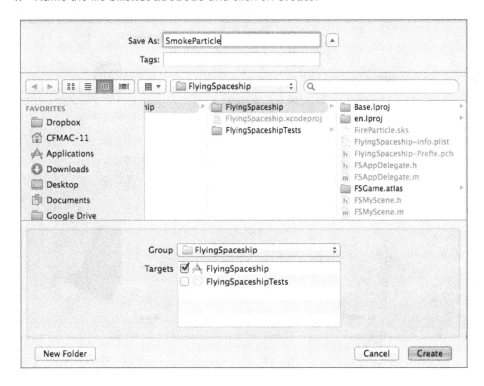

5. As a result, a `SmokeParticle.sks` file is created and the `spark.png` file imported explicitly will be used by this particle file also.

6. In the particle editor of the `SmokeParticle` file, the default effect that is created will look like this:

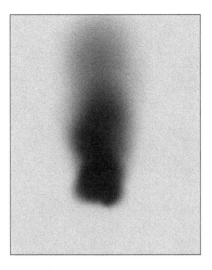

7. Now to produce a white smoke effect change, we will be changing the properties of the particle file. Set the following values to create the required effect:

   ❑ **Color Blend Factor** to 0

   ❑ **LifeTime** to 2

   ❑ **Particles** to 20

   ❑ **Angle** to 0

   ❑ **Speed** to 20

   ❑ **Maximum Particles** to 1

   ❑ **Scale** to 0.2

As a result, a small white smoke effect that will be displayed on the collision of coin and spaceship looks like this in the particle editor:

And the editor inspector of the particle editor will look like this after all the changes have been made:

Emitter Node		
Background		
Particle Texture	spark.png	
Particles	20 Birthrate	1 Maximum
Lifetime	2 Start	0 Range
Position Range	40 X	5 Y
Angle	0° Start	20.054° Range
Speed	20 Start	40 Range
Acceleration	0 X	10 Y
Alpha	0.4 Start	0.3 Range	−0.15 Speed
Scale	0.2 Start	0.3 Range	0.5 Speed
Rotation	0° Start	359.818° Range	171.887° Speed

As of now, both the `FireParticle` and `SmokeParticle` files are ready to be added to the game, but we should know about some classes used to add these files as a node to some node or scene. The node class to be used is `SKEmitterNode`.

A `SKEmitterNode` is a subclass of `SKNode` that automatically creates small particles as sprites and renders them on the screen. These emitter nodes can be used to create smoke, fire sparks, rain, and many other particle effects.

For instance, an object of `SKEmitterNode`, either we can use an sks particle file with properties set from the particle editor or directly create an object of the `SKEmitterNode` class and change the properties programmatically in the code. This means there are two ways to do so:

- Create an object of `SKEmitterNode` by getting the path of the particle file from the bundle with predefined property values and then adding to any other node or scene

> ‣ Create an object of SKEmitterNode just like any other node is created, setting all the properties such as particle image, lifetime, speed, and so on and then adding it to any other node or scene

How it works

Whenever a SpriteKit particle file is created, a default image that is imported, such as spark. png, is used as a particle in that particle system. We can also import any image of ours externally to make a personalized particle system.

As depicted earlier in the making of the thrust of the spaceship, we changed some values of the FireParticle file to have a fire thrust:

> ‣ We changed the angle value to 180 so that the direction of the thrust can be correct as per the spaceship that is, it moves right to left

> ‣ We reduced the lifetime and birthrate to match the capacity of the spaceship so that it can emit as per its size

> ‣ We also changed the initial size of the particles to match the machinery by which the thrust is released

> ‣ We tweaked the speed, alpha, and so on

As depicted earlier in the making of the collision effect, we changed some values of the SmokeParticle file to have a smoke effect:

> ‣ To make it white, we changed **Color Blend** to 0

> ‣ To make it disappear fast, change **LifeTime** to 2 and **Speed** to 20

> ‣ To reduce the intensity of particles, assign the number of **Particles** to 20, and to play it once, assign maximum particles to 1

> ‣ Set the angle to 0 and scale to 0.2 to make the smoke move subtile from left to right

So it's all on us how we want the emitter particle system to behave, to be put, and build according to that.

Talking about the class that helps to add this particle system that is, SKEmitterNode, which is used to add the particle system in the game by a file or in the code itself. Both options we would be doing at the code level in the upcoming section.

There's more

After using the particle editor thoroughly, we can really build some particle systems, which can be added as a change to the environment, such as making a snow effect and then adding them randomly onto the scene giving a feel of snowfall. Many more cool changes like this can be built using the particle system editor.

In the upcoming section, we will add the thrust of the spaceship we built earlier in our game giving a better feel and liveliness of the spaceship.

See also

For better documentation about the SKEmitterNode and its related properties, you can visit the following link `https://developer.apple.com/library/ios/documentation/SpriteKit/Reference/SKEmitterNode_Ref/index.html`.

Particle emitter integration

Now we are ready and equipped for the particle system to be added to our game FlyingSpaceship. In this section, we will take the `FireParticle` and `SmokeParticle` files, create a `SKEmitterNode` object for the respective file and add it to the respective entity on some event.

After all this, a thrust for the spaceship will be visible in the game making our character more empowered. Also, a collision smoke effect will be seen when a coin is picked by the spaceship.

Getting ready

We will start by adding emitters in the games. We should also go through the documentation of the `SKEmitterNode` class provided in the preceding sections. And then we can continue adding the code for the addition of the spaceship's thrust in the starter kit of this chapter.

How to do it

Continuing with the same Xcode project, now we will create our solution kit for this chapter that is, Chapter 4.

The following are the steps to add the spaceship's thrust in our game:

1. Open the `FSMyScene` class and add a method called `addSpaceShipThrust`.

   To get a particle file, first we need the file's path to pick it from the bundle. The method to find the path will require the name of the particle file and its type.

   ```
   NSString *emitterPath =
     [[NSBundle mainBundle] pathForResource:
       @"FireParticle" ofType:@"sks"];
   ```

2. After this, we can instantiate a new object of `SKEmitterNode` with the file path that is, `emitterPath` used in preceding code. This is accomplished by using `NSKeyedUnarchiver`, which will return an object of `SKEMitterNode` for a path that is provided.

```
SKEmitterNode *emitterNode =
  [NSKeyedUnarchiver
    unarchiveObjectWithFile:emitterPath];
```

3. Once the object of emitter is created, specify its position which has to be given according to the center of the spaceship as it's its thrust.

```
emitterNode.particlePosition =
  CGPointMake
    (-self.spaceShipSprite.frame.size.width/2,0);
```

4. Lastly, after all the configuration is done, just add the `emitterNode` object to SpaceShipSprite.

```
[self.spaceShipSprite addChild:emitterNode];
```

5. Call the `addSpaceShipThrust` method in the `init` method just after the `addSpaceShip` method.

6. The preceding `SKEmitterNode` was fully created using the **SpriteKit Particle** file. But we can tweak the properties of `SKEmitterNode` in the code itself.

7. As we want to increase the speed of the thrust after adding the emitter node, similarly, for this, we can edit the speed property of the emitter node object.

```
emitterNode.speed = 500.0f;
```

8. As output of all above creation of `FireParticle` file using particle editor and adding it in the code using `SKEmitterNode` class on the spaceship, the thrust appears at the back side of our character of game that is, spaceship.

The following are the steps to add the smoke effect on collision of the coin and the spaceship in our game:

1. Open the `FSMyScene` class and add a method called `addCoinCollisionEffectWithSpaceShip`.

2. Repeat the steps we performed while creating the thrust of the spaceship. Specify the filename and its type to get the path.

```
NSString *emitterPath =
  [[NSBundle mainBundle]
    pathForResource:@"SmokeParticle" ofType:@"sks"];
```

3. After this, we can instantiate a new object of `SKEmitterNode` using `NSKeyedUnarchiver`, which will return an object of `SKEMitterNode` for a path that is provided.

```
SKEmitterNode *emitterNode =
    [NSKeyedUnarchiver
        unarchiveObjectWithFile:emitterPath];
```

4. Once the object of the emitter is created, specify its position, which will be the center of spaceship.

```
emitterNode.particlePosition =  CGPointMake(0,0);
```

5. Lastly, after all the configuration is done, just add the `emitterNode` object (that is, `SmokeEffect` object) to `SpaceShipSprite`.

```
[self.spaceShipSprite addChild:emitterNode];
```

6. Add all these lines to the `addCoinCollisionEffectWithSpaceShip` method and it looks like this.

7. Now call this method when the coin collides with the spaceship that is, in method named `spaceShipCollidedWithCoin`.

```
[self addCoinCollisionEffectWithSpaceShip];
```

8. `spaceShipCollidedWithCoin` looks like this after a call is made to add `Coin CollisionEffect`.

As output of all above creating of `SmokeParticle` file using particle editor and adding it in the code using `SKEmitterNode` class on the spaceship, the smoke collision effect appears at the collision point of coin and the spaceship.

How it works

This is how it works when we add `SKEmitterNode` to `SKSprite` and the result of the preceding steps is depicted in the following screenshot, a thrust added to the spaceship:

Similarly, to add a collision smoke effect, we need the `ParticleSystem` file, which has been created in previous sections. For this effect also, the process works similar as depicted earlier for thrust of the spaceship. The following are the two snapshots after implementing the collision smoke effect.

▶ Coin collides with the spaceship:

▶ Collision smoke effect produced:

There's more

As the thrust of the spaceship is made, we can make a variety of such small particle effects to be added on such entities or when any sort of event occurs. Similarly, we can also add a particle effect when a coin is picked by the spaceship. And if needed, we can build a particle effect that can change the whole feel of an environment such as creating a rain or snowfall as discussed in previous sections.

See also

There are a variety of things to do using the Particle Editor of Xcode. To explore more about the particle system visit `https://developer.apple.com/library/ios/documentation/SceneKit/Reference/SCNParticleSystem_Class/index.html`.

Game performance analysis

While building games, a lot of intense processing and analysis is done to create a real-time environment of the game, so there is a huge requirement of game performance analysis to be done for the smooth functioning of a game or it can be a software product also.

From a user's perspective, if the game becomes slow or stops responding, technically decreasing the frame rate, users are likely to get frustrated by the game they are playing and will look for an alternative. So there has to be a good level of performance of games, which can be achieved by a game developer by doing performance analysis, which also helps in identifying problems easily and then fixing them.

So in the field of software performance analysis, developers need to use specific tools and the performance documentation so that they can identify and fix common performance issues thereby building a game with a stable and better performance.

In this recipe, we look at some performance tools for an application, how to use them, determine the lose pools, and fix them, thereby maintaining a better performance level for the application.

Getting ready

For doing performance analysis, we should go through and have a knowledge of some terminologies such as drawing code, launch time initialization code, file access code, application footprint, memory allocation code, basic optimizing tips, event-based handlers, improving concurrency of program's tasks, using accelerate framework, modernizing the application, and many more.

How to do it

Xcode includes tools with several graphical applications and command-line tools to collect performance metrics. There are many available tools such as instruments, analysis tools, monitoring tools, hardware analysis tools, additional command-line tools, and many more.

All are used to gather performance data, but there are a few of the them used more frequently such as the in-built debug navigator inspector, instruments, and many more. So in this section, you will learn about the debug navigator and the instrument's tools.

Debug navigator

In the project navigator of the Xcode project, there is a debug navigator at the sixth position of the panel, which shows the **CPU** utilization and the **Memory** utilization of the running application.

The following are the steps involved in analyzing the utilization types of the app:

1. First of all, open any project or we can open our own project the Solution kit of this chapter and press *command + R* to run the application FlyingSpaceship.

2. Click on the debug navigator; a panel like this appears:

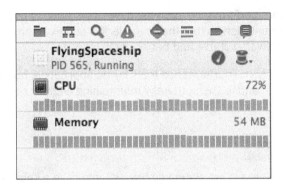

3. Here, the total **CPU** utilization in percentage that is, **72%** and **Memory** used that is, **54 MB** is shown in the panel. For further analysis of these metrics, we can click on the respective rows to view the proper graphs.

In **CPU** there are three different graphs of sections shown:

▶ The CPU Utilization section:

▶ The Utilization Over Time section:

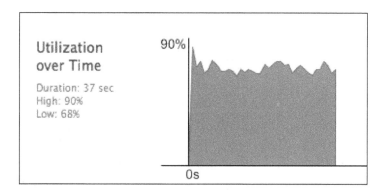

▶ The Threads section:

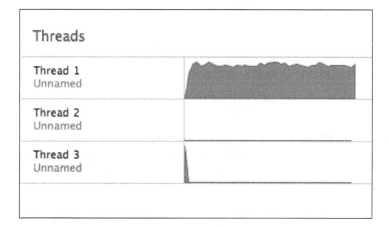

In **Memory**, two different graphs of sections are shown:

▶ Memory utilization:

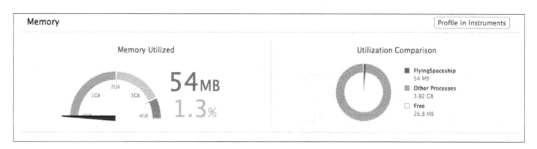

▶ Memory time-based graph:

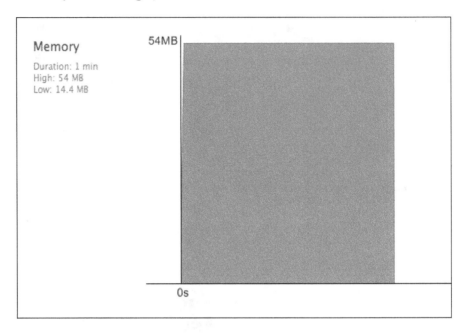

Instruments

Instruments is a collection of powerful analysis tools with an graphical user interface. Instruments help in knowing the runtime behavior of our application. It shows only one aspect of our program at a time, thereby we can configure each performance analysis session with multiple instruments each collecting a specific performance metric.

Talking about user interface, all data is shown side by side so that the data can be correlated from one instrument to another, identifying the trends followed in our application behavior. These metrics can be gathered using instruments:

▶ Core data based applications

▶ Read/write operation about filesystems

▶ Stats corresponding to memory-related allocations and objects

▶ Memory leaks information

▶ Information about events dispatched by Cocoa

▶ Samples of our app during runtime

▶ Stats related to garbage collected code

The following are the steps to use instruments:

1. First of all, open any project or we can open our own project from the solution kit of this chapter and press *command + R* to run the application FlyingSpaceship.

2. Click on the **CPU** utilization section of debug navigator.

3. Then click on the **Profile in Instruments** button, which is at the topmost right position in this section. Xcode will show a pop up asking us to transfer the same session to instruments or to restart. We can select the one we wish to analyze.

4. Suppose we say transfer, then Xcode will open the instruments with a time profiler inserted in its user interface by default showing running time of different threads.

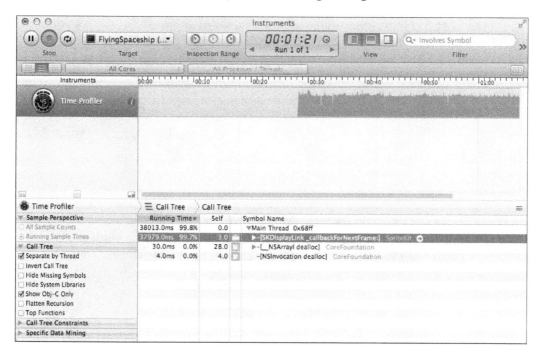

We can also run the instruments by pressing *command + i* and it will open instruments to select the metrics to be analyzed similar to this:

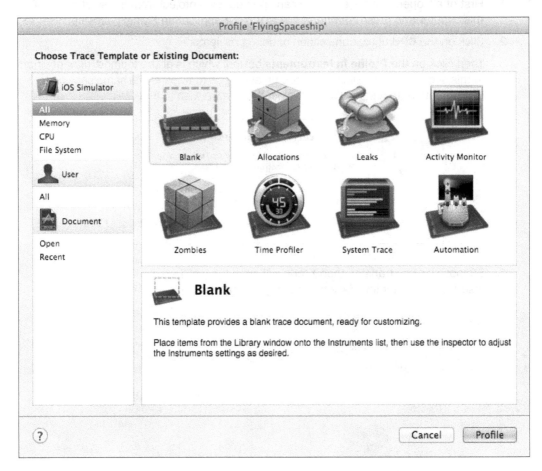

Now perform the following steps:

1. Now suppose we select the **Allocations** category to view these allocations of the app.
2. But the allocations are not in readable format; hence, click on the **Statistics** button and select **Call Trees** so that the calls are arranged in the sequence of calls.

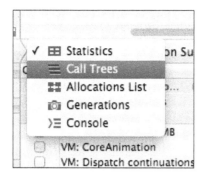

3. After that, for better readability, check the **Show Obj-C Only** checkbox.

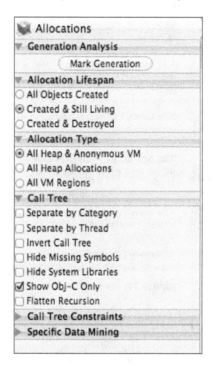

4. After clicking on these two buttons, we can really look at how the allocations are happening in the application. You can see and analyze your allocations using these methods.

5. For further analysis, there many more metrics that can be included with the help of a library by clicking on the top bar button **Library**.

This is what the library looks like with many options of selecting other metrics:

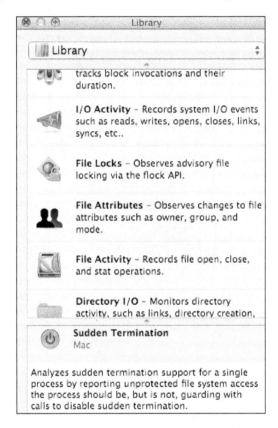

By using this library, we can include multiple metrics such as leaks, time profiler, and view them collectively at the side panel of instruments.

There's more

For better understanding of how the performance varies with your change in code, use tools listed in this section, such as instruments. And also, for better understanding of the preceding terminologies discussed, read the documentation provided at:

```
https://developer.apple.com/library/mac/documentation/Performance/
Conceptual/PerformanceOverview/BasicTips/BasicTips.html#//apple_ref/
doc/uid/TP40001410-CH204-BBCGCFGF.
```

See also

To check the level of performance for any application thereby improving that, use the tools and initial performance evaluation process documented at the following links:

- ▶ ```
  https://developer.apple.com/library/mac/documentation/
  Performance/Conceptual/PerformanceOverview/PerformanceTools/
  PerformanceTools.html#//apple_ref/doc/uid/TP40001410-CH205-
  BCIIHAAJ.
  ```

- ▶ ```
  https://developer.apple.com/library/mac/documentation/
  Performance/Conceptual/PerformanceOverview/InitialEvaluation/
  InitialEvaluation.html#//apple_ref/doc/uid/TP40001410-CH206-
  CJBFHBDB.
  ```

5
Adding Music to iOS Games and an Introduction to iCloud

In this chapter, we will be focusing on the following recipes:

- ▶ Adding music to games
- ▶ Adding background and sound effects
- ▶ Introduction to iCloud
- ▶ Integration of iCloud with iOS games

Introduction

In *Chapter 4, Particle System and Game Performance*, we created a full game of collecting coins by FlyingSpaceship containing sprites, scenes, parallax infinite scrolling background, particle effects, and many more except music. Now we are moving forward to add the most interesting part to the game, which is music. Music and sound effects brings a sense of engagement and fun to the game; no game exists without music. So we will be integrating some cool and awesome background music and sound effects into the FlyingSpaceship game built in the previous chapters. Moreover, we will be enlightening a new technology called iCloud and its framework recently released by Apple. Using iCloud, we can easily and securely store and retrieve the app data like a database from the iCloud, which is provided by Apple.

Adding music to games

No video or movie is complete without music and neither is a game. Our end goal in this topic is to integrate some smoothing and awesome sound effects to make it look like a complete game that can be enjoyed by the user. So, in iOS development, there are many ways to integrate and play audio in an app or in a game. Some are system sound services, AVAudioPlayer, audio queue services, and OpenAL. All are used for some or the other purpose and utility in an app.

In this recipe, we will be discussing different ways of integrating music and sound effects provided by iOS. And in the upcoming section, we will integrate background music and some sound effects at specific events happening in our FlyingSpaceship game, which will be the starter kit for this chapter.

Getting ready

Before starting with the technical ways of integrating music and sound effects in the game, we should have an understanding of how audio is added in videos, movies, or wherever audio is required. In a game, there has to be background music and some sound effects at the events that need the attention of the user. All these music and sound effects are to be decided on the basis of the theme of the game. So the prerequisite for this section is to have a common sense of music and sound effects.

How to do it...

Now we will look at some of the ways to implement sound services in our app.

System Sound Services

This is an easy way of playing audio files. For playing an audio sound using System Sound Services and to see how it works, the following are the steps involved:

1. Add an audio file to the project, and using `mainBundle` get the path of the audio file:

   ```
   NSString *samplePath = [[NSBundle mainBundle]
     pathForResource:@"sample-sound" ofType:@"caf"];
   ```

2. Here we have used the `.caf` format for the audio files. This is the recommended Apple format.

3. Using the path, form a `NSURL`, which will be used to create a `SystemSoundID`:

   ```
   NSURL *sampleURL = [NSURL fileURLWithPath:samplePath];
   ```

4. Then create a `systemSoundID` using the `NSURL` formed earlier and a property declared as `SystemSoundID` named `sampleSound` in the code:

   ```
   AudioServicesCreateSystemSoundID((__bridge
     CFURLRef)sampleURL, &self.sampleSound);
   ```

5. Finally, using the `systemSoundID` that is, `self.sampleSound`, play the audio file.

   ```
   AudioServicesPlaySystemSound(self.sampleSound);
   ```

6. For playing an audio sound using AVAudioPlayer AVFoundation framework is needed so it has to be imported and then add an audio file to the project and using `mainBundle` get the path of the audio file. To import the framework add the following line of code:

   ```
   #import <AVFoundation/AVFoundation.h>
   ```

7. Now create an instance of AVAudioPlayer with content as the `NSURL` of the file to be played with error.

   ```
   NSError *error;
   AVAudioPlayer *backgroundAudioPlayer = [AVAudioPlayer
      alloc] initWithContentsOfURL:file error:&error];
   ```

8. After that call a `prepareToPlay` method on the `AVAudioPlayer` object so that it prepares the audio file to be played.

   ```
   [backgroundAudioPlayer prepareToPlay];
   ```

9. Before playing the audio file, we can set the `volume` and `numberOfLoops` and lastly we can play the audio file.

   ```
   backgroundAudioPlayer.volume = 1.0;
   backgroundAudioPlayer.numberOfLoops = -1;
   [backgroundAudioPlayer play];
   ```

AVAudioPlayer

AVAudioPlayer is a modern way of playing and doing more things with audio. It supports audio files encoded with AAC and MP3, which are not supported by System Sound Services. Moreover, there is an easy way to play music through a class name `AVAudioPlayer`, which is treated as a player for every music or sound effect.

To accomplish this, perform the following steps:

1. First we have to import `AVFoundation`:

   ```
   @import AVFoundation;
   ```

2. Then use this snippet to play a sample sound using an object of AVAudioPlayer:

   ```
   NSString *samplePath = [[NSBundle mainBundle]
      pathForResource:@"sample-sound.caf" ofType:nil];
   NSURL *file = [NSURL fileURLWithPath:samplePath];
   NSError *error;
   AVAudioPlayer *backgroundAudioPlayer = [[AVAudioPlayer
      alloc] initWithContentsOfURL:file error:&error];
   ```

```
[backgroundAudioPlayer prepareToPlay];
backgroundAudioPlayer.numberOfLoops = -1;
backgroundAudioPlayer.volume = 1.0;
[backgroundAudioPlayer play];
```

Audio Queue Services

Audio Queue Services is high-level audio stuff as it is a way to record and play audios. It lets your app use hardware recording and playback using microphones and loudspeakers without the knowledge of the hardware interface. It provides fine-grained timing control for scheduling playback and synchronization. For further information on Audio Queue Services see the *There's more* section.

Above all are not suitable where there is a need for fine-grained control of audio with low latency; in such cases, only OpenAL is appropriate to be used, which is a cross-platform audio library supported by iOS. Learning OpenAL is a steep learning curve. So, to understand and implement it see, the *There's more* section.

How it works...

System Sound Services is particularly used for playing audio alerts and simple game sound effects such as click sound for moving a character in the game. Every sound that is played using this is assigned a systemSoundID. All of the tracking is based on this ID, such as stopping, pausing, and different actions that can be applied on an audio. All we have to do is add this set of lines to play a sound:

```
NSString *samplePath = [[NSBundle mainBundle]
pathForResource:@"sample-sound" ofType:@"caf"];
NSURL *sampleURL = [NSURL fileURLWithPath:samplePath];
AudioServicesCreateSystemSoundID((__bridge
  CFURLRef)sampleURL, &self.sampleSound);
AudioServicesPlaySystemSound(self.sampleSound);
```

The sampleSound is declared as a SystemSoundID property so that the sound can be disposed later in the dealloc method. If the sound is disposed immediately after the AudioServicesPlaySystemSound method, then the sound will never play.

There are some disadvantages of System Sound Services, such as only .caf, .aif, and .wav audio file formats are supported, sounds cannot be more than 30 seconds, and only one sound can be played at a time.

There's more...

Other than System Sound Services and AVAudioPlayer, there are two more advanced ways of playing audio which are Audio Queue Services used for playback and recording and OpenAL for fine-grained control of timing. You can explore Apple's docs for Core Audio overview and Audio Session Programming Guide.

See also

For better understanding and learning of Audio Queue Services and OpenAL, you can visit the following links:

- ▶ `https://developer.apple.com/library/mac/documentation/MusicAudio/Conceptual/AudioQueueProgrammingGuide/Introduction/Introduction.html`
- ▶ `https://developer.apple.com/library/ios/documentation/audiovideo/conceptual/multimediapg/usingaudio/usingaudio.html`

Adding background and sound effects

After understanding some ways of integrating audio in the app, the most commonly used and easiest way is AVAudioPlayer. Basically, in this recipe, we will be adding background music, which will be running forever, and some sound effects on specific events where the user's attention is required or where the user has to be notified of some change. This adding of background music and sound effects will be done in our game FlyingSpaceship built in the previous chapters.

Getting ready

Before starting with the addition of background music and sound effects on some events, we should have a good understanding of the `AVAudioPlayer` class and the `AVFoundation` framework. So the prerequisite for this section is to have knowledge of how to play audio using the AVAudioPlayer class as discussed in the preceding recipe.

How to do it...

We have the full game FlyingSpaceship built in which the addition of background music and sound effects will be done as discussed in the upcoming steps. To accomplish both, add two audio files `background-music.caf` and `coin-collected-sound.caf` to the resources folder of the project. Now perform the following steps:

1. Now we will add background music to make it a complete game. First of all import the module `AVFoundation` in the `FSMyScene` file of FlyingSpaceship.

   ```
   @import AVFoundation;
   ```

2. Declare a property named `backgroundAudioPlayer` as an object of `AVAudioPlayer`.

   ```
   @property (nonatomic, strong) AVAudioPlayer
     *backgroundAudioPlayer;
   ```

3. As explained in the code snippet of the *AVAudioPlayer* section, create a path and `NSURL` file using the `background-music.caf` file.

   ```
   NSString *samplePath = [[NSBundle mainBundle]
     pathForResource:@"background-music.caf" ofType:nil];
   NSURL *file = [NSURL fileURLWithPath:samplePath];
   ```

4. Just initialize the property `self.backgroundAudioPlayer` with the new `AVAudioPlayerobject`. This will also need an error object and the audio file, which we created earlier. All the errors will be logged in the object that we have passed in the parameter..

   ```
   NSError *error;
   self.backgroundAudioPlayer = [[AVAudioPlayer alloc]
   initWithContentsOfURL:file error:&error];
   if (error)
   {
       NSLog(@"Error in audio play %@",[error userInfo]);
       return;
   }
   ```

5. After this, call `prepareToPlay` on that object, set some volume such as 1.0, and in order to play it infinitely set `numberOfLoops` to -1.

   ```
   [self.backgroundAudioPlayer prepareToPlay];
   self.backgroundAudioPlayer.numberOfLoops = -1;
   self.backgroundAudioPlayer.volume = 1.0;
   ```

6. Finally, after all of this, play the background music that never ends.

   ```
   [self.backgroundAudioPlayer play];
   ```

7. After this, gather the code in a function called `startBackgroundMusic` and it will look like this:

```
- (void)startBackgroundMusic
{
    NSString *samplePath =
    [[NSBundle mainBundle] pathForResource:@"background-music.caf"
                                    ofType:nil];
    NSURL *file =
    [NSURL fileURLWithPath:samplePath];

    NSError *error;

    self.backgroundAudioPlayer =
    [[AVAudioPlayer alloc] initWithContentsOfURL:file
                                           error:&error];

    if (error)
    {
        NSLog(@"Error in audio play %@",[error userInfo]);
        return;
    }

    [self.backgroundAudioPlayer prepareToPlay];
    self.backgroundAudioPlayer.numberOfLoops = -1;
    self.backgroundAudioPlayer.volume = 1.0;
    [self.backgroundAudioPlayer play];
}
```

8. To make it play the background music, call the `startBackgroundMusic` function in the `initWithSize` method of `FSMyScene`.

9. Now, compile and run the project; you should be able to listen to the background music in the game.

10. Now we will add a sound effect in the game when a coin is collected. For this, declare a property named `coinCollectedAudioPlayer` as an object of AVAudioPlayer.

```
@property (nonatomic, strong) AVAudioPlayer
*coinCollectedAudioPlayer;
```

11. As explained in the code snippet in the *AVAudioPlayer* section, create a path and a NSURL file using `coin-collected-sound.caf` file.

```
NSString *samplePath = [[NSBundle mainBundle]
  pathForResource:@"coin-collected-sound.caf" ofType:nil];
NSURL *file = [NSURL fileURLWithPath:samplePath];
```

12. Assign an `AVAudioPlayer` object with the preceding sound effect file with the error as the parameter to the `self.coinCollectedAudioPlayer` property. And after creating this, check for errors, if any, print an error message, and return from there.

```
NSError *error;
self.coinCollectedAudioPlayer = [[AVAudioPlayer alloc]
initWithContentsOfURL:file error:&error];
if (error)
{
    NSLog(@"Error in audio play %@",[error userInfo]);
    return;
}
```

13. After that, call `prepareToPlay` on that object, set some volume such as 1.0 and play it once you set `numberOfLoops` to 1.

```
[self.coinCollectedAudioPlayer prepareToPlay];
self.coinCollectedAudioPlayer.numberOfLoops = 1;
self.coinCollectedAudioPlayer.volume = 1.0;
```

14. Finally, after all of this, play the sound effect that has to be played when the coin is collected by the spaceship.

```
[self.coinCollectedAudioPlayer play];
```

15. After all of this, gather the code in a function called `playCoinCollectedSoundEffect` and it will look like this:

```
- (void)playCoinCollectedSoundEffect
{
    NSString *samplePath =
    [[NSBundle mainBundle] pathForResource:@"coin-collected-sound.caf"
                                ofType:nil];
    NSURL *file =
    [NSURL fileURLWithPath:samplePath];

    NSError *error;

    self.coinCollectedAudioPlayer =
    [[AVAudioPlayer alloc] initWithContentsOfURL:file
                                error:&error];

    if (error)
    {
        NSLog(@"Error in audio play %@",[error userInfo]);
        return;
    }

    [self.coinCollectedAudioPlayer prepareToPlay];
    self.coinCollectedAudioPlayer.numberOfLoops = 1;
    self.coinCollectedAudioPlayer.volume = 1.0;
    [self.coinCollectedAudioPlayer play];
```

16. To make it play when the coin collides with the spaceship, call the `playCoinCollectedSoundEffect` function when `spaceShipCollidedWithCoin` is called by the detection of a collision, which looks like this:

17. After all the integration of background music and sound effects, our starter kit for this chapter is ready.

How it works...

How the AVAudioPlayer works and how the background music and sound effects are played has been explained in the preceding topic. Here the difference between background music and sound effect was the `numberOfLoops` property of AVAudioPlayer object. It was `-1` for the background music and `1` for sound effect of collecting the coin by the spaceship.

There's more...

Using the same AVAudioPlayer, we can play multiple sound effects together such as playing a sound of movement when the spaceship moves and the coin is collected. So for further enhancement in music and sound effects, there is no limit.

See also

For better understanding and learning of Core Audio in iOS, visit the link `https://developer.apple.com/library/mac/documentation/MusicAudio/Conceptual/CoreAudioOverview/CoreAudioEssentials/CoreAudioEssentials.html`.

Introduction to iCloud

Apple has introduced a technology called iCloud that leverages the power of building apps using the new CloudKit framework. Using iCloud, we can easily and securely store and retrieve our app data in the form of a database in the cloud built by Apple. The CloudKit framework provides a way for users to anonymously sign into the apps with their iCloud Apple IDs without sharing their personal information. The most important part is that CloudKit makes the developer focus on the client-side app development and does the server-side application logic by iCloud itself. It also provides an authenticated, private, and public database storage services, which are for free with very high limits of storage.

In this recipe, we will be doing an introduction of iCloud and its framework CloudKit. We will understand how the iCloud services are enabled in Xcode, iTunes Connect, playing with provisioning profiles for development devices to integrate iCloud for apps. Later in this next section, we will integrate the iCloud service with our game FlyingSpaceship.

Getting ready...

Before starting to make a setup with iCloud and the CloudKit framework, we should know about some features of Xcode capabilities, iTunes Connect, and provisioning profiles. Also, we must have an understanding of core data, storing, and retrieving data in iOS for a smooth use and integration of the CloudKit framework. These are the prerequisites for starting to use the new technology iCloud and its framework.

To integrate iCloud in any app, the following steps are a must before starting with the setup to be done in Xcode:

- ▶ A Mac computer with Xcode 6 or later installed
- ▶ Membership in either iOS or Mac Developer Program
- ▶ Permission to create the code signing identities and provisioning profiles in Member Center
- ▶ Lastly, after all this, our Xcode project should be built without errors

How to do it...

In this recipe, we will learn about the steps to enable CloudKit in our app. CloudKit is an app service provided by Apple. It is only available for the apps distributed by the App Store or the Mac App Store. CloudKit requires some additional configuration to be done from our Xcode Project. Our app must be provisioned and code signed to access the CloudKit service. So we will enable CloudKit for our FlyingSpaceship game. Perform the following steps to enable CloudKit in the Xcode project for our game:

1. Open the Xcode Project (FlyingSpaceship) in which we want to enable and use CloudKit services.

2. Click on the **Project** in the Project Navigator and we can see the **General** section selected.

3. Select the **FlyingSpaceship** target and then select the next section **Capabilities**.

4. Now, click on the first row, that is, **iCloud** and a section similar to this will open:

5. Now, on the right-hand side, switch to iCloud and some loading will occur.

6. Once the loading has finished, the iCloud will be enabled and giving options as shown in the following screenshot:

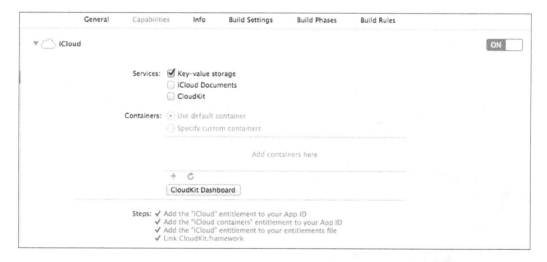

7. As we can see, there are are three services by iCloud; enable them as needed by the app. For now, we will enable CloudKit.

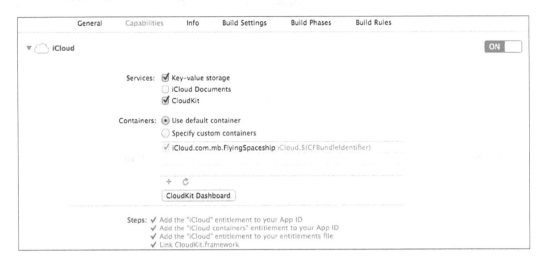

8. Also, a button called **CloudKit Dashboard** is visible. On clicking this button, we will be redirected to the CloudKit dashboard of the app FlyingSpaceship in Apple's iTunes Connect. The sidebar, record types to be added, and the container section of CloudKit dashboard look like this.

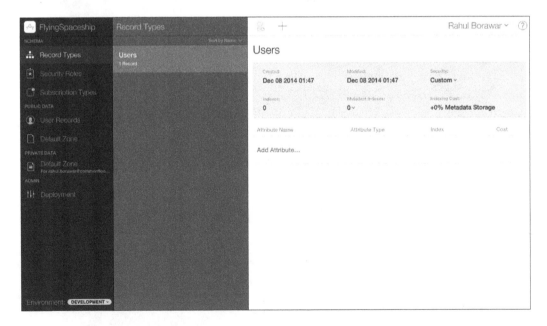

9. The dashboard is used to perform many database management tasks such as modifying schemas and records as shown in the preceding screenshot. A container's databases for an app exist both in the development and the production environment. Using the dashboard, we can play with the records creating, deleting, modifying, and so on.

10. To explore sign in to the dashboard and click on the options in the left column, which has many operations to do as depicted in the following screenshot:

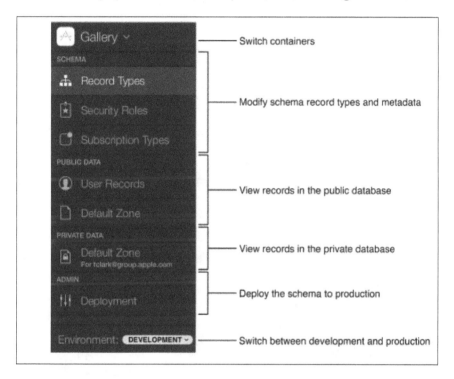

How it works...

The iCloud technology provides an easy and secure way of creating an app that stores a structured app and user data in a server called iCloud. Using the CloudKit framework, instances of an iCloud-enabled app, which is launched by different users on different devices, can access the assets stored in the app's database. After enabling iCloud for any app, we can make model objects for our app, which persist and are shared between multiple apps running on a large range of devices. These data or model objects are stored as records in the database and can be accessed by the authorized users.

iCloud is a free service provided by Apple that lets users access their personal data on all their devices by their Apple ID. It does all this by combining network-based storage dedicated APIs with full support of OS. Apple encourages building iCloud-enabled apps by providing server infrastructure, backups, and user accounts.

The following is a pictorial representation of iCloud's core idea, which addresses the problem of synchronization between multiple devices. A user using an iCloud app need not think about syncing his/her devices. When the user adopts iCloud storage, as depicted in the following diagram, all the changes appear automatically on all the devices that are attached to that iCloud account.

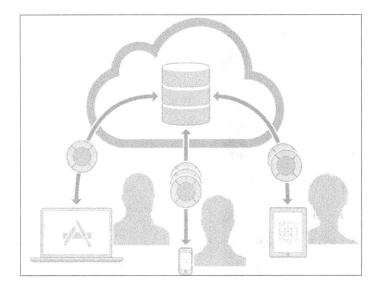

There's more...

iCloud supports many kinds of storage. The storage types are:

- ▶ Key-value storage such as user preferences, settings, and simple app state data
- ▶ iCloud document storage such as word-processing documents and drawings
- ▶ Core data storage for multidevice database solutions for structured content
- ▶ CloudKit storage for managing structured data ourselves and sharing among ourselves

To store data on iCloud, we can use any of these depending upon our requirement and capabilities. Moving forward, we can pick these storage types and make an iCloud app for sharing the storage on multiple devices.

See also...

For more information on storage types, visit the link `https://developer.apple.com/library/ios/documentation/Miscellaneous/Conceptual/CloudKitQuickStart/Introduction/Introduction.html#//apple_ref/doc/uid/TP40014987-CH1-SW1`.

Integration of iCloud with iOS games

In this recipe, you will learn the steps to integrate the iCloud with iOS games. iCloud integration plays an important role in the development of the application as it helps us to support various features and enhance interdevice synchronization. In this recipe, we will explore and integrate a few features of the iCloud in our game.

Getting ready

As of now, we have finished the initial setup for playing with iCloud. As a prerequisite to integrate iCloud in any app, we must be enrolled in membership for iOS or the Mac Developer Program, and have the device provisioning profile and AppID. To accomplish this and start with the integration part, we must take a look at these two links:

> ▸ `https://developer.apple.com/library/ios/documentation/IDEs/Conceptual/AppDistributionGuide/AddingCapabilities/AddingCapabilities.html#//apple_ref/doc/uid/TP40012582-CH26`

> ▸ `https://developer.apple.com/library/ios/documentation/IDEs/Conceptual/AppDistributionGuide/Introduction/Introduction.html#//apple_ref/doc/uid/TP40012582`

After all the configuration part is done, we can start with the integration of iCloud by CloudKit in our game FlyingSpaceship.

How to do it...

iCloud allows you to store and retrieve data easily from its secured server. This also provides an additional facility of sharing saved data among multiple applications. To save this data, our iCloud app places the data in a special local filesystem called the iCloud containers. It is also called **ubiquity container**, and serves as the local representation of the corresponding iCloud storage. This data is totally separate from the rest of our app data; it is kept by the operating system.

For some iCloud services, our app does not communicate directly to the iCloud servers, instead, the operating system manages all this uploading and downloading of data for the devices attached to the iCloud account. However, CloudKit provides the facility to manage these activities. The following are the steps required for using these services:

1. Configure the access to our app's iCloud containers. It involves requesting entitlements and programmatically initializing these containers.

2. Design the app to handle the responses of iCloud services accordingly, such as when the user signs out of iCloud and instances of our app on other devices can edit the data.

3. Read/write using the proper iCloud API.

4. The operating system coordinates the transition of data to and from iCloud when needed as per the design of the app.

We have briefly discussed the iCloud containers already, so this is the time to implement the iCloud containers in our app. To implement them, we will open the **Capabilities** tab of our Xcode project, which manages the entitlements and containers of our app. When we enable iCloud in the same tab, then Xcode configures our app to the default iCloud container whose name is based on the app's bundle ID. This default container is used by most apps as shown in the following screenshot:

If we want to build some app with data to be shared among each other, then we can enable the **Specify custom containers** option and it can be done using the following steps:

1. First of all, open `https://developer.apple.com/` in the browser, and click on **Member Center**.

2. Out of the six sections in the member center, go to the **Certificates**, **Identifiers**, and **Profiles** sections and then in the **iOS** section, go to **Identifiers** where a list of identifier types is present.

3. Click on the **iCloud containers** tab and we can see a default container there.

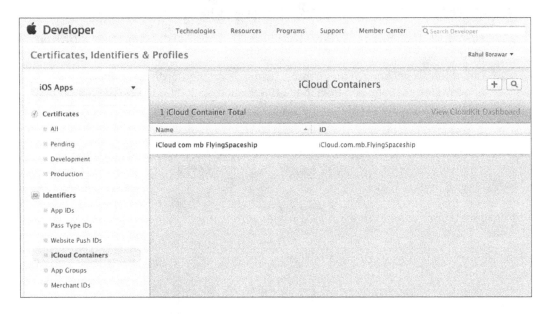

4. Now, to add another specific iCloud Container, click on the plus button at the top right of the page and then enter the ID `iCloud.com.mb.FlyingSpaceshipShared`. Add some description for the container.

5. After executing all the preceding steps, we can find our custom AppIDs in the member center.

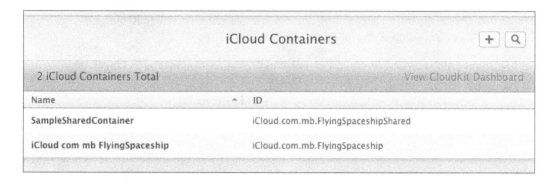

6. As the specific container is created, now go to the **Capabilities** tab of our app Xcode project. We can see an extra container visible in the **iCloud** section.

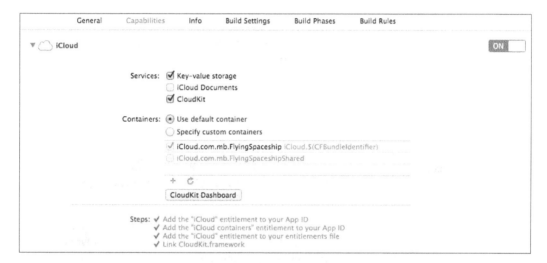

7. Now to use the specific container, select the **Specify custom containers** radio button then select the iCloud.com.mb.FlyingSpaceshipShared container.

Now we will prepare our code for iCloud. We will be incorporating some initial setup in the code for iCloud services to be used by the app. Firstly, when the user launches an iCloud-enabled FlyingSpaceship game for the first time, we should invite them to use iCloud. The choice should be all or none. Hence, to invite the user to use iCloud, the following are the steps of the initial setup:

1. In our app launch in the `application:didFinishLauchingWithOptions` method, get `ubiquityIdentityToken` from `NSFileManager`.

   ```
   NSFileManager* fileManager = [NSFileManager
    defaultManager];
   id currentiCloudToken =
    fileManager.ubiquityIdentityToken;
   ```

2. Then archive the iCloud availability in the user defaults database by the `ubiquityIdentityToken` property fetched using `NSFileManager`.

   ```
   if (currentiCloudToken)
     {
     NSData *newTokenData =
       [NSKeyedArchiver
         archivedDataWithRootObject:currentiCloudToken];
       [[NSUserDefaults standardUserDefaults]
         setObject:newTokenData
   forKey:@"com.mb.FlyingSpaceship.UbiquityIdentityToken"];
     }
     else
     {
       [[NSUserDefaults standardUserDefaults]
       removeObjectForKey:
         @"com.mb.FlyingSpaceship.UbiquityIdentityToken"];
     }
   ```

3. Now the `currentiCloudToken` function saved is the unique token representing the currently active iCloud account. Using this we can compare to detect whether the current account is different from the previous one.

4. When the user will enables airplane mode, iCloud will itself become inaccessible, but the current iCloud account will remain signed in and `ubiquityIdentityToken` contains the token of the current iCloud account.

5. For the user who signs out of iCloud, the value of `ubiquityIdentityToken` sets to `nil`. So to receive notification, we should register as an observer of the `NSUbiquityIdentityDidChangeNotification` notification where the token is received. This is a notification for iCloud availability change and we can handle it accordingly in the notification selector `iCloudAccountAvailabilityChanged`.

   ```
   [[NSNotificationCenter defaultCenter] addObserver:self
     selector:@selector(iCloudAccountAvailabilityChanged:)
       name:NSUbiquityIdentityDidChangeNotification object:nil];
   ```

6. After archiving the iCloud token and registering the iCloud notification, our app is ready to show an alert view in order to show invites to the user iCloud with two options: local only and use iCloud. For this, first of all save a Boolean variable for FirstLaunchWithiCloudAvailable when the token is retrieved:

```
BOOL firstLaunchWithiCloudAvailable =
  [[NSUserDefaults standardUserDefaults]
    objectForKey:@"FirstLaunchWithiCloudAvailable"];
if (firstLaunchWithiCloudAvailable == NO)
  {
    [[NSUserDefaults standardUserDefaults]
      setObject:[NSNumber numberWithBool:YES]
    forKey:@"FirstLaunchWithiCloudAvailable"];
  }
[[NSUserDefaults standardUserDefaults] synchronize];
```

7. Also, call a method showiCloudInviteAlertView always in didFinishLauchingWithOptions. In this method, show the alert view to invite the user to use iCloud if a current token exists (it will exist only if the user is logged in to the iCloud Account, otherwise NIL will be returned) and also if the FirstLaunchWithiCloudAvailable bool is YES.

```
- (void)showiCloudInviteAlertView
{
    BOOL firstLaunchWithiCloudAvailable =
      [[NSUserDefaults standardUserDefaults]
        objectForKey:@"FirstLaunchWithiCloudAvailable"];

    if (currentiCloudToken &&
      firstLaunchWithiCloudAvailable)
    {
    UIAlertView *alertView =
      [[UIAlertView alloc]  initWithTitle: @"Choose Storage
        Option" message: @"Should documents be stored in
          iCloud and available on all your devices?"
            delegate: self
              cancelButtonTitle: @"Local Only"
            otherButtonTitles: @"Use iCloud", nil];
          [alertView show];
    }
}
```

After all these changes, the `didFinishLauchingWithOptions:` method will look like this:

```objc
- (BOOL)application:(UIApplication *)application didFinishLaunchingWithOptions:(NSDictionary *)launchOptions
{
    // Override point for customization after application launch.

    NSFileManager* fileManager = [NSFileManager defaultManager];
    currentiCloudToken = fileManager.ubiquityIdentityToken;

    if (currentiCloudToken)
    {
        NSData *newTokenData =
        [NSKeyedArchiver archivedDataWithRootObject:currentiCloudToken];

        [[NSUserDefaults standardUserDefaults]
         setObject:newTokenData
         forKey:@"com.mb.FlyingSpaceship.UbiquityIdentityToken"];

        BOOL firstLaunchWithiCloudAvailable =
        [[NSUserDefaults standardUserDefaults] objectForKey:@"FirstLaunchWithiCloudAvailable"];

        if (firstLaunchWithiCloudAvailable == NO)
        {
            [[NSUserDefaults standardUserDefaults] setObject:[NSNumber numberWithBool:YES]
                                          forKey:@"FirstLaunchWithiCloudAvailable"];
        }

        [[NSUserDefaults standardUserDefaults] synchronize];
    }
    else
    {
        [[NSUserDefaults standardUserDefaults]
         removeObjectForKey: @"com.mb.FlyingSpaceship.UbiquityIdentityToken"];
    }

    [[NSNotificationCenter defaultCenter] addObserver:self
                                        selector:@selector(iCloudAccountAvailabilityChanged:)
                                            name:NSUbiquityIdentityDidChangeNotification
                                          object:nil];
    [self showiCloudInviteAlertView];
    return YES;
}
```

How it works...

If we start exploring iCloud Containers, then we will notice that depending on the design of the app in respect to iCloud integration, either the default container is selected or a custom container is created; the iCloud services are to be configured accordingly. If we do not make any custom container, then the default container will be configured, whose name will be based on the app's bundle ID.

And in order to share the data, the **Specify custom container identifiers** checkbox in the **Capabilities** tab of iCloud is used to add one or more container IDs. We need to specify the ID for the custom container created. For multiple container IDs, the first ID is the app's primary iCloud container.

With respect to custom iCloud containers, the sharing will be available on devices that are signed in to the iCloud account of the same app.

Now we will discuss the ways to prepare the code for iCloud. If the user is logged in to the iCloud account for the app, then only `ubiquityIdentityToken` will be returned; otherwise `nil` will be returned. And this token is retrieved using the `NSFileManager` object. It is also saved if it exists for further use in the app according to the design of the app with respect to iCloud integration.

We are subscribing to notifications using `NSUbiquityIdentityDidChangeNotification` to get a callback of all the changes in `ubiquityIdentityToken`. For example, it will give a callback whenever the user is logged out.

Sometimes iCloud may not be available to our app; at that time, the account becomes unavailable while the app is running in the background. So the app must remove all the references to user-specific iCloud storage and refresh the user interface that is dependent on the iCloud Storage.

After the token is saved and the notification for `UbiquityIdentityChange` is registered, the app becomes ready to show an alert to use iCloud. According to the selection of the user, the relevant iCloud APIs such as key-value storage, iCloud document storage, and CloudKit storage are used in the code for further handling of iCloud data.

There's more...

As described in preceding sections, there are many iCloud Storage APIs available in iCloud technology such as key-value storage, iCloud document storage, and CloudKit storage. From all of these, the proper selection of APIs depends upon the purpose that has to be accomplished. Hence, as a trial, the user data of the FlyingSpaceship game can be used to store in the iCloud servers and share it by using any suitable APIs mentioned previously.

To study more and for proper decision making, we can take a look at the link:

```
https://developer.apple.com/library/ios/documentation/General/
Conceptual/iCloudDesignGuide/Chapters/iCloudFundametals.html#//apple_
ref/doc/uid/TP40012094-CH6-SW28.
```

See also

For more information and integration of iCloud in any app, we can visit the link:

```
https://developer.apple.com/library/ios/documentation/General/
Conceptual/iCloudDesignGuide/Chapters/Introduction.html#//apple_ref/
doc/uid/TP40012094-CH1-SW1.
```

6

Physics Simulation

In this chapter, we will cover the following topics:

- ▶ Introduction to physics simulation
- ▶ Integrating physics engine with games
- ▶ Adding real-world simulation

Introduction

In *Chapter 5, Adding Music to iOS Games and an Introduction to iCloud* we learned various ways to add music to our games along with iCloud integration. Now in this chapter, our major focus will be on adding reality to the games by introducing physics simulation. SpriteKit has a seamlessly bundled physics engine and in this chapter we will be exploring and working to add physics to our games. Basically, the SpriteKit has been divided into the following two major components:

- ▶ The graphical interface that you see on the screen including UI interface, animations, sound effects, and so on
- ▶ The second is the physical physics world, which determines the interaction and behaviors of game objects

Introduction to physics simulation

We all like games that have realistic effects and actions. In this chapter we will learn about the ways to make our games more realistic. Have you ever wondered how to provide realistic effect to game objects? It is physics that provides a realistic effect to the games and their characters. In this chapter, we will learn how to use physics in our games.

While developing the game using SpriteKit, you will need to change the world of your game frequently. The world is the main object in the game that holds all the other game objects and physics simulations. We can also update the gravity of the gaming world according to our need. The default world gravity is 9.8, which is also the earth's gravity, World gravity makes all bodies fall down to the ground as soon as they are created.

More about SpriteKit can be explored using the following link:

```
https://developer.apple.com/library/ios/documentation/
GraphicsAnimation/Conceptual/SpriteKit_PG/Physics/Physics.html
```

Getting ready

The first task is to create the world and then add bodies to it, which can interact according to the principles of physics. You can create game objects in the form of sprites and associate physics bodies to them. You can also set various properties of the object to specify its behavior.

How to do it...

In this section, we will learn about the basic components that are used to develop games. We will also learn how to set game configurations, including the world settings such as gravity and boundary.

1. The initial step is to apply the gravity to the scene. Every scene has a physics world associated with it. We can update the gravity of the physics world in our scene using the following line of code:

   ```
   self.physicsWorld.gravity = CGVectorMake(0.0f, 0.0f);
   ```

   Currently we have set the gravity of the scene to 0, which means the bodies will be in a state of free fall. They will not experience any force due to gravity in the world.

2. In several games we also need to set a boundary to the games. Usually, the bounds of the view can serve as the bounds for our physics world. The following code will help us to set up the boundary for our game, which will be as per the bounds of our game scene:

   ```
   // 1 Create a physics body that borders the screen
   SKPhysicsBody* gameBorderBody = [SKPhysicsBody
     bodyWithEdgeLoopFromRect:self.frame];
   // 2 Set physicsBody of scene to gameBorderBody
   self.physicsBody = gameBorderBody;
   // 3 Set the friction of that physicsBody to 0
   self.physicsBody.friction = 0.0f;
   ```

In the first line of code we are initializing a SKPhysicsBody object. This object is used to add the physics simulation to any SKSpriteNode. We have created the gameBorderBody as a rectangle with the dimensions equal to the current scene frame.

Then we assign that physics object to the physicsBody of our current scene (every SKSpriteNode object has the physicsBody property through which we can associate physics bodies to any node).

After this we update the physicsBody.friction. This line of code updates the friction property of our world. The friction property defines the friction value of one physics body with another physics body. Here we have set this to 0, in order to make the objects move freely, without slowing down.

3. Every game object is inherited from the SKSpriteNode class, which allows the physics body to hold on to the node. Let us take an example and create a game object using the following code:

```
// 1
SKSpriteNode* gameObject = [SKSpriteNode
  spriteNodeWithImageNamed: @"object.png"];
gameObject.name = @"game_object";
gameObject.position = CGPointMake(self.frame.size.width/3,
  self.frame.size.height/3);
[self addChild:gameObject];

// 2
gameObject.physicsBody = [SKPhysicsBody
  bodyWithCircleOfRadius:gameObject.frame.size.width/2];
// 3
gameObject.physicsBody.friction = 0.0f;
```

We are already familiar with the first few lines of code wherein we are creating the sprite reference and then adding it to the scene. Now in the next line of code, we are associating a physics body with that sprite. We are initializing the circular physics body with radius and associating it with the sprite object.

Then we can update various other properties of the physics body such as friction, restitution, linear damping, and so on.

4. The physics body properties also allow you to apply force. To apply force you need to provide the direction where you want to apply force.

```
[gameObject.physicsBody applyForce:CGVectorMake(10.0f,
  -10.0f)];
```

In the code we are applying force in the bottom-right corner of the world. To provide the direction coordinates we have used CGVectorMake, which accepts the vector coordinates of the physics world.

5. You can also apply impulse instead of force. Impulse can be defined as a force that acts for a specific interval of time and is equal to the change in linear momentum produced over that interval.

```
[gameObject.physicsBody applyImpulse:CGVectorMake(10.0f,
  -10.0f)];
```

6. While creating games, we frequently use static objects. To create a rectangular static object we can use the following code:

```
SKSpriteNode* box = [[SKSpriteNode alloc]
  initWithImageNamed: @"box.png"];
box.name = @"box_object";
box.position = CGPointMake(CGRectGetMidX(self.frame),
  box.frame.size.height * 0.6f);
[self addChild:box];
box.physicsBody = [SKPhysicsBody
  bodyWithRectangleOfSize:box.frame.size];
box.physicsBody.friction = 0.4f;
// make physicsBody static
box.physicsBody.dynamic = NO;
```

So all the code is the same except one special property, which is dynamic. By default this property is set to YES, which means that all the physics bodies will be dynamic by default and can be converted to static after setting this Boolean to NO. Static bodies do not react to any force or impulse. Simply put, dynamic physics bodies can move while the static physics bodies cannot .

Integrating physics engine with games

From this section onwards, we will develop a mini game that will have a dynamic moving body and a static body. The basic concept of the game will be to create an infinite bouncing ball with a moving paddle that will be used to give direction to the ball.

Getting ready...

To develop a mini game using the physics engine, start by creating a new project. Open Xcode and go to **File** | **New** | **Project** and then navigate to **iOS** | **Application** | **SpriteKit Game**. In the pop-up screen, provide the **Product Name** as PhysicsSimulation, navigate to **Devices** | **iPhone** and click on **Next** as shown in the following screenshot:

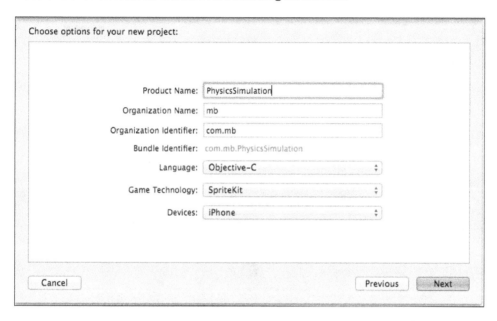

Click on **Next** and save the project on your hard drive.

Once the project is saved, you should be able to see something similar to the following screenshot:

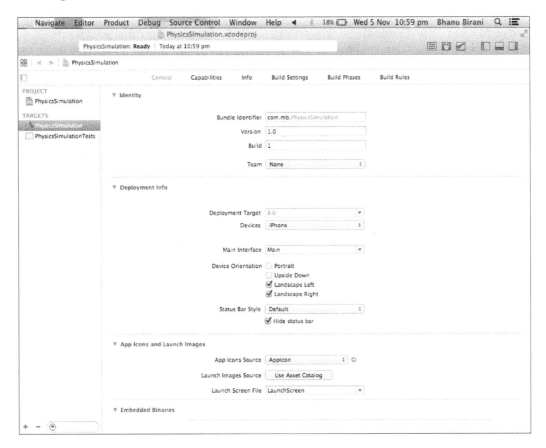

In the project settings page, just uncheck the **Portrait** from **Device Orientation** section as we are supporting only landscape mode for this game.

Graphics and games cannot be separated for long; you will also need some graphics for this game. Download the graphics folder, drag it and import it into the project. Make sure that the **Copy items into destination group's folder (if needed)** is checked and then click on **Finish** button. It should be something similar to the following screenshot:

```
//
//  GameScene.m
//  PhysicsSimulation
//
//  Created by Bhanu Birani on 05/11/14.
//  Copyright (c) 2014 mb. All rights reserved.
//

#import "GameScene.h"

@implementation GameScene

-(id)initWithSize:(CGSize)size {
    if (self = [super initWithSize:size]) {
        SKSpriteNode* background = [SKSpriteNode spriteNodeWithImageNamed:@"bg.png"];
        background.position = CGPointMake(self.frame.size.width/2, self.frame.size.height/2);
        [self addChild:background];
    }
    return self;
}

@end
```

How to do it...

Now your project template is ready for a physics-based mini game. We need to update the game template project to get started with code game logic. Take the following steps to integrate the basic physics object in the game.

1. Open the file GameScene.m .This class creates a scene that will be plugged into the games. Remove all code from this class and just add the following function:

    ```
    -(id)initWithSize:(CGSize)size {
        if (self = [super initWithSize:size]) {
            SKSpriteNode* background = [SKSpriteNode
              spriteNodeWithImageNamed:@"bg.png"];
            background.position =
             CGPointMake(self.frame.size.width/2,
               self.frame.size.height/2);
            [self addChild:background];
        }
    }
    ```

    This initWithSize method creates an blank scene of the specified size. The code written inside the init function allows you to add the background image at the center of the screen in your game.

2. Now when you compile and run the code, you will observe that the background image is not placed correctly on the scene. To resolve this, open `GameViewController.m`. Remove all code from this file and add the following function;

```
-(void)viewWillLayoutSubviews {
    [super viewWillLayoutSubviews];

    // Configure the view.
    SKView * skView = (SKView *)self.view;
    if (!skView.scene) {
        skView.showsFPS = YES;
        skView.showsNodeCount = YES;

        // Create and configure the scene.
        GameScene * scene = [GameScene
           sceneWithSize:skView.bounds.size];
        scene.scaleMode = SKSceneScaleModeAspectFill;

        // Present the scene.
        [skView presentScene:scene];
    }
}
```

To ensure that the view hierarchy is properly laid out, we have implemented the `viewWillLayoutSubviews` method. It does not work perfectly in `viewDidLayoutSubviews` method because the size of the scene is not known at that time.

3. Now compile and run the app. You should be able to see the background image correctly. It will look something similar to the following screenshot:

4. So now that we have the background image in place, let us add gravity to the world. Open `GameScene.m` and add the following line of code at the end of the `initWithSize` method:

```
self.physicsWorld.gravity = CGVectorMake(0.0f, 0.0f);
```

This line of code will set the gravity of the world to 0, which means there will be no gravity.

5. Now as we have removed the gravity to make the object fall freely, it's important to create a boundary around the world, which will hold all the objects of the world and prevent them to go off the screen. Add the following line of code to add the invisible boundary around the screen to hold the physics objects:

```
// 1 Create a physics body that borders the screen
SKPhysicsBody* gameborderBody = [SKPhysicsBody
bodyWithEdgeLoopFromRect:self.frame];
// 2 Set physicsBody of scene to borderBody
self.physicsBody = gameborderBody;
// 3 Set the friction of that physicsBody to 0
self.physicsBody.friction = 0.0f;
```

In the first line, we are are creating an edge-based physics boundary object, with a screen size frame. This type of a physics body does not have any mass or volume and also remains unaffected by force and impulses. Then we associate the object with the physics body of the scene. In the last line we set the friction of the body to 0, for a seamless interaction between objects and the boundary surface. The final file should look something like the following screenshot:

6. Now we have our surface ready to hold the physics world objects. Let us create a new physics world object using the following line of code:

```
// 1
SKSpriteNode* circlularObject = [SKSpriteNode
spriteNodeWithImageNamed: @"ball.png"];
circlularObject.name = ballCategoryName;
circlularObject.position = CGPointMake(self.frame.size.width/3,
self.frame.size.height/3);
[self addChild:circlularObject];

// 2
circlularObject.physicsBody = [SKPhysicsBody bodyWithCircleOfRadiu
s:circlularObject.frame.size.width/2];
// 3
circlularObject.physicsBody.friction = 0.0f;
// 4
circlularObject.physicsBody.restitution = 1.0f;
// 5
circlularObject.physicsBody.linearDamping = 0.0f;
// 6
circlularObject.physicsBody.allowsRotation = NO;
```

Here we have created the sprite and then we have added it to the scene. Then in the later steps we associate the circular physics body with the sprite object. Finally, we alter the properties of that physics body.

7. Now compile and run the application; you should be able to see the circular ball on the screen as shown in screenshot below:

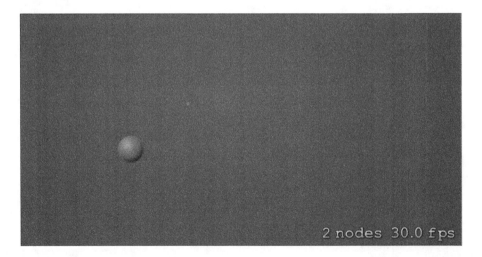

8. The circular ball is added to the screen, but it does nothing. So it's time to add some action in the code. Add the following line of code at the end of the `initWithSize` method:

```
[circlularObject.physicsBody applyImpulse:CGVectorMake(10.0f,
-10.0f)];
```

This will apply the force on the physics body, which in turn will move the associated ball sprite as well.

9. Now compile and run the project. You should be able to see the ball moving and then collide with the boundary and bounce back, as there is no friction between the boundary and the ball. So now we have the infinite bouncing ball in the game.

How it works...

There are several properties used while creating physics bodies to define their behavior in the physics world. The following is a detailed description of the properties used in the preceding code:

- ▸ **Restitution property** defines the bounciness of an object. Setting the restitution to `1.0f`, means that the ball collision will be perfectly elastic with any object. This means that the ball will bounce back with a force equal to the impact.

- ▸ **Linear Damping property** allows the simulation of fluid or air friction. This is accomplished by reducing the linear velocity of the body. In our case, we do not want the ball to slow down while moving and hence we have set the restitution to `0.0f`.

There's more...

You can read about all these properties in detail at Apple's developer documentation:
`https://developer.apple.com/library/IOs/documentation/SpriteKit/`
`Reference/SKPhysicsBody_Ref/index.html`.

Adding real-world simulation

Now we will be adding some real simulation in the game. We will add more physics bodies and make them interact with each other. This will help us to understand the physics interaction between various physics objects.

How to do it...

Now we have the infinite bouncing ball in place. To add more fun to the game, let us add some more elements to the it.

1. First we will add the static block to the game. To accomplish this, add the following line of code at the end of the `initWithSize` method:

    ```
    SKSpriteNode* block = [[SKSpriteNode alloc] initWithImageNamed:
    @"block.png"];
    block.name = paddleCategoryName;
    block.position = CGPointMake(CGRectGetMidX(self.frame), block.
    frame.size.height * 0.6f);
    [self addChild:block];
    block.physicsBody = [SKPhysicsBody bodyWithRectangleOfSize:block.
    frame.size];
    block.physicsBody.restitution = 0.1f;
    block.physicsBody.friction = 0.4f;
    // make physicsBody static
    block.physicsBody.dynamic = NO;
    ```

    First we create the block sprite. After that we associate a physics body to it and change the various parameters of the physics body object as well. The most important thing to note here is `block.physicsBody.dynamic = NO`. By default all the physics bodies are dynamic; so to create static bodies, we just need to set the `physicsBody.dynamic` Boolean to `NO`.

2. After adding the code, the final file should look something similar to the following screenshot:

```
Navigate   Editor   Product   Debug   Source Control   Window   Help        ◀  ⌁  34% ⎕  Fri 7 Nov 9:22 pm   Bhanu Birani   Q  ≔
                                    m  GameScene.m
        Running PhysicsSimulation on iPhone 5                                              ▤ ⬚ ✐      ▯▭▯

◀  ▶  | 🗎 PhysicsSimulation ⟩ ▢ PhysicsSimulation ⟩ m GameScene.m ⟩ Ⓜ –initWithSize:
29          self.physicsBody = gameborderBody;
30          // 3 Set the friction of that physicsBody to 0
31          self.physicsBody.friction = 0.0f;
32
33
34          // 1
35          SKSpriteNode* circlularObject = [SKSpriteNode spriteNodeWithImageNamed: @"ball.png"];
36          circlularObject.name = ballCategoryName;
37          circlularObject.position = CGPointMake(self.frame.size.width/3, self.frame.size.height/3);
38          [self addChild:circlularObject];
39
40          // 2
41          circlularObject.physicsBody = [SKPhysicsBody bodyWithCircleOfRadius:circlularObject.frame.size.
                width/2];
42          // 3
43          circlularObject.physicsBody.friction = 0.0f;
44          // 4
45          circlularObject.physicsBody.restitution = 1.0f;
46          // 5
47          circlularObject.physicsBody.linearDamping = 0.0f;
48          // 6
49          circlularObject.physicsBody.allowsRotation = NO;
50
51          [circlularObject.physicsBody applyImpulse:CGVectorMake(10.0f, -10.0f)];
52
53          SKSpriteNode* block = [[SKSpriteNode alloc] initWithImageNamed: @"block.png"];
54          block.name = paddleCategoryName;
55          block.position = CGPointMake(CGRectGetMidX(self.frame), block.frame.size.height * 0.6f);
56          [self addChild:block];
57          block.physicsBody = [SKPhysicsBody bodyWithRectangleOfSize:block.frame.size];
58          block.physicsBody.restitution = 0.1f;
59          block.physicsBody.friction = 0.4f;
60          // make physicsBody static
61          block.physicsBody.dynamic = NO;
62      }
63      return self;
64  }
```

3. Now compile and run the code. You should be able to see the block on the screen
    with a static body. Observe closely that when the ball collides with the block,
    it bounces back and you can play with it endlessly.

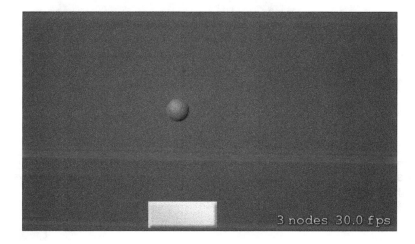

4. It's time to add some more action to make the game exciting. Now we will make the block paddle move based on touch. The following functions will help us to accomplish this:

```
- (void) touchesBegan: (NSSet*) touches
    withEvent: (UIEvent*) event;
- (void) touchesMoved: (NSSet*) touches
    withEvent: (UIEvent*) event;
- (void) touchesEnded: (NSSet*) touches
    withEvent: (UIEvent*) event;
```

These methods provide the callback when you touch the screen and also provide the list of the objects which were touched. There are three callbacks for touch begin, touch move and touch end action.

5. Now add the following code just before the `@implementation` line in `GameScene.m` file:

```
@interface GameScene ()

@property (nonatomic) BOOL isPaddleTapped;

@end
```

We have thus created a property to hold the user's state of touch on the paddle.

6. Now we will implement `touchesBegan:withEvent` function in our `GameScene.m` file. Add the following function just next to the `init` method:

```
- (void) touchesBegan: (NSSet*) touches
  withEvent: (UIEvent*) event {

    UITouch* touch = [touches anyObject];
    CGPoint touchLocation = [touch locationInNode:self];

    SKPhysicsBody* body = [self.physicsWorld
        bodyAtPoint:touchLocation];
    if (body && [body.node.name isEqualToString:
        paddleCategoryName]) {
        NSLog(@"touch began on paddle");
        self.isPaddleTapped = YES;
    }
}
```

This function will listen for the touch begin event and use it to find the body at the location where the user taps on the scene. In the next line, we get the physics body at the touch location.

7. Now compile and run the code. When you touch on the paddle, you should be able to see the logs demonstrating the touch working on the paddle.

```
71
72   -(void)touchesBegan:(NSSet*)touches withEvent:(UIEvent*)event {
73
74       UITouch* touch = [touches anyObject];
75       CGPoint touchLocation = [touch locationInNode:self];
76
77       SKPhysicsBody* body = [self.physicsWorld bodyAtPoint:touchLocation];
78       if (body && [body.node.name isEqualToString: paddleCategoryName]) {
79           NSLog(@"touch began on paddle");
80           self.isPaddleTapped = YES;
81       }
82   }
83
84   @end
85
```

```
2014-11-07 22:24:14.078 PhysicsSimulation[1673:52375] touch began on paddle
2014-11-07 22:24:16.332 PhysicsSimulation[1673:52375] touch began on paddle
2014-11-07 22:24:19.760 PhysicsSimulation[1673:52375] touch began on paddle
2014-11-07 22:24:20.820 PhysicsSimulation[1673:52375] touch began on paddle
```

All Output :

8. Now let us go ahead and implement `touchesMoved:withEvent` and add the following function just next to `touchesBegan`:

```
-(void)touchesMoved:(NSSet*)touches withEvent:(UIEvent*)event {

    if (self.isPaddleTapped) {
        // 2 Get touch location
        UITouch* touch = [touches anyObject];
        CGPoint touchLocation = [touch locationInNode:self];
        CGPoint previousLocation = [touch
previousLocationInNode:self];
        // 3 Get node for paddle
        SKSpriteNode* paddle = (SKSpriteNode*)[self
            childNodeWithName: paddleCategoryName];
        // 4 Calculate new position along x for paddle
        int paddleX = paddle.position.x + (touchLocation.x
            - previousLocation.x);
        // 5 Limit x so that the paddle will not leave the
            screen to left or right
        paddleX = MAX(paddleX, paddle.size.width/2);
        paddleX = MIN(paddleX, self.size.width -
            paddle.size.width/2);
        // 6 Update position of paddle
        paddle.position = CGPointMake(paddleX,
            paddle.position.y);
    }
}
```

Initially, check if the paddle is tapped. If yes, then update the paddle position based on the user's touch location. While repositioning, we just need to make sure that the position *y* of the paddle does not change.

9. Finally add the following function after `touchedMoved` in the `GameScene.m` file:

```
-(void)touchesEnded:(NSSet*)touches
   withEvent:(UIEvent*)event {
      self.isPaddleTapped = NO;
}
```

Just turn the `isPaddleTapped` flag off in the touch end function.

10. Now compile and run the game. You should be able to move the paddle block to hit the ball and keep it moving. You should tap on the paddle to move it to the left and right sides of the screen.

7
Adding Reality to Games

In this chapter, we will cover the following recipes:

- ▸ Creating physics bodies in the world
- ▸ Physics joints
- ▸ Detecting contact and collisions

Introduction

In the previous chapters, you learned about the anatomy of physics simulation in games. We have explored various sections of the Physics engine, including its integration with games and playing with the basics of the game engine. You have learned the ways to create static and dynamic bodies as well. Now, in this chapter, our major focus will be on adding some more reality to games by the advanced level of physics integration. This includes playing with lots of physics bodies tied together with joints. You will also learn the ways to detect the collision between two physics bodies. The overall agenda will be to create a mini game in the chapter, which will hold together all the recipes and will help in better understanding of these sections. The game will be divided into three the following parts:

- ▸ Creating the game holding a physics world with some physics bodies
- ▸ Then we will move forward and join those physics bodies with various types of joints
- ▸ Then, finally, you will learn various ways to detect the collision and contact between the various physics bodies in the world

Creating physics bodies in the world

In this recipe, we will be creating a fresh game project and will set it up to be used in all the recipes. The game project will hold together the creation of a physics world along with some physics body objects. We will be using these physics objects to add joints between them.

Getting ready

To develop a mini game using the physics engine, start by creating a new project. Open Xcode and go to **File | New | Project** and navigate to **iOS | Application | SpriteKit Game**. In the popup, provide the product name as `Physics Joints` and navigate to **Devices | iPhone** and click on **Next** as shown in the following screenshot:

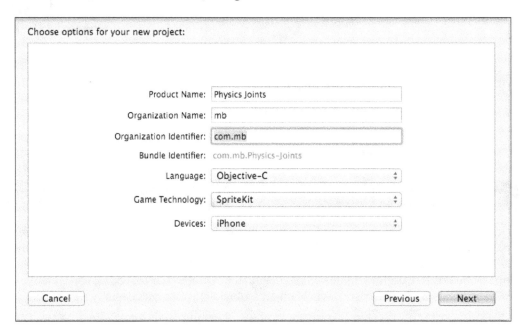

Click on **Next** and save the project on your hard drive.

Once the project is saved, you should be able to see project settings. In this project settings page, just uncheck the **Portrait** from the **Device Orientation** section as we are supporting only landscape mode for this game. The final screen should look something similar to following screenshot:

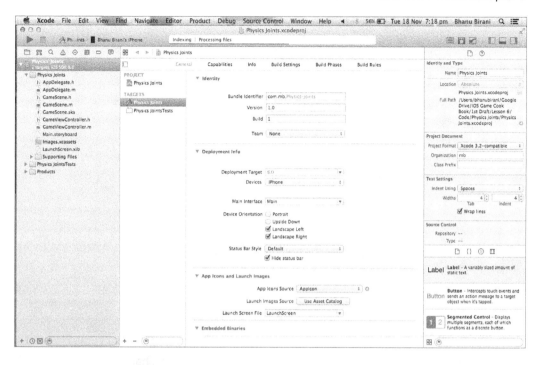

How to do it...

Now our project template is ready to hold together some advanced physics behaviors. To accommodate these behaviors, we also need to tweak some code in the project. Perform the following steps to update the project as per our requirements:

1. Open the `GameScene.m` file available with the code bundle of this chapter; this class creates a scene that will be plugged into the game. Remove all the code from this class and just add the following function:

    ```
    -(id)initWithSize:(CGSize)size {
        if (self = [super initWithSize:size]) {
            self.backgroundColor = [SKColor colorWithRed:0.15
                green:0.15 blue:0.3 alpha:1.0];
        }
        return self;
    }
    ```

    This `initWithSize` method creates an empty scene with specified size. The code written inside the `init` function changes the background color of the scene. We can tweak the rgb to get the desired background color.

2. Now open `GameViewController.m`. Remove all the code from this file and add the following function:

```objc
- (void)viewWillLayoutSubviews {
    [super viewWillLayoutSubviews];

    // Configure the view.
    SKView * skView = (SKView *)self.view;
    if (!skView.scene) {
        skView.showsFPS = YES;
        skView.showsNodeCount = YES;

        // Create and configure the scene.
        GameScene * scene = [GameScene
            sceneWithSize:skView.bounds.size];
        scene.scaleMode = SKSceneScaleModeAspectFill;

        // Present the scene.
        [skView presentScene:scene];
    }
}
```

3. Now compile and run the app. You should be able to see the background color correctly. This will look something similar to following screenshot:

4. Now we have the background color in place, so let's add the gravity to the world. Open `GameScene.m` and add the following line of code in the end of the `initWithSize` method:

```objc
self.physicsWorld.gravity = CGVectorMake(0.0f, -0.5f);
```

This line of code will set the gravity of the world to -0.5, which means all the physics objects will experience a force towards the ground in the game scene.

5. Now we have applied some gravitational force to make the objects pulled towards the ground. So it's important to make some boundary to the world, which will hold all the objects of the world and prevent them from going off the screen. Add the following line of code to add the invisible boundary around the screen to hold the physics objects:

```
self.PhysicsBody = [SKPhysicsBody
  bodyWithEdgeLoopFromRect:self.frame];
self.physicsBody.friction = 0.0f;
```

6. In the first line, we are creating an edge-based physics boundary object with a screen-size frame. This type of physics body does not have any mass or volume and they also remain unaffected by forces and impulses. Then we associate the object with the physics body of the scene. In the last line, we change the friction of the body to 0, to make interaction between objects and the boundary surface lossless.

7. Now we are all set to create physics bodies in the world. Add the following method just after the `initWithSize` method:

```
-(void)update:(CFTimeInterval)currentTime {
    /* Called before each frame is rendered */
}
```

This is the update method that will be called in each frame of the game execution. So all the actions that need regular updates will be coded inside this method.

8. It's time to create physics objects in the world. All the physics objects are referred to as bodies. Now add the following method to create the bodies in the physics world.

```
-(void)createPhysicsBodiesOnScene:(SKScene*)scene
{
    //Adding Rectangle
    SKSpriteNode* backBone = [[SKSpriteNode alloc]
      initWithColor:[UIColor whiteColor]
        size:CGSizeMake(20, 200)];
    backBone.position =
      CGPointMake(CGRectGetWidth(self.frame)/2.0,
        CGRectGetHeight(self.frame)/2.0);
    backBone.physicsBody = [SKPhysicsBody
      bodyWithRectangleOfSize:backBone.size];
    [scene addChild:backBone];


    //Adding Square
    SKSpriteNode* head = [[SKSpriteNode alloc]
      initWithColor:[SKColor grayColor] size:CGSizeMake(40,
        40)];
```

```
head.position = CGPointMake(backBone.position.x,
   backBone.position.y-40);
head.physicsBody = [SKPhysicsBody
   bodyWithRectangleOfSize:head.size];
[scene addChild:head];

}
```

The preceding code will create two physics bodies, one rectangle and one square. We have adjusted the bodies' positions relative to each other.

9. Now, add the following line of code at the end of the `initWithSize` method to add the physics bodies in the game scene:

```
[self createPhysicsBodiesOnScene:self];
```

Here we are creating the bodies by calling the instance method inside `initWithSize`.

10. Now, compile and run the app. You should be able to see the two physics bodies created in the world and they will fall to the ground because of gravity. This will look something similar to following screenshot:

Physics joints

We have already seen lots of interesting features of the physics engine. However, we can make our games even more interesting by connecting the physics bodies with each other using joints. All the physics simulation and forces will be applied on the bodies after considering the way they are joined together.

Getting ready

There are various ways of joining two physics bodies together. They vary based on the places and the location of the bodies that are joined. Joints are divided into the following types based on the ways they connect bodies with each other:

- **Pin Joint**: This type of joint joins/pins two physics together such that they both can independently rotate around their anchor point. The joint will look something similar to following diagram:

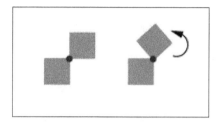

- **Limit Joint**: In this type of joints the bodies always maintain the fix maximum distance from each other. This is something like the bodies are connected to each other with a rote with a fixed maximum distance which is the length of the rope.

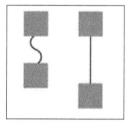

- **Spring Joint**: This type of joint attaches two bodies as if they were connected to each other with a spring. This makes them behave in a perfectly elastic manner. The length of the spring can be defined by the initial distance between two bodies.

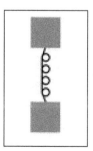

▶ **Sliding Joint**: This type of joint allows to bodies to slide with respect to each other. The sliding axis can be explicitly defined by the user.

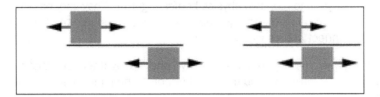

▶ **Fixed Joint**: This type of joint fuses the two physics bodies with each other through a provided reference point. These joints can be used to create complex objects, which can be broken into pieces later.

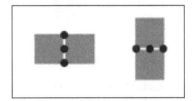

How to do it...

Now we will open our working project again to integrate and implement all types of joints in our project. The following steps will provide the step-by-step ways to implement the joints and understand them in more depth.

1. To implement the pin joint, open the `GameScene.m` file and add the following function in it:

```
- (void) createPinJointOnScene: (SKScene*) scene
{
    //Adding Rectangle
    SKSpriteNode* backBone = [[SKSpriteNode alloc]
        initWithColor: [UIColor whiteColor]
            size:CGSizeMake(20, 200)];
    backBone.position =
        CGPointMake(CGRectGetWidth(self.frame)/2.0,
            CGRectGetHeight(self.frame)/2.0);
    backBone.physicsBody = [SKPhysicsBody
        bodyWithRectangleOfSize:backBone.size];
    backBone.physicsBody.categoryBitMask =
        GFPhysicsCategoryRectangle;
    backBone.physicsBody.collisionBitMask =
        GFPhysicsCategoryWorld;
```

```
[scene addChild:backBone];

//Adding Square
SKSpriteNode* head = [[SKSpriteNode alloc]
  initWithColor:[SKColor grayColor] size:CGSizeMake(40,
    40)];
head.position = CGPointMake(backBone.position.x+5,
  backBone.position.y-40);
head.physicsBody = [SKPhysicsBody
  bodyWithRectangleOfSize:head.size];
head.physicsBody.categoryBitMask =
  GFPhysicsCategorySquare;
head.physicsBody.collisionBitMask =
  GFPhysicsCategoryWorld;
[scene addChild:head];

//Pinning Rectangle and Square
NSLog(@"Head position %@",
  NSStringFromCGPoint(head.position));
SKPhysicsJointPin* pin =[SKPhysicsJointPin
  jointWithBodyA:backBone.physicsBody
    bodyB:head.physicsBody
      anchor:CGPointMake(head.position.x-5,
        head.position.y)];
[scene.physicsWorld addJoint:pin];
}
```

In the first five lines of code, we are creating a rectangular sprite with a physics body. We have also specified the collision and the category mask for this sprite.

Similarly, in the following lines of code, we will create square sprite with the physics body attached. For this sprite also, we are specifying the category and the collision masks.

Then, finally, in last three lines of code, we are attaching the two bodies to each other through a pin joint. We've created an object of the SKPhysicsJointPin class and provided both the rectangle and square bodies to it along with the anchor point from which they will be rotating around each other.

2. Now, replace the createPhysicsBodiesOnScene function call with createPinJointOnScene. Add the following code at the end of the init function:

```
[self createPinJointOnScene:self];
```

The final function should look something similar to following screenshot:

```objectivec
-(id)initWithSize:(CGSize)size {
    if (self = [super initWithSize:size]) {
        self.backgroundColor = [SKColor colorWithRed:0.15 green:0.15 blue:0.3 alpha:1.0];
        self.physicsWorld.gravity = CGVectorMake(0, -0.5);
        self.physicsBody = [SKPhysicsBody bodyWithEdgeLoopFromRect:self.frame];
        self.physicsBody.friction = 0.0f;

        [self createPinJointOnScene:self];
    }
    return self;
}
```

3. Now, compile and run the project and you should be able to see both the physics bodies attached with the pin joint. You can see them attached to each other through the anchor point.

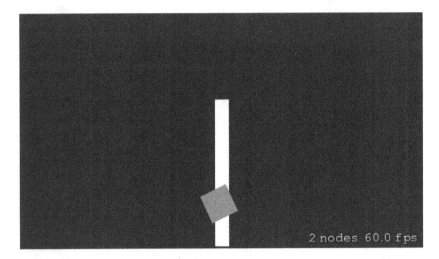

4. Now we will implement the fixed joint; open the GameScene.m file, and add the following function to implement the fixed joint:

```objectivec
- (void)createFixedJointOnScene:(SKScene*)scene
{
    //Adding Rectangle
    SKSpriteNode* backBone = [[SKSpriteNode alloc]
        initWithColor:[UIColor whiteColor]
            size:CGSizeMake(20, 200)];
    backBone.position =
        CGPointMake(CGRectGetWidth(self.frame)/2.0,
            CGRectGetHeight(self.frame)/2.0);
```

```objc
backBone.physicsBody = [SKPhysicsBody
   bodyWithRectangleOfSize:backBone.size];
backBone.physicsBody.categoryBitMask =
   GFPhysicsCategoryRectangle;
backBone.physicsBody.collisionBitMask =
   GFPhysicsCategoryWorld;
[scene addChild:backBone];


//Adding Square
SKSpriteNode* head = [[SKSpriteNode alloc]
   initWithColor:[SKColor grayColor] size:CGSizeMake(40,
      40)];
head.position = CGPointMake(backBone.position.x+5,
   backBone.position.y-40);
head.physicsBody = [SKPhysicsBody
   bodyWithRectangleOfSize:head.size];
head.physicsBody.categoryBitMask =
   GFPhysicsCategorySquare;
head.physicsBody.collisionBitMask =
   GFPhysicsCategoryWorld;
[scene addChild:head];


//Pinning Rectangle and Square
NSLog(@"Head position %@",
   NSStringFromCGPoint(head.position));
SKPhysicsJointFixed* pin =[SKPhysicsJointFixed
   jointWithBodyA:backBone.physicsBody
      bodyB:head.physicsBody
         anchor:CGPointMake(head.position.x-5,
            head.position.y)];
[scene.physicsWorld addJoint:pin];
}
```

Now, we have attached two physics bodies together with a fixed joint. In the last function, we have provided two bodies and the anchor point to which they are attached.

5. Now, replace the `createPinJointOnScene` function call with `createFixedJointOnScene`. Add the following code in the end of the `init` function:

```objc
[self createFixedJointOnScene:self];
```

6. Now, compile and run the project and you should be able to see both the physics bodies attached by the fixed joint. You will observe that the bodies are attached together with the specified anchor point.

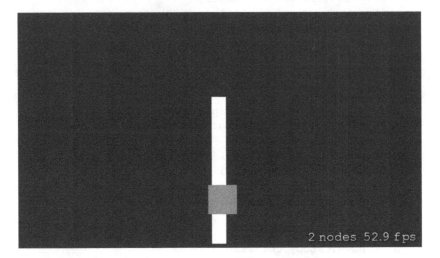

7. Now, to implement the sliding joint in our sample project, open the GameScene.m file and add the following function at the end:

```
-(void)createSlidingJointOnScene:(SKScene*)scene {
    //Adding Rectangle
    SKSpriteNode* backBone = [[SKSpriteNode alloc]
        initWithColor:[UIColor whiteColor]
            size:CGSizeMake(20, 200)];
    backBone.position =
        CGPointMake(CGRectGetWidth(self.frame)/2.0,
        CGRectGetHeight(self.frame)/2.0);
    backBone.physicsBody = [SKPhysicsBody
        bodyWithRectangleOfSize:backBone.size];
    backBone.physicsBody.categoryBitMask =
        GFPhysicsCategoryRectangle;
    backBone.physicsBody.collisionBitMask =
        GFPhysicsCategoryWorld;
    backBone.physicsBody.affectedByGravity = NO;
    backBone.physicsBody.allowsRotation = NO;
    [scene addChild:backBone];

    //Adding Square
    SKSpriteNode* head = [[SKSpriteNode alloc]
        initWithColor:[SKColor grayColor] size:CGSizeMake(40,
            40)];
```

```
head.position = CGPointMake(backBone.position.x,
   backBone.position.y-40);
head.physicsBody = [SKPhysicsBody
   bodyWithRectangleOfSize:head.size];
head.physicsBody.categoryBitMask =
   GFPhysicsCategorySquare;
head.physicsBody.collisionBitMask =
   GFPhysicsCategoryWorld;
[scene addChild:head];

//Pinning Rectangle and Square
NSLog(@"Head position %@",
   NSStringFromCGPoint(head.position));
SKPhysicsJointSliding* pin =[SKPhysicsJointSliding
   jointWithBodyA:backBone.physicsBody
     bodyB:head.physicsBody anchor:head.position
       axis:CGVectorMake(0, 1)];
pin.shouldEnableLimits = YES;
pin.upperDistanceLimit = 200;
pin.lowerDistanceLimit = -100;

[scene.physicsWorld addJoint:pin];
}
```

8. Now you will observe that we are creating two physics bodies and in the last section we are joining both of them using the slide joint. However, to see slide joint in action, we will have to apply impulses on the square body. Add the following function to apply an impulse:

```
-(void)applyImpulseUpwards:(NSTimer*)timer {
   NSDictionary* dict = [timer userInfo];
   SKPhysicsBody* body = dict[@"body"];

   CGVector impulse = CGVectorMake(0, [dict[@"impulse"]
     intValue]);

   [body applyImpulse:impulse];
}
```

9. To add the impulse implementation, we will have to add the following line of code at the end of the `createSlidingJointOnScene` function.

```
[NSTimer scheduledTimerWithTimeInterval:5 target:self
   selector:@selector(applyImpulseUpwards:)
     userInfo:@{@"body":head.physicsBody,@"impulse":@(25)}
       repeats:YES];
```

Now the square body will experience the impulse every 5 seconds.

10. Now, replace the `createFixedJointOnScene` function call with `createSlidingJointOnScene`. Add the following code at the end of the `init` function:

    ```
    [self createSlidingJointOnScene:self];
    ```

11. Now, compile and run the project and you should be able to see both the physics bodies sliding over each other.

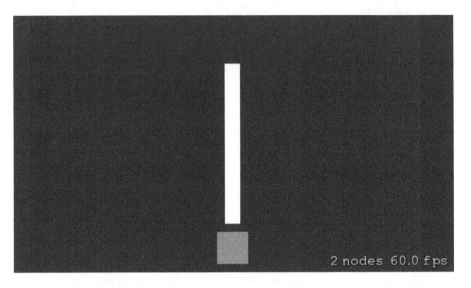

12. Now we will head towards implementing the spring joint in our sample project. Open the `GameScene.m` file and add the following function at the end of the file:

    ```
    - (void)createSpringJointOnScene:(SKScene*)scene
    {
        SKSpriteNode* backBone = [[SKSpriteNode alloc]
            initWithColor:[UIColor whiteColor]
              size:CGSizeMake(20, 200)];
        backBone.position =
            CGPointMake(CGRectGetWidth(self.frame)/2.0,
              CGRectGetHeight(self.frame)/2.0);
        backBone.physicsBody = [SKPhysicsBody
            bodyWithRectangleOfSize:backBone.size];
        backBone.physicsBody.categoryBitMask =
            GFPhysicsCategoryRectangle;
        backBone.physicsBody.collisionBitMask =
            GFPhysicsCategoryWorld;
    ```

```
[scene addChild:backBone];


//Adding Square
SKSpriteNode* head = [[SKSpriteNode alloc]
  initWithColor:[SKColor grayColor] size:CGSizeMake(40,
    40)];
head.position = CGPointMake(backBone.position.x,
  backBone.position.y+backBone.size.height/2.0+40);
head.physicsBody = [SKPhysicsBody
  bodyWithRectangleOfSize:head.size];
head.physicsBody.categoryBitMask =
  GFPhysicsCategorySquare;
head.physicsBody.collisionBitMask =
  GFPhysicsCategoryWorld;
[scene addChild:head];


//Pinning Rectangle and Square
NSLog(@"Head position %@",
  NSStringFromCGPoint(head.position));
SKPhysicsJointSpring* pin =[SKPhysicsJointSpring
  jointWithBodyA:backBone.physicsBody
    bodyB:head.physicsBody anchorA:head.position
      anchorB:CGPointMake(backBone.position.x,
        backBone.position.y+backBone.size.height/2.0)];
pin.damping = 0.5;
pin.frequency = 0.5;
[scene.physicsWorld addJoint:pin];
}
```

To apply a spring joint between two physics bodies, we have provided two physics bodies along with two anchor points as the function parameters. We can also provide additional parameters such as damping and frequencies.

13. Now, replace the `createSlidingJointOnScene` function call with `createSpringJointOnScene`. Add the following code at the end of the `init` function:

```
[self createSpringJointOnScene:self];
```

14. Now compile and run the project and you should be able to see both the physics bodies sliding over each other.

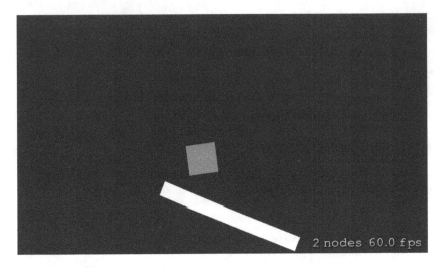

15. Our next type of joint is the limit joint in our sample project. Now open the GameScene.m file and add the following function at the end of the file:

```
-(void)createLimitJointOnScene:(SKScene*)scene {
    SKLabelNode* label = [SKLabelNode
        labelNodeWithFontNamed:@"Futura-Medium"];
    label.text = @"An upward impulse is applied to the
        square every few seconds.";
    label.fontSize = 14;
    label.position = CGPointMake(220,
        scene.view.frame.size.height-100);
    [scene addChild:label];

    SKSpriteNode* backBone = [[SKSpriteNode alloc]
        initWithColor:[UIColor whiteColor]
            size:CGSizeMake(20, 200)];
    backBone.position =
        CGPointMake(CGRectGetWidth(self.frame)/2.0,
            CGRectGetHeight(self.frame)/2.0);
    backBone.physicsBody = [SKPhysicsBody
        bodyWithRectangleOfSize:backBone.size];
    backBone.physicsBody.categoryBitMask =
        GFPhysicsCategoryRectangle;
    backBone.physicsBody.collisionBitMask =
        GFPhysicsCategoryWorld;
    [scene addChild:backBone];
```

```
//Adding Square
SKSpriteNode* head = [[SKSpriteNode alloc]
  initWithColor:[SKColor grayColor] size:CGSizeMake(40,
    40)];
head.position = CGPointMake(backBone.position.x,
  backBone.position.y+backBone.size.height/2.0+40);
head.physicsBody = [SKPhysicsBody
  bodyWithRectangleOfSize:head.size];
head.physicsBody.categoryBitMask =
  GFPhysicsCategorySquare;
head.physicsBody.collisionBitMask =
  GFPhysicsCategoryWorld;
[scene addChild:head];

//Pinning Rectangle and Square
NSLog(@"Head position %@",
  NSStringFromCGPoint(head.position));
SKPhysicsJointLimit* pin =[SKPhysicsJointLimit
  jointWithBodyA:backBone.physicsBody
    bodyB:head.physicsBody anchorA:head.position
      anchorB:CGPointMake(backBone.position.x,
        backBone.position.y+backBone.size.height/2.0)];
pin.maxLength = 100;
[scene.physicsWorld addJoint:pin];

[NSTimer scheduledTimerWithTimeInterval:5 target:self
  selector:@selector(applyImpulseUpwards:)
  userInfo:@{@"body":head.physicsBody,@"impulse":@(50)}
    repeats:YES];
}
```

In the second last section, we are applying the limit joint on both the physics bodies that we have created. To apply a limit joint, we have to pass both the bodies along with the anchor points that create the joint. Now, when the joint object is initialized, we can add the joint to the physics world.

As we have seen earlier in sliding joint, an extra impulse has been applied on one of the bodies. Similarly, here also we have to apply the impulse on the square body to test the limit joint behavior.

16. Now, replace the `createSpringJointOnScene` function call with `createLimitJointOnScene`. Add the following code at the end of the `init` function:

```
[self createLimitJointOnScene:self];
```

17. Now compile and run the project and you should be able to see both the physics bodies sliding over each other.

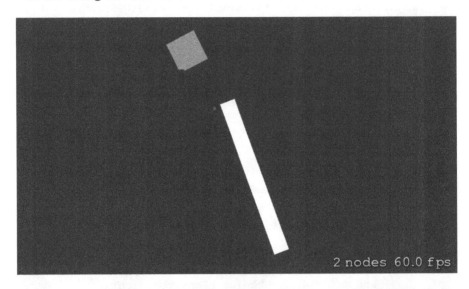

2 nodes 60.0 fps

Detecting contact and collisions

We apply physics simulation to the bodies by adding the `SKPhysicsBody` function to a node. While the scene processes each frame, it performs all the physics-related calculations for all the bodies in the scene. It also calculates all the custom forces that are applied on any body in the scene, which eventually gives the realistic effects in the game. Collision detection is an important part while developing any game in the real world because in almost all games we check for the collision of two bodies. For example, in any warfare game, we may need to check whether a bullet has collided with the player.

Getting ready

There are various shapes for the physics bodies that can be used to apply physics to a scene. These shapes are defined as the personal space of the node. When the shape of one node intersects with the shape of another node, the `-didBeginContact` method is invoked and physics may be applied. Now, to implement the collision detection, we will have to understand the following properties of the physics bodies:

- ▶ `categoryBitMask`: This property defines the category of the physics body. We can have custom categories depending on our requirement. For example, in a warfare game, we can have player, bullets, and enemies as the categories. All the physics bodies can be based on these categories.

> ▸ collisionBitMask: This property adds a mask that defines which physics bodies can collide with this physics body. This will help the physics engine to evaluate and throw only the required results in the delegate methods. For example, the bullets can only collide with enemies, not with any player.

> ▸ contactTestBitMask: This property defines the mask to specify which categories of physics bodies cause intersection notifications with this physics body.

How to do it...

Now, we will open our working project again to implement an example dealing with collision and contact detection. The following steps will provide the step-by-step ways to implement and understand collision detection in our project:

1. To implement the collision detection, open the GameScene.m file and add the following function at the end of the file:

```
- (void)createCollisionDetectionOnScene:(SKScene*)scene {
    collisionLabel = [SKLabelNode labelNodeWithFontNamed:@"Futura-
Medium"];
    collisionLabel.text = @"Collision detected";
    collisionLabel.fontSize = 18;
    collisionLabel.fontColor = [SKColor whiteColor];
    collisionLabel.position = CGPointMake(CGRectGetWidth(self.
frame)/2.0,
  CGRectGetHeight(self.frame)/1.2);
    collisionLabel.alpha = 0.0f;
    [scene addChild:collisionLabel];

    SKSpriteNode* backBone = [[SKSpriteNode alloc]
      initWithColor:[UIColor whiteColor]
        size:CGSizeMake(20, 200)];
    backBone.position =
      CGPointMake(CGRectGetWidth(self.frame)/2.0,
        CGRectGetHeight(self.frame)/2.0);
    backBone.physicsBody = [SKPhysicsBody
      bodyWithRectangleOfSize:backBone.size];
    backBone.physicsBody.categoryBitMask =
      GFPhysicsCategoryRectangle;
    backBone.physicsBody.collisionBitMask =
      GFPhysicsCategorySquare;
    backBone.physicsBody.contactTestBitMask =
      GFPhysicsCategorySquare;
    backBone.physicsBody.dynamic = YES;
    [scene addChild:backBone];
```

```
//Adding Square
SKSpriteNode* head = [[SKSpriteNode alloc]
    initWithColor:[SKColor grayColor] size:CGSizeMake(40,
        40)];
head.position = CGPointMake(backBone.position.x,
    backBone.position.y+backBone.size.height/2.0+40);
head.physicsBody = [SKPhysicsBody
    bodyWithRectangleOfSize:head.size];
head.physicsBody.categoryBitMask =
    GFPhysicsCategorySquare;
head.physicsBody.collisionBitMask =
    GFPhysicsCategoryRectangle;
head.physicsBody.contactTestBitMask =
    GFPhysicsCategoryRectangle;
head.physicsBody.dynamic = YES;
[scene addChild:head];

[NSTimer scheduledTimerWithTimeInterval:5 target:self
    selector:@selector(applyImpulseUpwards:)
    userInfo:@{@"body":head.physicsBody,@"impulse":@(50)}
     repeats:YES];
}
```

Now we are familiar with code in this function. We will create two physics bodies and add them on the scene. Finally, in the last section, we will apply an impulse every 5 seconds on the physics body.

Here we are updating three additional parameters for each of the physics bodies. We are updating `categoryBitMask`, `collisionBitMask`, and `contactTestBitMask` for the bodies. As explained, we are updating `categoryBitMask` to provide the specific categories to the physics bodies. Along with that, we provide the information to define which bodies it can detect collision with.

2. Now we have to add the delegate method, which will be invoked when both the bodies collide with each other. We have added logs to check the bodies that are colliding. We can identify bodies using their `categoryBitMask`.

```
- (void)didBeginContact:(SKPhysicsContact *)contact
{
    NSLog(@"did %u, %u", contact.bodyA.categoryBitMask, contact.bodyB.categoryBitMask);

}
```

3. Now, replace the `createLimitJointOnScene` function call with `createCollisionDetectionOnScene`. Add the following code at the end of the `init` function:

   ```
   [self createCollisionDetectionOnScene:self];
   ```

4. Also we have to subscribe to the delegate callbacks for contact detection. To subscribe, add the following line of code:

   ```
   self.physicsWorld.contactDelegate = self;
   ```

5. We will also have to declare the contact delegate in the interface file. So open `GameScene.h` and add the following code at the end of interface declaration line:

   ```
   <SKPhysicsContactDelegate>
   ```

6. The final code file should look something similar to following screenshot:

   ```
   #import <SpriteKit/SpriteKit.h>

   @interface GameScene : SKScene <SKPhysicsContactDelegate>

   @end
   ```

7. Now compile and run the project and you should be able to see both the physics bodies on the screen and logs on the Xcode debug window. You can see that the collision has been detected and printed in the logs. You can also notice that the collision has been detected between the bodies with category mask as 2 and 4. We have a rectangular body with mask as 2 and square body with mask as 4, which are colliding with each other.

```
No Selection
2014-12-11 20:57:12.840 Physics Joints[4599:1056521] did 2, 4
2014-12-11 20:57:13.707 Physics Joints[4599:1056521] did 2, 4
2014-12-11 20:57:13.840 Physics Joints[4599:1056521] did 2, 4
2014-12-11 20:57:17.340 Physics Joints[4599:1056521] did 4294967295, 4
2014-12-11 20:57:17.840 Physics Joints[4599:1056521] did 2, 4
2014-12-11 20:57:18.707 Physics Joints[4599:1056521] did 2, 4
2014-12-11 20:57:18.840 Physics Joints[4599:1056521] did 2, 4
2014-12-11 20:57:22.340 Physics Joints[4599:1056521] did 4294967295, 4
2014-12-11 20:57:22.841 Physics Joints[4599:1056521] did 2, 4
2014-12-11 20:57:23.707 Physics Joints[4599:1056521] did 2, 4
2014-12-11 20:57:23.841 Physics Joints[4599:1056521] did 2, 4
2014-12-11 20:57:27.341 Physics Joints[4599:1056521] did 4294967295, 4
2014-12-11 20:57:27.840 Physics Joints[4599:1056521] did 2, 4
2014-12-11 20:57:28.707 Physics Joints[4599:1056521] did 2, 4
2014-12-11 20:57:28.841 Physics Joints[4599:1056521] did 2, 4
2014-12-11 20:57:32.341 Physics Joints[4599:1056521] did 4294967295, 4
2014-12-11 20:57:32.841 Physics Joints[4599:1056521] did 2, 4

All Output
```

8. Now we will make the collision detection more intuitive. For this, let's add a label on the screen, which will blink when the bodies collide with each other. To do this, add the following line of code at the top just before the `@implementation` GameScene code:

```
SKLabelNode* collisionLabel;
```

9. Now, add the following lines of code at the start of the `createCollisionDetectionOnScene` function:

```
collisionLabel = [SKLabelNode labelNodeWithFontNamed:@"Futura-
Medium"];
collisionLabel.text = @"Collision detected";
collisionLabel.fontSize = 18;
collisionLabel.fontColor = [SKColor whiteColor];
collisionLabel.position =
  CGPointMake(CGRectGetWidth(self.frame)/2.0,
    CGRectGetHeight(self.frame)/1.2);
collisionLabel.alpha = 0.0f;
[scene addChild:collisionLabel];
```

10. Now, for fade-in and fade-out of the label on collision, add the following line of code at the end of the `didBeginContact` method:

```
SKSpriteNode *firstNode, *secondNode;

firstNode = (SKSpriteNode *)contact.bodyA.node;
secondNode = (SKSpriteNode *) contact.bodyB.node;

if (firstNode.physicsBody.categoryBitMask ==
  GFPhysicsCategoryRectangle &&
    secondNode.physicsBody.categoryBitMask ==
      GFPhysicsCategorySquare) {

    SKAction *fadeIn = [SKAction fadeAlphaTo:1.0f
      duration:0.2];
    SKAction *fadeOut = [SKAction fadeAlphaTo:0.0f
      duration:0.2];
    [collisionLabel runAction:fadeIn completion:^{
        [collisionLabel runAction:fadeOut];
    }];
}
```

11. Here we are checking for the rectangular and square bodies. Once we get a callback for the collision of these two bodies, we can fade in the label for a fraction of a second and then fade it out again. This will give a nice effect to show when the bodies have collided with each other.

12. Now compile and run the project and you should be able to see both the physics bodies attached with the pin joint. You can see them attached to each other through the anchor point.

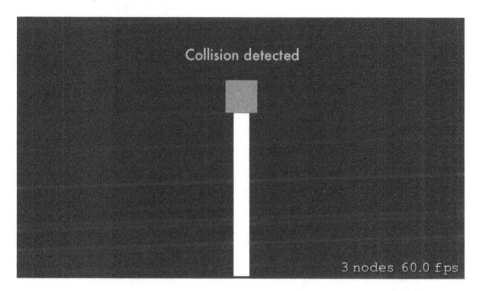

8
Introduction to Game Math and Physics

In this chapter, we will cover the following recipes:

- ▸ The Pythagorean theorem
- ▸ Using vectors
- ▸ Physics

Introduction

In this chapter, we will learn all the basic mathematical concepts that we will be using in the next few chapters of this book. While learning game physics, it's always good to have some basic command over mathematics and physics, as they are the main key components in making realistic games. For example, when we drop a ball on the ground, it keeps bouncing back and forth before coming to rest. To implement such conditions, we have to apply certain conditions to physical bodies by updating their physical parameters, such as restitution, force, bounce, friction, and so on. In the next chapter, we will use all the physics and mathematical concepts that we will learn in this chapter.

The Pythagorean theorem

The most widely used triangles are right-angled triangles. There are many interesting properties of right-angled triangles that can be used in games to make life easier. One of the famous properties is that the square of the hypotenuse of a right-angled triangle is equal to the sum of the squares of the other two sides.

Getting ready

The hypotenuse of a triangle is the longest side of a right-angled triangle, as shown in the following diagram:

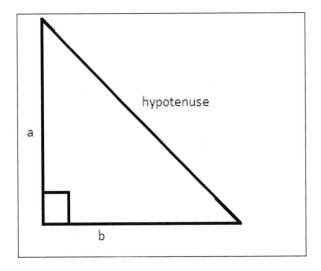

If the hypotenuse is denoted as h, the Pythagorean theorem can be written as follows:

$h^2 = a^2 + b^2$

If you take the square root of both the sides, you will get the following:

$h = sqrt(a^2+b^2)$

This means that if we know the length of any two sides of a right-angled triangle, we can easily find the length of the third side.

When working with the game's Artificial Intelligence (AI), we will be using the Pythagorean theorem frequently to calculate which agent is closer to the object. If side A is bigger than side B, then it will always be bigger, irrespective of whether the lengths are squared or not. Now, we can avoid taking the square roots to compare the distance. Instead, we can just compare the squared values.

How to do it

Here's a practical usage of the Pythagorean theorem:

Let's say we have a gunman at position X (8, 4) and his target at position Y (2, 1). The gunman can only fire a bullet a maximum distance of 10 units. Consequently, to determine whether he can hit the target, the distance between them must be calculated. This is easy to determine using the Pythagorean theorem. First, the lengths of the sides YZ and XZ shown in the following figure are calculated:

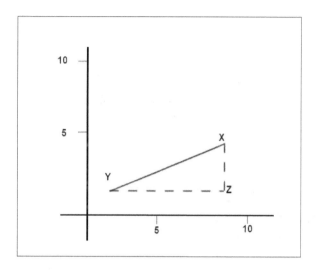

To find the distance XZ, the y component of the gunman's position is subtracted from the y component of the target's position as follows:

XZ = 4 - 1 = 3

To find the distance YZ, we do the same, but with the x components:

YZ = 8 - 2 = 6

Now that YZ and XZ are known, the distance from the gunman to the target can be calculated using the Pythagorean theorem as follows:

$$XY = \sqrt{XZ^2 + YZ^2}$$
$$= \sqrt{3^2 + 6^2}$$
$$= 6.71$$

Well within target range. Let the target be hit!

If you know the length of one of the sides of a right-angled triangle and one of the remaining two angles, you can determine everything else about the triangle using trigonometry. First, take a look at the following figure. It shows the names of each side of a right-angled triangle.

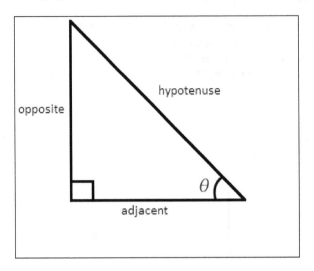

The following is what the figure represents:

▶ *Sin(θ) = opposite/hypotenuse*

▶ *Cos(θ) = adjacent/hypotenuse*

▶ *Tan(θ) = opposite/adjacent*

The best way to see how the sine, cosine, and tangent functions can be utilized is by taking a look at the following example:

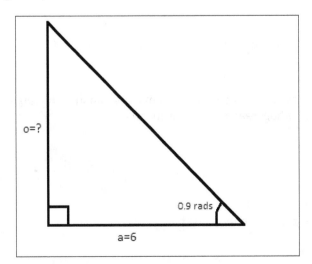

We want to calculate the length of the opposite side, given the length of the adjacent side and the angle. From here, we know that the tangent of an angle is equal to the opposite side divided by the adjacent side. Rearranging the equation a little gives us the following:

$o = aTan(\theta)$

So, all we have to do in order to get **o** is to pick up a calculator (to determine the tangent) and plug in the numbers, as follows:

$o = 6Tan(0.9)$

$\quad = 7.56$

Using vectors

We will be using vector math frequently when designing the AI for our games. Vectors are used everywhere, from calculating which direction a game agent should shoot its gun in, to expressing the inputs and outputs of an artificial neural network. You should know them well.

Let's take a point P as follows:

$P = (x, y)$

A two-dimensional vector looks almost the same when written, as follows:

$V = (x, y)$.

However, although similar, a vector represents two components: direction and magnitude. The right-hand side of the following diagram shows the vector (9, 6) situated at the origin:

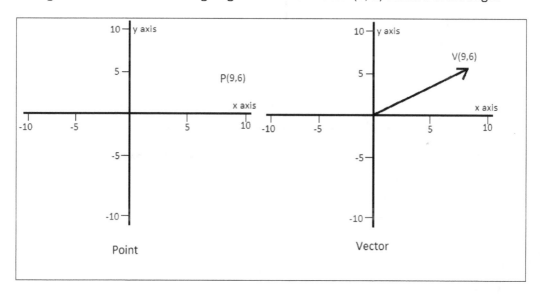

The bearing of the arrow shows the direction of the vector, and the length of the line represents the magnitude of the vector. A vector can represent the velocity of a vehicle. The magnitude of the vector represents the speed of the vehicle, and the direction represents the heading of the vehicle.

That's quite a lot of information from just two numbers (x, y). Vectors aren't restricted to two dimensions either. They can be any size at all. You would use a three-dimensional vector, (x, y, z), for example, to represent the velocity of a vehicle that moves in three dimensions, like a helicopter. Let's take a look at some of the things you can do with vectors.

How to do it

Vectors can be used in multiple ways, few of them are listed as follows:

- Multiplying vectors is a cinch. You just multiply each component by the value. For example, the vector V (4, 5) multiplied by 2 is (8, 10).

- The magnitude of a vector is its length. In the previous example, the magnitude of the vector V (4, 5) is the distance from the start point to the point P(4, 5) which is illustrated in the following figure:

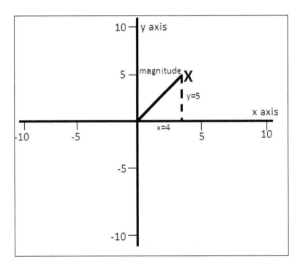

This is easy to calculate using the Pythagorean theorem as follows:

magnitude = $\sqrt{4^2 + 5^2} = 6.403$

If you had a three-dimensional vector, then you would use the similar equation:

magnitude = $\sqrt{x^2+y^2+z^2}$

Mathematicians place two vertical bars around a vector to denote its length, as shown in the following:

magnitude = $|V|$

▸ **Normalizing Vectors**: When a vector is normalized, it retains its direction but its magnitude is recalculated so that it is of unit length (a length of 1). To do this you divide each component of the vector by the magnitude of the vector. Mathematicians write the formula as follows:

$N = V/|V|$

Therefore, to normalize the vector (4, 5), you would do the following:

new X = 4 /6.403 = 0.62

new Y = 5 /6.403 = 0.78

▸ **Resolving Vectors**: It's possible to use trigonometry to resolve a vector into two separate vectors, one parallel to the x axis and one to the y axis. Take a look at the vector, V, representing the thrust of a jet fighter at point V, as shown in the following figure:

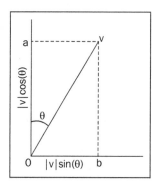

To resolve V into its x/y components, we need to find **Oa** and **Ob**. This will give us the component of the aircraft's thrust that is acting along the y axis, and the component along the x axis. Another way of putting it is that **Oa** is the amount of thrust acting along the x axis, and **Ob** is the amount along the y axis.

First, let's calculate the amount of thrust along the y axis: **Oa**. From trigonometry, we know that:

cos(θ) = adjacent / hypotenuse = Oa / |V|

Rearranged, this gives:

Oa = |V| Cos(θ) = y component

To calculate Ob, the following equation is used:

sin(θ) = opposite / hypotenuse = Ob / |V|

Giving:

Ob = |V| sin(θ) = x component

The Dot Product: The dot product gives the angle between two vectors—something you will need to calculate often when programming AI. Given the two two-dimensional vectors, u and v, the equation looks like the following:

u.v = ux vx + uy uy //Equation (1)

The . (dot) symbol denotes the dot product. Equation (1) doesn't give us an angle though. I promised an angle, so you'll get one! Here's another way of calculating the dot product:

u.v = |u| |v| cos(θ)

Rearranging, we get:

cos(θ) = u.v / |u| |v|

Remember, the vertical lines surrounding a vector indicate its magnitude. Now is the time when you discover one of the useful uses for normalizing vectors. If v and u are both normalized, then the equation simplifies enormously to:

*cos(θ) = u.v / 1*1*

    = u.v

Substituting in the equation from Equation (1) for the right-hand side gives:

cos(θ) = u.v = ux vx + uy uy

This gives us an equation for the angle between the vectors.

How it works

Here's an example of some of the vector methods you've just learned about working together. Let's say you have a game agent, Eric the Troll, who stands at position T (the origin) and facing in the direction given by the normalized vector H (for heading). He can smell a helpless princess at position P and would very much like to throw his club at her, to tenderize her a little, before he rips her to pieces. To do this, he needs to know how many radians he must rotate to face her. The following figure shows the situation:

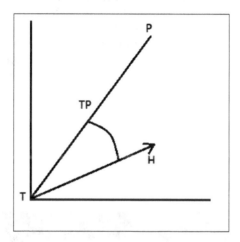

You've discovered that you can calculate the angle between two vectors using the dot product. However, in this problem you only have one vector to start with, **H**. Therefore, we need to determine a vector—the vector **TP** that points directly at the princess. This is calculated by subtracting point **T** from point **P**. Because **T** is at the origin (0, 0), in this example, P−T= P. However, the answer P−T is a vector, so let's show this by typing it in bold and calling it **P**.

We know that the cosine of the angle the troll needs to turn to face the princess is equivalent to the dot product of **H** and **P**, provided both vectors are normalized. **H** is already normalized, so we only need to normalize **P**. Remember, to normalize a vector, its components are divided by its magnitude.

Consequently, the normal of P (NP) is:

$Np = P / |P|$ // Equation (2)

The dot product can now be used to determine the angle:

cos(θ) = Np.H // Equation (3)

So:

θ = cos⁻¹(Np.H) // Equation (4)

To clarify the process, let's do the whole thing again, but with some numbers. Let's say, the troll is situated at the origin T (0, 0) and has a heading of H (1, 0). The princess is standing at the point P (4, 5). How many radians does the troll have to turn to face the princess? We know that we can use Equation (4) to calculate the angle, but first we need to determine the vector, TP, between the troll and the princess and normalize it. To obtain TP, we subtract T from P, resulting in the vector (4,5). To normalize TP, we divide it by its magnitude, resulting in NTP (0.62,0.78). Finally, we plug the numbers into Equation (4), which is illustrated as follows:

θ = cos⁻¹(Ntp.H)

θ = cos⁻¹ ((0.62 *1) + (0.78 * 0))

θ = cos⁻¹ (0.62)

θ = 0.902 radians

Physics

Physics is the branch of science concerned with the nature and properties of matter and energy. The subject matter of physics includes mechanics, heat, light and other radiation, sound, electricity, magnetism, and the structure of atoms.

How to do it

- **Time**: Time is a scalar quantity (completely specified by its magnitude and with no direction) measured in seconds:

  Time = Distance / Speed

- **Distance**: The standard unit of distance—a scalar quantity—is the meter, abbreviated to m:

  Distance=Speed * Time

- **Mass**: Mass is a scalar quantity measured in kilograms, abbreviated to kg. Mass is the measure of an amount of something.

- **Velocity**: Velocity is a vector quantity (a quantity that has magnitude and direction) that expresses the rate of change of distance over time. The standard unit of measurement of velocity is meters per second, abbreviated to m/s. This can be expressed mathematically as:

  $v = \Delta x / \Delta t$

  The Greek capital letter Δ, read as delta, is used in mathematics to denote a change in quantity.

- **Acceleration**: Acceleration is a vector quantity that expresses the rate of change of velocity over time and is measured in meters per second square, written as m/s^2. Acceleration can be expressed mathematically as:

  $a = \Delta v / \Delta t$

How it works

The above physics properties are used in the following ways:

- **Time**: In games often we have to evaluate the time required for the player to reach a object with a given speed. In such cases, we use the Pythagorean theorem to evaluate the distance between the object and the player, then we will use the *Time = Distance/Speed* formula to evaluate the time that the player will need to cover a certain distance with a given speed.

- **Distance**: Similarly, to evaluate the distance between the player and the object, we can use the *Distance = Speed * Time* formula to evaluate the distance between the object and the player, considering the speed and time as known factors.

- **Mass**: This is a property that is frequently used while dealing with the physics engine. Whenever we want to demonstrate both the objects with different behavior in terms of movement, we can change their mass property. Consider a situation in which we want to have two physics objects such as bullet and a ball. In this case, the mass of the bullet will be very low as compared to the ball, so as to make the bullet travel with a high speed, even with a very little applied force or impulse.

- **Velocity**: Whenever we apply any force to any physics body by using a vector, we are changing the velocity of the object by providing the magnitude and the direction to the physics object.

9
Autonomous Moving Agents

In this chapter, we will cover the following recipes:

- ▶ Introduction to steering behaviors
- ▶ Implementing seek
- ▶ Implementing flee
- ▶ Implementing arrive
- ▶ Implementing evade
- ▶ Implementing wander
- ▶ Implementing wall avoidance
- ▶ Obstacle avoidance

Introduction

Games are interesting as they are challenging in each and every level. To make a game interesting, it's important to increase the difficulty of the game at each level. It's always interesting to defeat something in the game. In this chapter, we will learn about various ways to create the autonomous behavior for game objects. This chapter has a bunch of recipes to demonstrate the artificially intelligent game objects. To understand all the concepts in detail, it is recommended to read the previous chapter, which gives you a grip on mathematics and physics. Each recipe will allow you to understand and learn a specific autonomous behavior. By the end of this chapter, you will be able to understand and implement various autonomous game behaviors.

Introduction to steering behaviors

AI characters are a type of autonomous agent that is intended to be used in computer games for showing virtual reality. These agents represent a character in a story or game and have some ability to follow some pre-set actions. Actions of these characters are directed in real time by a human player or participant. In games, autonomous characters are sometimes called non-player or artificially intelligent characters. An AI character always has some aspects of an autonomous robot with some predefined skills such as either they will be seeking some characters in the game or they will evade themselves from the playing character. All these behaviors are called steering behaviors.

Getting ready

In this chapter, we will create a new game to demonstrate all the steering behaviors. To get started with the implementation, let us create a new project. Open Xcode and go to **File** | **New** | **Project**, and then select **iOS** | **Application** | **SpriteKit Game**. In the pop up provide the **Product Name** as SteeringBehaviors, select **Devices** | **iPhone**, and click on **Next**, as shown in the following screenshot:

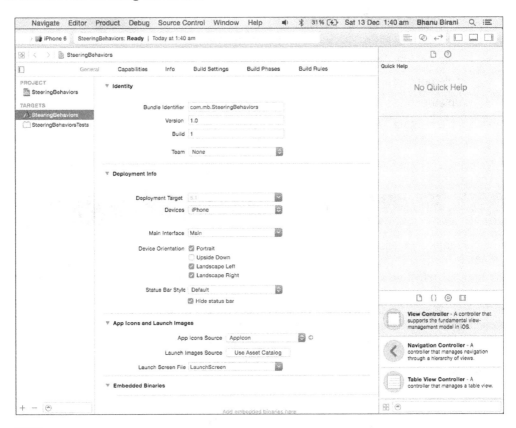

How to do it

Now we have our working sample project and we need to update the game template project to get started with code game logic. Perform the following steps to start working with the basic code flow for the game:

1. Open the `GameViewController.m` file and update the `viewDidLoad` method; remove all the code from this class and make it look something similar to the following lines of code:

```
- (void)viewDidLoad {
    [super viewDidLoad];

    // Configure the view.
    SKView * skView = (SKView *)self.view;
    skView.showsFPS = YES;
    skView.showsNodeCount = YES;

    // Create and configure the scene.
    SKScene * scene = [GameScene
      sceneWithSize:skView.bounds.size];
    scene.scaleMode = SKSceneScaleModeAspectFill;

    // Present the scene.
    [skView presentScene:scene];
}
```

2. Open the `GameScene.m` file; this class creates a scene, which will be plugged inside the game. Now, remove all the codes from this class and just add the following function:

```
- (id)initWithSize:(CGSize)size {
if (self = [super initWithSize:size]) {
    self.backgroundColor = [SKColor colorWithRed:0.15
      green:0.15 blue:0.3 alpha:1.0];
}
}
```

3. Now, compile and run the app; you should be able to see the background image correctly. This will look something similar to the following screenshot:

4. Now we will need one AI character on which we will be implementing all our AI behaviors. So, we will create a new subclass of SKSpriteNode with the name Player. Go to **File | New | File**, then select **iOS | Source | Cocoa Touch Classes**, and click on **Next**. Now, change the **Subclass of** to **SKSpriteNode**, and **Class** name as Player. The final screen should look something similar to the following screenshot:

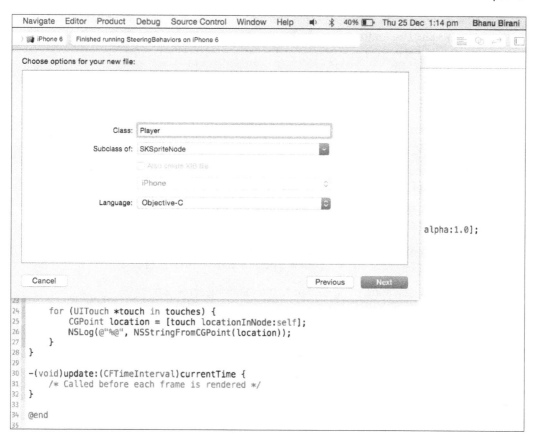

```
for (UITouch *touch in touches) {
    CGPoint location = [touch locationInNode:self];
    NSLog(@"%@", NSStringFromCGPoint(location));
}
}

-(void)update:(CFTimeInterval)currentTime {
    /* Called before each frame is rendered */
}

@end
```

5. Now, open the `Player.m` file, and add the following code after `@implementation`:

```objc
+ (Player*) playerObject {
    // Create a new critter, and give it a name
    Player* obj = [Player spriteNodeWithColor:[SKColor
        whiteColor] size:CGSizeMake(30, 30)];
    obj.name = @"GamePlayer";
    return obj;
}


- (void) update:(float)deltaTime {

}
```

6. Now, add the declaration of both the methods in the `Player.h` file using the following code:

```objc
+ (Player*) playerObject;
- (void) update:(float)deltaTime;
```

7. Now, open your `GameScene.m` file and add the following code right after your `initWithSize` method:

```
- (Player *)createPlayer
{
    Player *plyr = [Player playerObject];
    [self addChild:plyr];

    return plyr;
}
```

8. Now, add the `touchesBegan` method just after the `createPlayer` method. This method will give you all the touch events.

9. So, nothing happened till now. Let's make the game work for the first state. Now, add the following code:

```
Player *newPlayer = [self createPlayer];
newPlayer.position = [touch locationInNode:self];
```

The final file should look something similar to the following screenshot:

Now, compile and run the project. Touch on any location and you will see the square box is created on that location. Multiple sprites are added to the scene on the tap action. The output should look something similar to the following screenshot:

Now we have a separate class for our player. This approach will help us to isolate all the features of the game character. Similarly, when we take the games to next levels, these are very useful as we can isolate the behaviors for various types of AI characters.

Implementing the seek

To implement the seek behavior for our player, we will need a derive force that will redirect the agent toward a target position. In the seek behavior, our character will overshoot the target because the force applied on the player will be more, which will make the player overshoot the target and then return to the target. It will take a finite amount of time before coming to rest.

Getting ready

Seek behavior is something similar to the following screenshot:

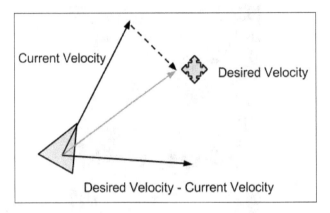

The preceding image explains the algorithm that will be used to implement the seek behavior. In our case, we will need to seek to the target and have to follow the following algorithm:

Vector desiredVelocity = targetVector – player.locationVector;

desiredVelocity.normalize;

*desiredVelocity *= player.maxSpeed;*

return (desiredVelocity – agent.locationVector);

How to do it

Now we will start again on the project to implement the seek behaviors. Now, follow the steps below to implement the seek behavior:

1. Open the `Player.m` file and add the `enum` function on the top, after the import statements:

    ```
    typedef enum : NSUInteger {
        Seek,
        Arrive,
        Flee,
        Wander,
        Evade
    } SteeringBehaviorType;
    ```

2. Then, add the following code after your interface:

```
@property (assign) SteeringBehaviorType behaviourType;
@property (assign) CGPoint target;
```

The enum holds the behavior we want to implement. Whenever we add any behavior, we will have to add it to this enum.

The target property will hold the location where we want the player to seek and behaviourType will tell us which behavior we want to implement.

3. Now, to implement the seek, add the following function:

```
- (void) seek:(CGPoint )target deltaTime:(float)deltaTime {

    // Work out the direction to this position
    GLKVector2 myPosition = GLKVector2Make(self.position.x,
        self.position.y);
    GLKVector2 targetPosition = GLKVector2Make(target.x,
        target.y);

    GLKVector2 offset = GLKVector2Subtract(targetPosition,
        myPosition);

    // Reduce this vector to be the same length as our
        movement speed
    offset = GLKVector2Normalize(offset);
    offset = GLKVector2MultiplyScalar(offset, 10);

    [self.physicsBody applyForce:CGVectorMake(offset.x,
        offset.y)];
}
```

4. Now, add the following code in the update function:

```
if (self.behaviourType == Seek) {
    [self seek:self.target deltaTime:deltaTime];
}
```

This function will be executed if the player behavior is set as seek.

5. Now we are all set to test the function we have written in the previous few steps. So, open the GameScene.m file and create the instance of the newPlayer object at the top of the implementation file. The implementation code should look like the following:

```
@implementation GameScene {
    float lastTime;
    Player * newplayer;
    SteeringBehaviorType behaviourType;
}
```

6. Also, add the following line of code in the `init` method we have written earlier:

```
self.physicsWorld.gravity = CGVectorMake(0, 0);

newplayer = [self createPlayer];
newplayer.position = CGPointMake(size.width/2, size.height/2);

behaviourType = Seek;
newplayer.behaviourType = behaviourType;

if (behaviourType == Seek) {
    newplayer.physicsBody = [SKPhysicsBody bodyWithRectangleOfSize
:CGSizeMake(30, 30)];
    newplayer.physicsBody.friction = 1.0f;
    newplayer.physicsBody.linearDamping = 1.0f;
}
```

The final init function should look something similar to the following screenshot:

We have created a `newPlayer` object and have also associated the physics body with it.

7. Now we have our player ready to seek the target. Wherever we tap on the screen, the player will seek to that location. In the `touchesBegain:withEvent` method, add the following line of code:

```
for (UITouch *touch in touches) {
    CGPoint location = [touch locationInNode:self];
    NSLog(@"%@", NSStringFromCGPoint(location));

    newplayer.target = location;
}
```

8. So, now we are all set for the seek behavior. So, finally, we will call the player's update method on every update of the scene, so that the player can seek to the location a user has tapped on. To perform this add the following code:

```
- (void)update:(CFTimeInterval)currentTime {
    /* Called before each frame is rendered */

    if (!CGPointEqualToPoint(newplayer.target,
      CGPointZero)) {
        float deltaTime = currentTime - lastTime;
        [newplayer update:deltaTime];
        lastTime = currentTime;
    }
}
```

In the above line of code, we are calling the update function on each and every `newPlayer` object.

9. Now, compile and run the project; you will see the player in the center of the screen and it will seek the location that you will tap on the screen. The output should look something similar to the following screenshot:

This completes our seek behavior for the player object.

There's more

You can read all these properties in more detail at Apple's developer documentation at `https://developer.apple.com/library/IOs/documentation/SpriteKit/Reference/SKPhysicsBody_Ref/index.html`.

Implementing flee

Flee is the opposite of the seek behavior, which steers the vehicle in the opposite direction from the target. Instead of producing the force toward target, we will push the player off to the target as the object has to flee from the target.

Getting ready

To implement the flee behavior, we need to flee to the target and follow the following algorithm:

```
Vector desiredVelocity = player.locationVector - targetVector;
desiredVelocity.normalize;
desiredVelocity *= player.maxSpeed;
return (desiredVelocity - agent.locationVector);
```

In the preceding algorithm, we are calculating the force that will be needed to flee the object off from the screen. First, we will calculate the direction vector to determine the direction opposite to the player, so that our object can flee from the target in that location. Now, in the second step, we normalize the vector and increase its magnitude to its max speed. Using this algorithm, we will implement the flee behavior for our object.

How to do it

Perform the following steps to implement the flee behavior in the game:

1. Open the Player.m file and add the following line of code just after the seek function:

    ```
    - (void) flee:(CGPoint )target deltaTime:(float)deltaTime {

        // Work out the direction to this position
        GLKVector2 myPosition = GLKVector2Make(self.position.x,
            self.position.y);
        GLKVector2 targetPosition = GLKVector2Make(target.x,
            target.y);

        GLKVector2 offset = GLKVector2Subtract(targetPosition,
            myPosition);

        // Reduce this vector to be the same length as our
            movement speed
        offset = GLKVector2Normalize(offset);
        offset = GLKVector2MultiplyScalar(offset, -10);

        [self.physicsBody applyForce:CGVectorMake(offset.x,
            offset.y)];
    }
    ```

2. Now, add the following code in the update function after the seek code:

```
if (self.behaviourType == Flee) {
    [self flee:self.target deltaTime:deltaTime];
}
```

3. Now, our function is ready to flee the player. This function will accept a target from which it will flee. So, once again, we will be using the same approach, and when the user will tap on the screen, we will make the object flee from the tapped point. The final `Player.m` file should look something similar to the following screenshot:

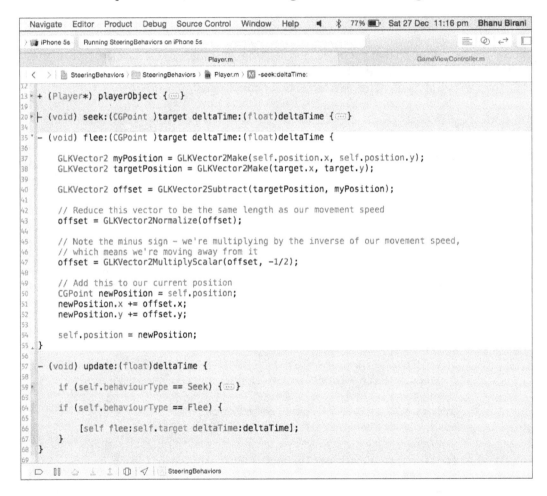

4. Now our `Player.m` class is ready to execute the flee behavior. So, open the `GameScene.m` file and take the following line of code:

```
behaviourType = Seek;
```

Then, replace this with the following line of code:

```
behaviourType = Flee;
```

And also, add the following code:

```
if (behaviourType == Seek)
```

Then, update the `if` condition from the above code to:

```
if (behaviourType == Seek || behaviourType == Flee)
```

5. The `init` function should look something similar to the following screenshot:

```objc
-(id)initWithSize:(CGSize)size {
    if (self = [super initWithSize:size]) {

        self.backgroundColor = [SKColor colorWithRed:0.15 green:0.15 blue:0.3 alpha:1.0];
        self.physicsWorld.gravity = CGVectorMake(0, 0);

        newplayer = [self createPlayer];
        newplayer.position = CGPointMake(size.width/2, size.height/2);

        behaviourType = Flee;
        newplayer.behaviourType = behaviourType;

        if (behaviourType == Seek || behaviourType == Flee) {
            newplayer.physicsBody = [SKPhysicsBody bodyWithRectangleOfSize:CGSizeMake(30, 30)];
            newplayer.physicsBody.friction = 1.0f;
            newplayer.physicsBody.linearDamping = 1.0f;
        }

        if (behaviourType == Wander) {
            newplayer.physicsBody = [SKPhysicsBody bodyWithRectangleOfSize:CGSizeMake(30, 30)];
            SKPhysicsBody* borderBody = [SKPhysicsBody bodyWithEdgeLoopFromRect:self.frame];
            self.physicsBody = borderBody;
            self.physicsBody.friction = 0.0f;
        }
    }
    return self;
}
```

6. That's all. Now compile and run the project. You should be able to see the player and when you tap anywhere near to the player, you will see the player will flee from the tapped location.

There's more

You can read all these properties in more detail at Apple's developer documentation at `https://developer.apple.com/library/IOs/documentation/SpriteKit/Reference/SKPhysicsBody_Ref/index.html`.

Implementing arrive

Arrive is similar to seek. The only difference between seek and arrive is that in arrive the player will stop at the target location. However, in seek, it overshoots the target location and then seeks again.

Getting ready

The technical definition of arrive is to reach the goal with zero velocity. The arrival behavior will remain the same as the seek behavior, the only difference is that it will not overshoot the target.

In this approach, when the player is outside the stopping radius, it will follow the maximum speed toward the target, while as soon as the player is inside the stopping radius, the desired velocity of the player will be ramped down to zero.

How to do it

Perform the following steps to implement the arrive behavior:

1. Open the Player.m file, and add the following line of code in the end of the file:

```
- (void) arrive:(CGPoint )target deltaTime:(float)deltaTime {

    // Work out the direction to this position
    GLKVector2 myPosition = GLKVector2Make(self.position.x, self.
position.y);
    GLKVector2 targetPosition = GLKVector2Make(target.x,
target.y);

    GLKVector2 offset = GLKVector2Subtract(targetPosition,
myPosition);

    // Reduce this vector to be the same length as our movement
speed
    offset = GLKVector2Normalize(offset);
    offset = GLKVector2MultiplyScalar(offset, 5);

    // Add this to our current position
    CGPoint newPosition = self.position;
    newPosition.x += offset.x;
    newPosition.y += offset.y;

    self.position = newPosition;
}
```

2. Now, we have to call this function till our player is not in the stopping radius. So, we will create a box around our target point, and as soon as the player is inside this box, we will stop calling the arrive function. To implement this, add the following line of code in the update method:

```
if (self.behaviourType == Arrive) {
    int boxWidth = 20;

    CGRect targetRect = CGRectMake(self.target.x - boxWidth, self.
target.y - boxWidth, boxWidth*2, boxWidth*2);

    if (!CGRectContainsPoint(targetRect, self.position)) {
        [self arrive:self.target deltaTime:deltaTime];
    }
}
```

The final update function should look something similar to the following screenshot:

```
- (void) update:(float)deltaTime {

    if (self.behaviourType == Arrive) {
        int boxWidth = 20;

        CGRect targetRect = CGRectMake(self.target.x - boxWidth, self.target.y - boxWidth, boxWidth*2,
            boxWidth*2);

        if (!CGRectContainsPoint(targetRect, self.position)) {
            [self arrive:self.target deltaTime:deltaTime];
        }
    }

    if (self.behaviourType == Seek) {

        [self seek:self.target deltaTime:deltaTime];
    }

    if (self.behaviourType == Flee) {

        [self flee:self.target deltaTime:deltaTime];
    }
}
```

3. Now, it's time to check the arrive function we have written in the `Player.m` file. Open the `GameScene.m` file. Take the following line of code:

```
behaviourType = Flee;
```

Then, replace this with the following line of code:

```
behaviourType = Arrive;
```

4. Now, compile and run the project; you should see our player in the center of the screen. Now, click anywhere on the screen to provide the target for the player. After you have tapped, the player will arrive at the target location you have tapped on with overshooting the target. The output should look something similar to the following screenshot:

The red pointer shows the target location where the player has to arrive.

There's more

You can read all these properties in more detail at Apple's developer documentation at https://developer.apple.com/library/IOs/documentation/SpriteKit/ Reference/SKPhysicsBody_Ref/index.html.

Implementing evade

Evade is similar to flee. The only difference between flee and evade is that in evade, the player will stop after fleeing to a safe location from the target location selected for evade. However, in flee, it just runs out of the screen from the target location and never comes back.

Getting ready

Technically, evade is to flee from the target to the safe location. The evade behavior will remain the same as the flee behavior, the only difference is that it will not run away infinitely from the target.

In this approach, when the target location is inside the safe range of the player, then the player will flee till the target location is not outside its safe range. So, in our case, we will make the player flee till the player is far from the target, and then its velocity will be ramped down to zero.

How to do it

Perform the following steps to implement the evade behavior:

1. Open the `Player.m` file and add the following line of code in the end of the file:

   ```
   - (void) evade:(CGPoint )target deltaTime:(float)deltaTime {

       GLKVector2 myPosition = GLKVector2Make(self.position.x, self.
   position.y);
       GLKVector2 targetPosition = GLKVector2Make(target.x,
   target.y);

       GLKVector2 offset = GLKVector2Subtract(targetPosition,
   myPosition);

       // Reduce this vector to be the same length as our movement
   speed
       offset = GLKVector2Normalize(offset);

       // Note the minus sign - we're multiplying by the inverse of
   our movement speed,
       // which means we're moving away from it
       offset = GLKVector2MultiplyScalar(offset, -5);
   ```

```
    // Add this to our current position
    CGPoint newPosition = self.position;
    newPosition.x += offset.x;
    newPosition.y += offset.y;

    self.position = newPosition;
}
```

2. Now, add the following code in the `update` method:

```
if (self.behaviourType == Evade) {

    int boxWidth = 100;

    CGRect targetRect = CGRectMake(self.target.x - boxWidth, self.
target.y - boxWidth, boxWidth*2, boxWidth*2);

    if (CGRectContainsPoint(targetRect, self.position)) {

        [self evade:self.target deltaTime:deltaTime];
    }
}
```

3. After this, the update function should look something similar to the following screenshot:

In the preceding function, we are drawing a rectangle on the target location vector. Whenever the player is inside this rectangle, it's not safe. So, it will flee to get the player outside into the safe location. So, we will execute our evade function till the player is in the rectangle.

4. Now, it's time to test the evade function we have written in `Player.m`. So, open the `GameScene.m` file. Enter the following line of code:

   ```
   behaviourType = Arrive;
   ```

   Then, replace this with the following line of code:

   ```
   behaviourType = Evade;
   ```

5. The final `init` method should look something similar to the following screenshot:

```
Navigate   Editor   Product   Debug   Source Control   Window   Help   ◀)   ✷   100% ▣   Sun 28 Dec 10:58 am   Bhanu Birani   Q

⟩ 🖳 iPhone 5s    Running SteeringBehaviors on iPhone 5s                                                          ≣  ⦿  ↩  ◻  ◻

                                      GameScene.m                                    GameViewController.m

🗒 ⟨ ⟩  📄 SteeringBehaviors ⟩ 🗂 SteeringBehaviors ⟩ m GameScene.m ⟩ Ⓜ -initWithSize:
   //
8
9   #import "GameScene.h"
10  #import "Player.h"
11
12  @implementation GameScene {
13      float lastTime;
14      Player * newplayer;
15      SteeringBehaviorType behaviourType;
16  }
17
18  -(id)initWithSize:(CGSize)size {
19      if (self = [super initWithSize:size]) {
20
21          self.backgroundColor = [SKColor colorWithRed:0.15 green:0.15 blue:0.3 alpha:1.0];
22          self.physicsWorld.gravity = CGVectorMake(0, 0);
23
24          newplayer = [self createPlayer];
25          newplayer.position = CGPointMake(size.width/2, size.height/2);
26
27          behaviourType = Evade;
28          newplayer.behaviourType = behaviourType;
29
30          if (behaviourType == Seek || behaviourType == Flee) {
31              newplayer.physicsBody = [SKPhysicsBody bodyWithRectangleOfSize:CGSizeMake(30, 30)];
32              newplayer.physicsBody.friction = 1.0f;
33              newplayer.physicsBody.linearDamping = 1.0f;
34          }
35
36          if (behaviourType == Wander) {
37              newplayer.physicsBody = [SKPhysicsBody bodyWithRectangleOfSize:CGSizeMake(30, 30)];
38              SKPhysicsBody* borderBody = [SKPhysicsBody bodyWithEdgeLoopFromRect:self.frame];
39              self.physicsBody = borderBody;
40              self.physicsBody.friction = 0.0f;
41          }
42      }
43      return self;

▣ ▷ ‖ ⌂ ↓ ↑ ❶ ◁  ▢ SteeringBehaviors
```

6. Now, compile and run the project to see the object player in action. Click anywhere near the player, and it will flee to maintain a certain distance from the location you have tapped, as shown in the following screenshot:

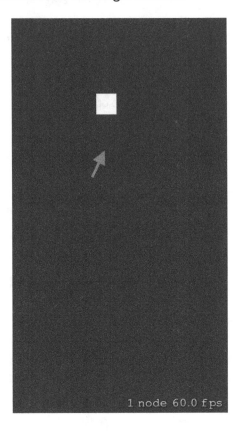

There's more

You can read about all these properties in more detail at Apple's developer documentation at `https://developer.apple.com/library/IOs/documentation/SpriteKit/Reference/SKPhysicsBody_Ref/index.html`.

Implementing wander

You might have observed very often in the game that few characters are just randomly moving around in their environment. These characters are waiting for some event to happen. For example, in any warfare game, the enemy soldiers are just wandering around in the castle to catch the player and they will keep on wandering till they find the player. Once the player is in the vicinity, then they will change their behavior to seek. So, the wandering ability of the characters makes them visually pleasant and realistic.

Making a game object follow the path will make it unrealistic and will affect the overall game play by making it more predictive. So these wandering behaviors add much more fun and realistic behavior to the game.

The wander steering behavior produces a realistic movement, which makes the players think that the character is just walking and to feel the whole environment more alive.

Getting ready

There are various ways to implement the wander behaviors. They are as follows:

- Implementing wander using seek and randomness. In this approach, wander brings together two behaviors, seek and randomness. This means technically wander is just seeking to some random points and targets in the world.

- The second way is to evaluate a virtual point in front of the character and draw a circle in front of it, and get point on it circumference. Now, make the object seek that location. The following image will explain the approach a little better:

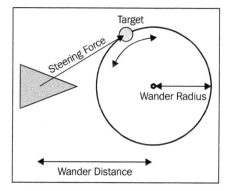

We will implement the first approach, so we will follow the following approach:

```
Get targetVector
while (true) {
  Seek (targetVector);
  get anotherTargetVector;
}
```

How to do it

Now we will implement the wander behavior and will take our project a little more further. Perform the following steps to implement the wander behavior:

1. Open the `Player.m` file and add the following line of code in the end of the file:

```
int myRandom() {
    return (arc4random() % 2 ? 1 : -1);
}


- (void)wanderWithDeltaTime:(float)deltaTime
{
    int boxWidth = 20;

    CGRect targetRect = CGRectMake(self.target.x - boxWidth, self.
target.y - boxWidth, boxWidth*2, boxWidth*2);
        if (!CGRectContainsPoint(targetRect, self.position)) {

        [self seek:self.target deltaTime:deltaTime];

    } else {
        int offsetX = self.scene.size.width;
        int offsetY = self.scene.size.height;

        self.target = CGPointMake(arc4random() % offsetX,
arc4random() % offsetY);
    }
}
```

We have implemented the algorithm that we have seen in the start of this section. In this code, we are getting a random local point in front of the player, and then make the player to seek that location. This will make a wander behavior.

2. Now, add the following line of code in the `update` method:

```
if (self.behaviourType == Wander) {
    [self wanderWithDeltaTime:deltaTime];
}
```

The final `update` function should look something similar to the following screenshot:

```objc
- (void) update:(float)deltaTime {

    if (self.behaviourType == Arrive) {
        int boxWidth = 20;

        CGRect targetRect = CGRectMake(self.target.x - boxWidth, self.target.y - boxWidth, boxWidth*2,
            boxWidth*2);
        if (!CGRectContainsPoint(targetRect, self.position)) {
            [self arrive:self.target deltaTime:deltaTime];
        }
    }

    if (self.behaviourType == Seek) {

        [self seek:self.target deltaTime:deltaTime];
    }

    if (self.behaviourType == Flee) {

        [self flee:self.target deltaTime:deltaTime];
    }

    if (self.behaviourType == Evade) {
        int boxWidth = 100;
        CGRect targetRect = CGRectMake(self.target.x - boxWidth, self.target.y - boxWidth, boxWidth*2,
            boxWidth*2);
        if (CGRectContainsPoint(targetRect, self.position)) {

            [self evade:self.target deltaTime:deltaTime];
        }
    }

    if (self.behaviourType == Wander) {

        [self wanderWithDeltaTime:deltaTime];
    }
}
```

3. Now, it's time to test the `evade` function we have written in `Player.m`. So, open the `GameScene.m` file and add the following line of code:

```objc
behaviourType = Evade;
```

Then, replace it with the following line of code:

```objc
behaviourType = Wander;
```

Also, add the following if condition right after the if we had for the seek and flee:

```objc
if (behaviourType == Wander) {
    newplayer.physicsBody = [SKPhysicsBody bodyWithRectangleOfSize
:CGSizeMake(30, 30)];
    SKPhysicsBody* borderBody = [SKPhysicsBody
bodyWithEdgeLoopFromRect:self.frame];
    self.physicsBody = borderBody;
    self.physicsBody.friction = 0.0f;
    newplayer.physicsBody.friction = 1.0f;
    newplayer.physicsBody.linearDamping = 1.0f;
}
```

The final file should look something similar to the following screenshot:

```objc
-(id)initWithSize:(CGSize)size {
    if (self = [super initWithSize:size]) {

        self.backgroundColor = [SKColor colorWithRed:0.15 green:0.15 blue:0.3 alpha:1.0];
        self.physicsWorld.gravity = CGVectorMake(0, 0);

        newplayer = [self createPlayer];
        newplayer.position = CGPointMake(size.width/2, size.height/2);

        behaviourType = Wander;
        newplayer.behaviourType = behaviourType;

        if (behaviourType == Seek || behaviourType == Flee) {
            newplayer.physicsBody = [SKPhysicsBody bodyWithRectangleOfSize:CGSizeMake(30, 30)];
            newplayer.physicsBody.friction = 1.0f;
            newplayer.physicsBody.linearDamping = 1.0f;
        }

        if (behaviourType == Wander) {
            newplayer.physicsBody = [SKPhysicsBody bodyWithRectangleOfSize:CGSizeMake(30, 30)];
            SKPhysicsBody* borderBody = [SKPhysicsBody bodyWithEdgeLoopFromRect:self.frame];
            self.physicsBody = borderBody;
            self.physicsBody.friction = 0.0f;
            newplayer.physicsBody.friction = 1.0f;
            newplayer.physicsBody.linearDamping = 1.0f;
        }
    }
    return self;
}
```

4. Now, compile and run the project to see the object player in action. Click anywhere on the screen and the player will start wandering on the screen, as shown in the following screenshot:

You can read all these properties in more detail at Apple's developer documentation at
`https://developer.apple.com/library/IOs/documentation/SpriteKit/`
`Reference/SKPhysicsBody_Ref/index.html`.

Implementing wall avoidance

The AI characters will look a little odd if they collide with a wall while wandering. So, we have
to make them even more intelligent so that they can seek the wall and can respond or change
direction accordingly.

The wander behavior returns a force that steers the AI away from the wall to avoid collision.

Getting ready

The following approach will be used to implement the wall avoidance behavior:

- ▸ Create feelers to sense the wall
- ▸ We will use one feeler in front of the AI to sense the wall
- ▸ When wall is detected, apply the force at the reflected vector

How to do it

Follow the following algorithm to achieve the wall avoidance behavior in the project:

1. The visual explanation of the technique is shown in the following screenshot:

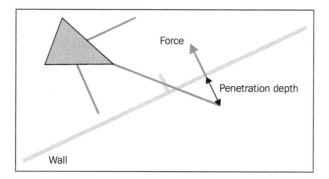

2. Create feelers that will sense the wall:

```
Front_Feeler = player->Get velocity; // vector
Front_Feeler = Front_Feeler.normalize(); // vector
```

This will project the feeler in front of the player.

```
Front_Feeler =  Front_Feeler *  FeelerLength; // vector
Front_Feeler =  Front_Feeler + player->location;
```

3. Now we have got the `Front_Feeler` so let's apply the force in the same direction. This force will push the player away from the wall.

4. To fine-tune the behavior even more, you can additionally add two more feelers on the either side of the player. This will help player to take a more smooth turn and look realistic.

Obstacle avoidance

If the game objects are exhibiting the group behaviors, then it's really important to make them avoid collision with each other. Also, there can be multiple obstacles on the way, which the characters have to avoid intelligently.

Getting ready

The following approach will be used to implement the obstacle avoidance behavior:

- ▶ Create three feelers in front of the player object
- ▶ Let all the three feelers sense the obstacles on the way
- ▶ Redirect the player in the opposite direction if the feeler has sensed any obstacles

How to do it

Follow the following algorithm to achieve the obstacle avoidance behavior in the project.

1. The visual explanation of the technique is shown in the following screenshot:

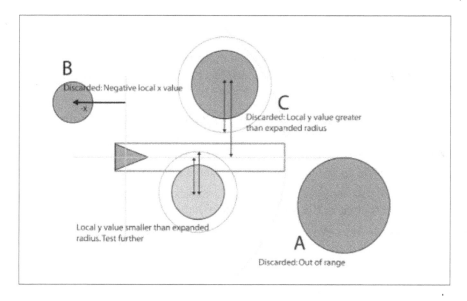

2. Create feelers that will sense the wall:

```
Front_Feeler = player->Get velocity; // vector
Front_Feeler = Front_Feeler.normalize(); // vector

Left_Feeler = player->Get velocity; // vector
Left_Feeler = Left_Feeler.normalize(); // vector

Right_Feeler = player->Get velocity; // vector
Right_Feeler = Right_Feeler.normalize(); // vector
```

This will project the feeler in front of the player.

```
Front_Feeler =  Front_Feeler *  FeelerLength; // vector
Front_Feeler =  Front_Feeler + player->location;

Left_Feeler =  Left_Feeler *  FeelerLength; // vector
Left_Feeler =  Left_Feeler + player->location;
Left_Feeler->x = Left_Feeler -> x - player-> width;

Right_Feeler =  Right_Feeler *  FeelerLength; // vector
Right_Feeler =  Right_Feeler + player->location;
Right_Feeler->x = Right_Feeler -> x + player-> width;
```

Now we have left, right, and front feelers. So whenever these feelers will sense any object in their way, they will push the player away from the obstacle.

There's more

There are a lot more steering behaviors that can make the games very interesting. There are various group behaviors as well, which can be explored after having a hands-on these behaviors. Few of the behaviors are as follows:

- **Flocking**: When the objects exhibit certain common behavior in groups, then that behavior is called flocking

- **Alignment**: When the objects exhibit some behavior that causes a particular character to line up with agents close by, then it's called alignment

- **Cohesion**: In this behavior, the objects are steered toward the center of the mass of all the objects—that is, the average position of the agents within a certain radius

- **Separation**: In this behavior, the objects are steered away from all of their neighbors

You can read more about these behaviors at:

- `http://gamedevelopment.tutsplus.com/tutorials/the-three-simple-rules-of-flocking-behaviors-alignment-cohesion-and-separation--gamedev-3444`

- `http://www.red3d.com/cwr/steer/gdc99/`

10

3D Game Programming with OpenGL

In this chapter, we will focus on the following recipes:

- ▶ Introducing OpenGL
- ▶ Building a mini three-dimensional animation game using OpenGL

Introduction

In the previous chapters, you learned about the anatomy of physics simulation in depth. Now, we will explore the most interesting part of the game, which is to add three-dimensional objects to your games. In this chapter, we will start exploring the basics of OpenGL. Then, step-by-step, we will explore OpenGL in depth by crafting some three-dimensional models. In this chapter, we will start learning by using the two-dimensional model project, and then we will enhance the project to accommodate three-dimensional models.

Introducing OpenGL

OpenGL stands for Open Graphics Library. This is a widely used library for visualizing two-dimensional and three-dimensional objects. This is a standard multipurpose two-dimensional and three-dimensional content creation graphics library. It is used in various streams, such as mechanical design, architectural design, gaming, prototyping, flight simulation, and many more. OpenGL is used to configure and submit three-dimensional graphics data to the device. All the data is prepared in the form of matrices and they are transformed to vertices, which are transformed and assembled to produce two-dimensional rasterized images. Two-dimensional graphics have two axes, which are x and y; however, in the case of three-dimensional graphics, we have three-dimensional axes, which are x, y, and z, where z is the depth.

This library is designed to compile normal function calls into graphical commands, which will get executed on the graphics rendering hardware. All the graphics hardware is designed to execute the graphics commands. OpenGL draws and renders views very fast.

Getting ready

Xcode provides a built-in OpenGL-ES project template; still, we think it will be confusing for beginners to start with that template. A typical approach is to write the code step-by-step, in order to understand how the code works and the functionality of each function.

Here, we will write all the code from scratch, which will help you to understand the nitty-gritty of each and every line of code written to render views using OpenGL. To add frameworks, perform the following steps:

1. Start up Xcode. Make a single-view application and click on **Next**. Name your project OpenGLSample, click on **Next**, choose a folder to save it in, and click on **Create**.

2. Now, we will add all the required frameworks in the project. To add the frameworks, the first step is to add the two required frameworks for our OpenGL project. They are `OpenGLES.frameworks` and `GLKit.framework`.

3. To add these frameworks in Xcode 6, click on your OpenGLSample project in the Groups & Files tree, and select the **OpenGLSample** target. Expand the **Link Binary with the Libraries** section, click on the plus button, and select **OpenGLES.framework**. Repeat for **GLKit.framework** as well, as shown in the following screenshot:

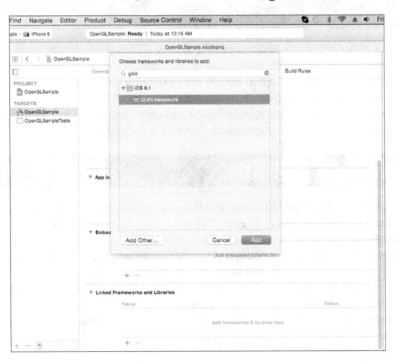

How to do it

To create three-dimensional textures in our app, perform the following steps:

1. Open the `Main.storyboard` file and select the view controller. You will see a view already added in the view controller.

2. Select the view, open the Identity inspector, and set the view's class to `GLKView`, as shown in the following screenshot:

3. Open `ViewController.h`, import `GLKit/GLKit.h`, and change the ViewController's parent class from `UIViewController` to `GLKViewController`. `GLKViewController` provides the OpenGL render loop in addition to all native view controller functionalities. The code will be as follows:

```
#import "GLKit/GLKit.h"
@interface ViewController : GLKViewController
```

4. Modify `viewController.m`. Add the following code to `viewDidLoad`:

```
GLKView* view = (GLKView*)self.view;

    view.context = [[EAGLContext alloc]
       initWithAPI:kEAGLRenderingAPIOpenGLES2];
```

5. Add the following methods:

```
(void)glkView:(GLKView *)view drawInRect:(CGRect)rect{
glClearColor(0.0, 0.5, 0.0, 1.0);
  glClear(GL_COLOR_BUFFER_BIT);
}
```

The first line of the code calls `glClearColor`, which effectively tells OpenGL that the clear color should be set to the RGBA value (0.0, 0.5, 0.0, 1.0)—that is, fully opaque, dark green. The next line instructs OpenGL to actually clear the color buffer—that is, it fills the entire screen with the clear color that was set on the previous line.

6. Now, compile and run the project. You should see something similar to the following screenshot:

7. Now, it's time to create OpenGL context. Drawing triangles in OpenGL is easier than drawing squares because triangles are always coplanar, that is, all of the points in the shape are on the same plane. So, to draw a square, we first draw two triangles that share an edge.

8. To inform OpenGL about where the vertices are, we use a structure for vertices and for making an array. This will later show on GLView as follows:

```
typedef struct {
GLKVector3 position;
} Vertex;
const Vertex SquareVertices[] = {
{-1, -1 , 0},// vertex 0: bottom left
{1, -1 , 0}, // vertex 1: bottom right
{1, 1 , 0}, // vertex 2: top right
{-1, 1 , 0}, // vertex 4: top left
};
```

9. Now we need to define which triangle uses which vertices. In OpenGL, we do this by numbering each vertex, and then describing triangles by giving OpenGL three numbers at a time:

```
const GLubyte SquareTriangles[] = {
0, 1, 2, // BL->BR->TR
2, 3, 0 // TR->TL->BL
};
```

In this case, Glubyte is the type in which the first triangle uses vertices 0, 1, and 2, and the second triangle uses vertices 2, 3, and 0. Note that both triangles use vertices 0 and 2. This means that they share an edge, which means that there won't be any gap between the two triangles.

10. Both the SquareVertices and SquareTriangles arrays need to be stored in a buffer so that OpenGL can use them for rendering as follows:

```
@interface ViewController () {
GLuint _vertexBuffer;
GLuint _indexBuffer;
GLKBaseEffect* _squareEffect;
}
@end
```

11. First, we set up the GLKView with an OpenGL context, as shown in the following code. Because, if we don't do this, none of our OpenGL commands will do anything.

```
GLKView* view = (GLKView*)self.view;
view.context = [[EAGLContext alloc]
   initWithAPI:kEAGLRenderingAPIOpenGLES2];
[EAGLContext setCurrentContext:view.context];
```

12. Next, we create the buffers starting with the vertex buffer:

```
glGenBuffers(1, &_vertexBuffer);
glBindBuffer(GL_ARRAY_BUFFER, _vertexBuffer);
```

13. The vertex buffer is then filled with the vertex information:

```
glBufferData(GL_ARRAY_BUFFER, sizeof(SquareVertices),
    SquareVertices, GL_STATIC_DRAW);
```

14. The same thing is then done for the index buffer, which you'll recall stores information on which vertices the two triangles will use:

```
glGenBuffers(1, &_indexBuffer);
glBindBuffer(GL_ELEMENT_ARRAY_BUFFER, _indexBuffer);
glBufferData(GL_ELEMENT_ARRAY_BUFFER,
    sizeof(SquareTriangles), SquareTriangles,
        GL_STATIC_DRAW);
```

Once this is done, all of the information has been passed to OpenGL. GLKit provide several effects, which are the objects that contain information such as color, position, orientation, and so on. In this activity, we will make one square to be red and to be present it in the middle of the screen.

15. The first step is to create the effect object, and then provide it with a projection matrix. The projection matrix controls the overall sizes of things on the screen. In this case, we create a projection matrix that uses the aspect ratio of the screen and uses a 60 degrees field of view:

```
_squareEffect = [[GLKBaseEffect alloc] init];
float aspectRatio =
    self.view.bounds.size.width/self.view.bounds.size.height;
float fieldOfViewDegrees = 60.0;

GLKMatrix4 projectionMatrix =
    GLKMatrix4MakePerspective(GLKMathDegreesToRadians
        (fieldOfViewDegrees),aspectRatio, 0.1, 10.0);
_squareEffect.transform.projectionMatrix =
    projectionMatrix;
```

16. Now, we need to provide a model view matrix. The model view matrix controls the position of the object, relative to the camera:

```
GLKMatrix4 modelViewMatrix =
    GLKMatrix4MakeTranslation(0.0f,   0.0f, -6.0f);
_squareEffect.transform.modelviewMatrix =
    modelViewMatrix;
//Set the constant color red for the effects.
_squareEffect.useConstantColor = YES;
_squareEffect.constantColor = GLKVector4Make(1.0, 0.0,
    0.0, 1.0);
```

17. Create the `drawInRect` method after the `viewDidLoad` method:

```
- (void)glkView:(GLKView *)view drawInRect:(CGRect)rect {
}
```

18. The actual work of rendering is done in the `glkView:drawInRect` method. The first thing that happens in this is that the view is cleared, by filling the screen with black:

```
glClearColor(0.0, 0.0, 0.0, 1.0);
glClear(GL_COLOR_BUFFER_BIT);
```

19. Now call `prepareToDraw`. It configures OpenGL in such a way that anything we draw will use the effect's setting:

```
[_squareEffect prepareToDraw];
```

20. We first tell OpenGL that we're going to be working with positions, and then tell OpenGL where to find the position information in the vertex data:

```
glEnableVertexAttribArray(GLKVertexAttribPosition);
glVertexAttribPointer(GLKVertexAttribPosition, 3,
    GL_FLOAT, GL_FALSE, 0, 0);
```

21. Finally, we need to know how many vertices we're asking OpenGL to draw. This can be figured out by taking the size of the entire index array, and dividing that by the size of one element in that array:

```
int numberOfTriangles =
    sizeof(SquareTriangles)/sizeof(SquareTriangles[0]);
glDrawElements(GL_TRIANGLES, numberOfTriangles,
    GL_UNSIGNED_BYTE, 0);
```

So, our final implementation class probably looks like the following code:

```
#import "ViewController.h"
typedef struct {
GLKVector3 position;
} Vertex;
const Vertex SquareVertices[] = {
{-1, -1 , 0}, {1, -1 , 0}, {1, 1 , 0}, {-1, 1 , 0}
};
const GLubyte SquareTriangles[] = {
0, 1, 2,
2, 3, 0
};
@interface ViewController () {
GLuint _vertexBuffer;
GLuint _indexBuffer;
GLKBaseEffect* _squareEffect;
}
@end
@implementation ViewController
- (void)viewDidLoad
{
```

```objc
[super viewDidLoad];
GLKView* view = (GLKView*)self.view;
view.context = [[EAGLContext alloc]
  initWithAPI:kEAGLRenderingAPIOpenGLES2];
[EAGLContext setCurrentContext:view.context];

glGenBuffers(1, &_vertexBuffer);
glBindBuffer(GL_ARRAY_BUFFER, _vertexBuffer);
glBufferData(GL_ARRAY_BUFFER, sizeof(SquareVertices),
  SquareVertices,
GL_STATIC_DRAW);
glGenBuffers(1, &_indexBuffer);
glBindBuffer(GL_ELEMENT_ARRAY_BUFFER, _indexBuffer);
glBufferData(GL_ELEMENT_ARRAY_BUFFER,
  sizeof(SquareTriangles),
SquareTriangles, GL_STATIC_DRAW);
_squareEffect = [[GLKBaseEffect alloc] init];
float aspectRatio =
self.view.bounds.size.width/self.view.bounds.size.height;
float fieldOfViewDegrees = 60.0;
GLKMatrix4 projectionMatrix =
GLKMatrix4MakePerspective(GLKMathDegreesToRadians
  (fieldOfViewDegrees),aspectRatio, 0.1, 10.0);
_squareEffect.transform.projectionMatrix =
  projectionMatrix;

GLKMatrix4 modelViewMatrix =
  GLKMatrix4MakeTranslation(0.0f, 0.0f, -6.0f);
_squareEffect.transform.modelviewMatrix = modelViewMatrix;

_squareEffect.useConstantColor = YES;
_squareEffect.constantColor =
  GLKVector4Make(1.0, 0.0, 0.0, 1.0);
}
- (void)glkView:(GLKView *)view drawInRect:(CGRect)rect {
glClearColor(0.0, 0.0, 0.0, 1.0);
glClear(GL_COLOR_BUFFER_BIT);

[_squareEffect prepareToDraw];
glEnableVertexAttribArray(GLKVertexAttribPosition);
glVertexAttribPointer(GLKVertexAttribPosition, 3, GL_FLOAT, GL_FALSE,
0, 0);
int numberOfVertices = sizeof(SquareTriangles)/
sizeof(SquareTriangles[0]);
glDrawElements(GL_TRIANGLES, numberOfVertices,
  GL_UNSIGNED_BYTE, 0);
}
@end
```

Run the project, and you will see the red square box on the black screen, as shown in the following screenshot:

Building a mini 3D animation game using OpenGL

In this recipe, we will load a texture and apply it to the square. Later, we will make a cube, and finally we will learn how to implement three-dimensional animation by rotating our cube in three-dimensions.

How to do it

Now we will start from the place we have left before and will load all the textures. To load the textures, follow the following steps:

1. First, in our vertex structure, we need to include texture coordinate information:

    ```
    typedef struct {
    GLKVector3 position; // the location of each vertex in
       space
    GLKVector2 textureCoordinates; // the texture coordinates
       for each vertex
    } Vertex;
    const Vertex SquareVertices[] = {
    {{-1, -1 , 0}, {0,0}}, // bottom left
    {{1, -1 , 0}, {1,0}}, // bottom right
    {{1, 1 , 0}, {1,1}}, // top right
    {{-1, 1 , 0}, {0,1}}, // top left
    };
    ```

2. Next, add an image (any) in our project, rename it as `Texture.png`, and then add the following code in `viewDidLoad`:

    ```
    NSString* imagePath = [[NSBundle mainBundle]
    pathForResource:@"Texture" ofType:@"png"];
    NSError* error = nil;
    GLKTextureInfo* texture = [GLKTextureLoader textureWithContentsOfF
    ile:imagePath options:nil error:&error];
    if (error != nil) {
    NSLog(@"Problem loading texture: %@", error);
    }
    _squareEffect.texture2d0.name = texture.name;
    ```

3. To modify the earlier square color, remove the following lines:

    ```
    _squareEffect.useConstantColor = YES;
    _squareEffect.constantColor =
       GLKVector4Make(1.0, 0.0, 0.0, 1.0);
    ```

4. Finally, when rendering in `glkView:drawInRect`, we indicate to OpenGL where to find texture coordinates in the vertex information:

    ```
    glEnableVertexAttribArray(GLKVertexAttribTexCoord0);
    glVertexAttribPointer(GLKVertexAttribTexCoord0, 2,
       GL_FLOAT, GL_FALSE,
    sizeof(Vertex), (void*)offsetof(Vertex,
       textureCoordinates));
    ```

When the square is rendered, you'll see your image appear on it, as shown in the following screenshot:

5. Now we will make it as a cube. The cube is made up of eight vertices, so we need to provide information for each vertex, including its position and texture coordinates. From now on, rename `SquareVertices` to `CubeVertices` to follow a better naming convention.

```
const Vertex CubeVertices[] = {
{{-1, -1, 1}, {0,0}}, // bottom left front
{{1, -1, 1}, {1,0}}, // bottom right front
{{1, 1, 1}, {1,1}}, // top right front
```

```
{{-1,  1,  1},  {0,1}},  // top left front
{{-1, -1, -1},  {1,0}},  // bottom left back
{{1, -1, -1},  {0,0}},  // bottom right back
{{1,  1, -1},  {0,1}},  // top right back
{{-1,  1, -1},  {1,1}},  // top left back
};

const GLubyte CubeTriangles[] = {
0, 1, 2, // front face 1
2, 3, 0, // front face 2
4, 5, 6, // back face 1
6, 7, 4, // back face 2
7, 4, 0, // left face 1
0, 3, 7, // left face 2
2, 1, 5, // right face 1
5, 6, 2, // right face 2
7, 3, 6, // top face 1
6, 2, 3, // top face 2
4, 0, 5, // bottom face 1
5, 1, 0, // bottom face 2
};
```

6. The next step is a purely aesthetic one: the cube will be rotated, in order to illustrate that it is in fact a three-dimensional object.

    Select the following lines:

```
GLKMatrix4 modelViewMatrix = GLKMatrix4MakeTranslation(0.0f, 0.0f,
-6.0f);
_squareEffect.transform.modelviewMatrix = modelViewMatrix;
```

    Replace them with the following:

```
GLKMatrix4 modelViewMatrix =
  GLKMatrix4MakeTranslation(0.0f, 0.0f, -6.0f);
modelViewMatrix = GLKMatrix4RotateX(modelViewMatrix,
  GLKMathDegreesToRadians(45));
modelViewMatrix = GLKMatrix4RotateY(modelViewMatrix,
  GLKMathDegreesToRadians(45));
_squareEffect.transform.modelviewMatrix = modelViewMatrix;
```

    However, to draw our cube, a depth buffer needs to be added and enabled. The depth buffer is needed to provide a three-dimensional and more realistic look to the object.

7. Add the following code immediately after the call to EAGLContext's `setCurrentContext` method:

```
view.drawableDepthFormat = GLKViewDrawableDepthFormat24;
glEnable(GL_DEPTH_TEST);
```

8. Finally, replace the `glClear(GL_COLOR_BUFFER_BIT);` line with the `glClear(GL_COLOR_BUFFER_BIT | GL_DEPTH_BUFFER_BIT);` line.

9. Compile and run the project to see the cube in three-dimensions, as shown in the following screenshot:

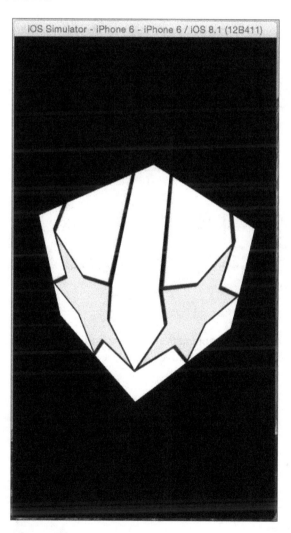

10. Now we will take it to the next level by adding a code to rotate a cube. Now we will animate movement in a view, such as rotation. Add the following instance variable to the `ViewController` class in the interface part:

```
float rotation;
```

11. Next, add the following method to the class:

```
- (void) update {
NSTimeInterval timeInterval = self.timeSinceLastUpdate;
float rotationSpeed = 15 * timeInterval;
rotation += rotationSpeed;
GLKMatrix4 modelViewMatrix = GLKMatrix4MakeTranslation(0.0f, 0.0f,
-6.0f);
modelViewMatrix = GLKMatrix4RotateX(modelViewMatrix,
GLKMathDegreesToRadians(45));
modelViewMatrix = GLKMatrix4RotateY(modelViewMatrix,
GLKMathDegreesToRadians(rotation));
_squareEffect.transform.modelviewMatrix = modelViewMatrix;
}
```

12. Now, the update function should look something similar to the following screenshot:

```
- (void) update {

    NSTimeInterval timeInterval = self.timeSinceLastUpdate;
    float rotationSpeed = 15 * timeInterval;
    rotation += rotationSpeed;
    GLKMatrix4 modelViewMatrix = GLKMatrix4MakeTranslation(0.0f, 0.0f, -6.0f);
    modelViewMatrix = GLKMatrix4RotateX(modelViewMatrix, GLKMathDegreesToRadians(45));
    modelViewMatrix = GLKMatrix4RotateY(modelViewMatrix, GLKMathDegreesToRadians(rotation));

    _squareEffect.transform.modelviewMatrix = modelViewMatrix;
}
```

13. Now compile and run the application. You will find your cube rotating at the angle we have specified, as shown in the following screenshot:

See also

So far we have learned various ways to create two-dimensional and three-dimensional models using OpenGL. OpenGL serves as the backbone of the three-dimensional game programming, and hence is a very vast topic to dive into. We have just taken a glance of OpenGL, to know more about it, you can refer to `https://developer.apple.com/opengl/`.

11
Getting Started with Multiplayer Games

In this chapter, we will be focusing on the following recipes:

- ▸ Anatomy of multiplayer games
- ▸ Setup for a multiplayer game
- ▸ Assigning roles to players

Introduction

So far in the book, we have done a lot of cool game-related stuff, such as SpriteKit, parallax scrolling background, physics simulation with autonomous moving agents, three-dimensional game programming using OpenGL, and much more. All these were done to make a single-player game, meaning only one person can play it at a time. But now, we will be moving forward to make a multiplayer game, which engages more than one person at the same time. Multiplayer is, in itself, more engaging and fun for the user, as live competition gets into the picture, making the gaming experience a lot more enjoyable for the users. So, it's time to understand things related to multiplayer games. In *Chapter 12, Implementing Multiplayer Games*, we will be creating a multiplayer game. For taking a tour of multiplayer game development, the overall agenda will be divided into the following sections:

1. Creating a sample multiplayer game to understand the anatomy and various states of a multiplayer game.

2. Doing the setup for the same multiplayer game using SpriteKit and Apple's Multipeer Connectivity framework. After that, handshaking or connection establishment between players using `MCBrowserViewController` of the same framework.

3. Assigning roles to players by sending and receiving network packets.

Anatomy of multiplayer games

In a single-player game, there is only one player, so talking about the game as an object that maintains all of the game behavior, whereas if we understand the anatomy of multiplayer games, we'll see that it's totally different. In multiplayer games, there are multiple players playing the same game, so technically for every device, there is a player who is actively driving the game on that device. This is called the local player, and all other players are treated as remotes players for that device. The local player's activities should ideally be updated on the remote players' devices, which is the foremost challenge in multiplayer development. The update of the local player is called syncing the game on some other device, and is done by the game object that resides in the game. It's the responsibility of the game object (that is, the instance of game running on the device) to make the game look the same on all devices as a live game is played.

So, moving further in this section, we will be creating a fresh multiplayer game, called TankRace, using SpriteKit, in which game sessions will be instantiated. We will incorporate multiplayer game states with their explanation and essentiality. All the session and multiplayer related processes will be done using the Multipeer Connectivity framework introduced in iOS 7, which was a part of GameKit in iOS 6.

Getting ready

To develop the TankRace multiplayer game using SpriteKit, start by creating a new project. Open Xcode and go to **File** | **New** | **Project** | **iOS** | **Application** | **SpriteKit Game**. In the pop-up, type the **Product Name** as `TankRace`, go to **Devices** | **iPhone**, and click on **Next**, as shown in the following screenshot:

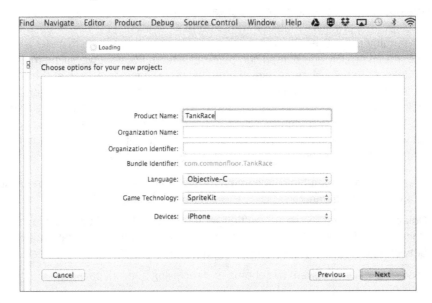

Click on **Next** and save the project on your hard drive.

Once the project is saved, you should be able to see the project settings. On the project settings page, just check in the **Portrait** from the **Device Orientation** section and uncheck all others, as we are supporting only the portrait mode for this game. Also set the deployment target to 7.0 so that a range of devices can be supported.

The changes are shown here:

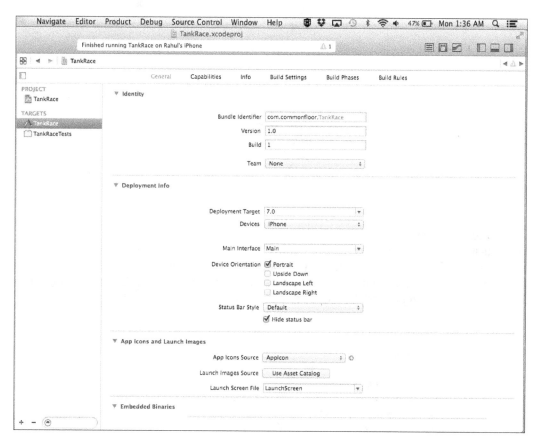

Let's take a closer view at what structure SpriteKit has provided:

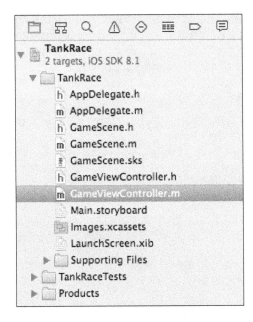

In the `viewDidLoad` method of `GameViewController` a piece of code is written that converts its view to `SKView` and a scene that is, `GameScene` is presented on the `SKView` as shown below. The `unarchiveFromFile` method is implemented by the project itself to fetch the `GameScene.sks` file, which we can see in the project created. For not showing the FPS and nodes, comment both the lines as shown in the following code:

```
- (void) viewDidLoad
{
    [super viewDidLoad];

    // Configure the view.
    SKView * skView = (SKView *) self.view;
//    skView.showsFPS = YES;
//    skView.showsNodeCount = YES;

    /* Sprite Kit applies additional optimizations to improve
rendering performance */
    skView.ignoresSiblingOrder = YES;

    // Create and configure the scene.
    GameScene *scene = [GameScene unarchiveFromFile:@"GameScene"];
    scene.scaleMode = SKSceneScaleModeAspectFill;

    // Present the scene.
    [skView presentScene:scene];
}
```

How to do it...

Before starting with the multiplayer code we should make the game ready for it. First, go in to the GameScene class and remove the sample SKLabelNode addition code in the overridden method didMoveToView of GameScene where we usually set up the scene. Secondly, remove the for loop of touches from the touchesBegan:withEvent method, which does the addition of SKSpriteNode and its action.

Our project is now ready to start with the multiplayer. Multiplayer games can be developed in several ways. They can be either played using Bluetooth, Wifi, Internet, or GameCenter. All these techniques allow us to interconnect devices and share data across devices. This allows us to show the movement of players in real time. You might have seen the responsiveness in multiplayer games. They are really seamless. In this section we will explore more about multiplayer games and their implementation in iOS. Here we will be instantiating a session (that is, MCSession) for the local player, which will further connect to another player in this recipe. Also, to instruct the user to touch we will add an info label saying Tap to connect and further will implement the delegates of MCSession following with the explanation of Multiplayer Game States. Stated below are the steps to accomplish this task:

1. Open GameScene.m file, and create an interface with properties of InfoLabel and all related session stuff. Also make GameScene follow MCSessionDelegate and the interface will look like this:

   ```
   @interface GameScene() <MCSessionDelegate>

   @property (nonatomic, strong) MCSession* gameSession;
   @property (nonatomic, strong) MCPeerID* gamePeerID;
   @property (nonatomic, strong) NSString* serviceType;
   @property (nonatomic, strong) MCAdvertiserAssistant* advertiser;

   @property (nonatomic, strong) SKLabelNode* gameInfoLabel;

   @end
   ```

   Here gameSession is the session that will be created for playing a multiplayer game, gamePeerID is the unique ID for the local player of this gameSession, which will be in future acting as the unique ID of the remote player to whom this device will be connected to. This is why it is called peerID. ServiceType is the unique ID assigned particularly to the game; here, the service type will be TankRace and advertiser is a class that handles all incoming invitations to the user and handles all user responses. A gameInfoLabel property is declared, which will be created to instruct the user to connect with other players.

2. Add a method called `addGameInfoLabelWithText`, which can be used to show any GameInfo with `pragma` mark.

```
#pragma mark - Adding Assets Methods

- (void)addGameInfoLabelWithText:(NSString*)labelText
{
    if (self.gameInfoLabel == nil) {
        self.gameInfoLabel = [SKLabelNode labelNodeWithFontNamed:@
"Chalkduster"];
        self.gameInfoLabel.text = labelText;
        self.gameInfoLabel.fontSize = 32;
        self.gameInfoLabel.position =
CGPointMake(CGRectGetMidX(self.frame),

CGRectGetMidY(self.frame));
        self.gameInfoLabel.zPosition = 100;

        [self addChild:self.gameInfoLabel];
    }
}
```

3. Declare hash defines for different GameInfo texts.

```
#define kConnectingDevicesText @"Tap to Connect"
#define kGameStartedText       @"Game Started"
#define kConnectedDevicesText @"Devices Connected"
```

4. Call `addGameInfoLabelWithText` from the `didMoveToView` method of `GameScene`. With text hash define `kConnectingDevicesText` and `pragma` mark as depicted below.

```
#pragma mark - Overridden Methods

- (void)didMoveToView:(SKView *)view {
    /* Setup your scene here */
    [self addGameInfoLabelWithText:kConnectingDevicesText];
}
```

5. Declare an `enum`, GameState, and a property corresponding to it in the private interface of `GameScene`. Also, set the initial state of game as `kGameStatePlayerToConnect`, as, to start a multiplayer game, players need to be connected first to play. Add these lines just above the hash defines:

```
typedef enum {

    kGameStatePlayerToConnect,
    kGameStatePlayerAllotment,
```

```
    kGameStatePlaying,
    kGameStateComplete,

} GameState;
```

6. Add this property of `gameState` in the private interface of `GameScene`:

```
@property (nonatomic, assign) GameState gameState;
```

7. Assign `gameState` to `kGameStatePlayerToConnect` in `didMoveToView` of `GameScene`:

```
self.gameState = kGameStatePlayerToConnect;
```

8. Create a method called `instantiateMCSession` and add the `pragma` mark as shown in the following code:

```
#pragma mark - Networking Related Methods

- (void)instantiateMCSession
{
  if (self.gameSession == nil)
  {
    UIDevice *device = [UIDevice currentDevice];
    MCPeerID* peerID = [[MCPeerID alloc]
      initWithDisplayName:device.name];
    self.gameSession = [[MCSession alloc]
       initWithPeer:peerID];
    self.gameSession.delegate = self;
      self.serviceType = @"TankFight"; // should be
        unique
    self.advertiser = [[MCAdvertiserAssistant alloc]
      initWithServiceType:self.serviceType
        discoveryInfo:nil session:self.gameSession];
        [self.advertiser start];
  }
}
```

Here, an object of `MCSession` is created using `peerID` with the display name as the device name and the `delegate` property of this object is set to the `GameScene` object to get the `delegate` methods implemented in this class. For invitations to the user and handling all user responses an object of `MCAdvertiserAssistant` is created using the `gameSession` and a `serviceType`, which should be unique.

In the fist line of the code snippet we have used the `pragma` marks. Using `pragma` marks we can make our code much more readable and also provide logical grouping to our methods. It is a good programming practice to follow.

9. Implement all delegates MCSessionDelegate with the pragma mark as shown below:

```
#pragma mark - MCSessionDelegate Methods

- (void)session:(MCSession *)session peer:(MCPeerID
  *)peerID
 didChangeState:(MCSessionState)state {
// A peer has changed state - it's now either
  connecting, connected, or disconnected.
   if (state == MCSessionStateConnected)
   {
     NSLog(@"state == MCSessionStateConnected");
   }
   else if (state == MCSessionStateConnecting)
   {
       NSLog(@"state == MCSessionStateConnecting");
   }
   else if (state == MCSessionStateNotConnected)
   {
       NSLog(@"state == MCSessionStateNotConnected");
   }
}

- (void)session:(MCSession *)session didReceiveData:(NSData
    *)data fromPeer:(MCPeerID *)peerID {
   // Data has been received from a peer.
   // Do something with the received data, on the main
     thread
   [[NSOperationQueue mainQueue]  addOperationWithBlock:^{

       // Process the data
   }];
}

- (void)session:(MCSession *)session
  didStartReceivingResourceWithName:
  (NSString *)resourceName fromPeer:(MCPeerID *)peerID
    withProgress:(NSProgress *)progress {
    // A file started being sent from a peer. (Not used in this
example.)
}
- (void)session:(MCSession *)session
  didFinishReceivingResourceWithName:(NSString
     *)resourceName fromPeer:(MCPeerID *)peerID
      atURL:(NSURL *)localURL withError:(NSError *)error {
```

```
    // A file finished being sent from a peer. (Not used in this
example.)
}


- (void)session:(MCSession *)session
  didReceiveStream:(NSInputStream *)stream
 withName:(NSString *)streamName fromPeer:(MCPeerID
  *)peerID {
    // Data started being streamed from a peer. (Not used
       in this example.)
}
```

These all are the delegate methods of `MCSession` implemented in the `GameScene` class, amongst which the former two are mostly used. The first one is used to determine the state of game changes, like, whether it is connected, connecting or not connected. And the latter one is used to receive data, hence to process that data under an operation queue block as shown in the above implementation.

10. Now add `instantiateMCSession` in `touchBegan:withEvent` according to `gameState` of GameScene with `pragma` mark.

```
#pragma mark - Touch Methods
- (void)touchesBegan:(NSSet *)touches withEvent:(UIEvent *)event {
    /* Called when a touch begins */

    if (self.gameState == kGameStatePlayerToConnect)
    {
        [self instantiateMCSession];
    }
    else if (self.gameState == kGameStatePlaying)
    {
    }
}
```

In the `touchesBegan` method if the state is `kGameStatePlayerToConnect` then it means that the user has touched to start the game that is, technically connecting of players to be done and in other states of game the handling would be done accordingly on touches.

After all these steps an initial session of game set up has been accomplished with an understanding of multiplayer games' architecture.

How it works...

In the preceding setup we used the Multipeer Connectivity framework for setting up a structure of a multiplayer game with an instance of `MCSession` to be there in every device that will be used to play the game. We also implemented all its delegate methods, which informs the `GameScene` about the changing of game states and will also be used for receiving data when incoming sections from some network packets are sent. For now, in this section, we have put a label `Tap to connect` and on clicking the screen a session is instantiated. Now build the project. First you will see the following launch screen and then the initial `GameScene` with a label **Tap to connect**:

Setup for a multiplayer game

In this recipe, we will write the code for setting up our multiplayer game. All the configurations and session managers will be the part of this section. We will dig into the various concepts of creating and maintaining sessions.

Getting ready

Before starting this recipe, MCSession, MCPeerId, advertiser and service type terms of Multipeer Connectivity framework should be known to us. In this recipe we will be establishing the connection between players, thereby, they can communicate in future, making the players play a game, which we will be doing in the next chapter.

How to do it

Now, on tapping the screen, a MCSession with a service type has been instantiated; we can use this session and service type to present a `MCBrowserViewController` and establish connection between players (that is, devices). `MCBrowserViewController` is fully equipped and designed for connecting multiple players for a session provided in the Multipeer Connectivity framework. These are the steps involved:

1. First of all, create a protocol of `GameScene` as `GameSceneDelegate` and its delegate object in `GameScene`, which will be set as `GameViewController` so that it uses its delegate method when the user touches the screen. `GameViewController` can be informed to present `MCBrowserViewController`. Declare the protocol code and `GameSceneDelegate` object, as follows:

   ```
   @protocol GameSceneDelegate <NSObject>

   - (void)showMCBrowserControllerForSession:(MCSession*)session
     serviceType:(NSString*)serviceType;
   @end

   @property (nonatomic, weak) id<GameSceneDelegate>
     gameSceneDelegate;
   ```

2. When the user touches the screen that has the `gameState` as `kGameStatePlayerToConnect`, where we are calling the method, `instantiateMCSession`, which also informs `gameSceneDelegate` to show `MCBrowserViewController` by passing `gameSession` that was created and the `serviceType` property:

   ```
   if (self.gameSceneDelegate && [self.gameSceneDelegate
   respondsToSelector:@selector(showMCBrowserControllerForSession:ser
   viceType:)])
     {
       [self.gameSceneDelegate
         showMCBrowserControllerForSession:self.gameSession
           serviceType:self.serviceType];
     }
   ```

3. The delegate method has to be called by `GameViewController`, and on the same controller, `MCBrowserViewController` has to be presented, which will also have its own delegate methods. Now, it's time to declare the private interface of `GameViewController` and follow both `MCBrowserViewControllerDelegate` and `GameSceneDelegate` as shown in this snippet:

```
@interface GameViewController() <MCBrowserViewControllerDelegate,
        GameSceneDelegate>
@property (nonatomic, strong) GameScene* gameScene;
@end
```

4. In `viewDidLoad` of `GameViewController`, replace the local scene object with `self.gameScene` and assign the `gameSceneDelegate` property of the `GameScene` object as the `GameViewController`, as shown here:

```
// Create and configure the scene.
self.gameScene = [GameScene
  unarchiveFromFile:@"GameScene"];
self.gameScene.scaleMode = SKSceneScaleModeAspectFill;

self.gameScene.gameSceneDelegate = self;

// Present the scene.
[skView presentScene:self.gameScene];
```

5. Implement the delegate method of `GameSceneDelegate`, like this:

```
- (void)showMCBrowserControllerForSession:
(MCSession*)session
serviceType:(NSString*)serviceType
{
    MCBrowserViewController* viewController =
      [[MCBrowserViewController alloc]
    initWithServiceType:serviceType session:session];

    viewController.minimumNumberOfPeers = 2;
    viewController.maximumNumberOfPeers = 2;

    viewController.delegate = self;

    [self presentViewController:viewController animated:YES
      completion:nil];
}
```

In this method, `MCBrowserViewController` is presented on `GameViewController` with its delegate set and restricted the peers to 2.

6. Add two public methods to `GameScene`, to be called the cancel and done actions of `MCBrowserViewController`.

   - In `GameScene.h`, declare the public methods, as follows:

     ```
     #pragma mark - Public Methods

     - (void)startGame;
     - (void)discardSession;
     ```

   - In `GameScene.m`, define the public methods, like this:

     ```
     - (void)startGame
     {
         self.gameInfoLabel.text = kConnectedDevicesText;
     }

     - (void)discardSession
     {
         self.gameState = kGameStatePlayerToConnect;

         self.gameSession = nil;
         self.gamePeerID = nil;
         self.serviceType = nil;
         self.advertiser = nil;
     }
     ```

7. Now we will add two public methods in the `GameScene` file. These methods will be invoked on the cancel and done actions of `MCBrowserViewControllerDelegate` respectively:

   ```
   #pragma mark - MCBrowserViewControllerDelegate Methods

   - (void)browserViewControllerDidFinish:
     (MCBrowserViewController *)browserViewController {
       // The MCSession is now ready to use.
       [self dismissViewControllerAnimated:YES
         completion:nil];
       if (self.gameScene)
       {
           [self.gameScene startGame];
       }
   }

   - (void)browserViewControllerWasCancelled:
     (MCBrowserViewController *)browserViewController{
       // The user cancelled.
       [self dismissViewControllerAnimated:YES
         completion:nil];
       if (self.gameScene)
   ```

```
        {
            [self.gameScene discardSession];
        }
    }
```

In both the delegate methods, first the MCBrowserViewController is dismissed and GameScene is informed to change accordingly.

Now when both the device players click on the screen, MCBrowserViewController opens and the players try to connect to each other using the default behavior provided by this controller, and when done we show the appropriate text to the player. Hence this entire implementation accomplishes our starter kit of this chapter.

How it works

Now we will understand how the connection using the MCBrowserViewController is established in the following steps (in the snapshots shown below, the left side is the simulator device and right side is iPhone 5s):

1. Both the players click on the screen and MCBrowserViewController opens, searching for peers nearby, with cancel and done buttons placed on the navigation bar. Here the done button is disabled, as initially no one is connected to the device.

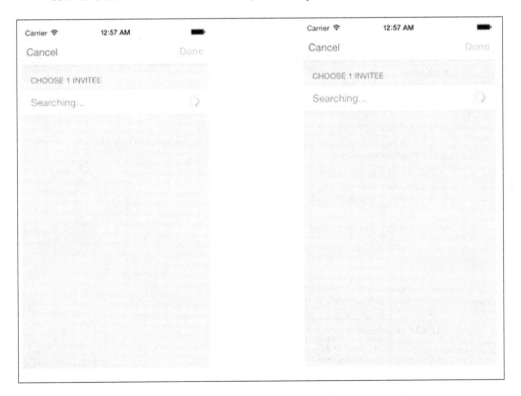

2. Once a peer is detected, it shows the name of the devices in the list.

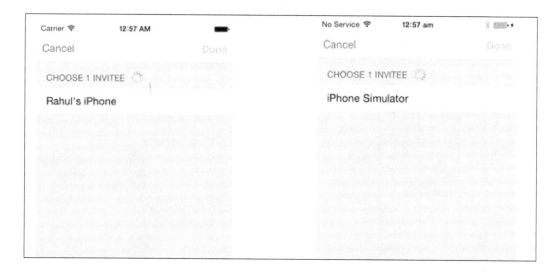

3. After that both the players press the device name with which they want to connect and the search of peers stop. Hence following this selection of device a request is sent to connect to it.

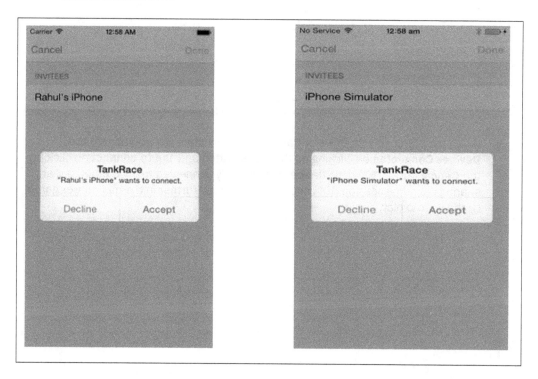

4. Depending on the reply of the other user the status of the peer at the right text of table row is updated; it can be **Connecting**, **Connected**. And when the devices are connected the status is changed to **Connected** and the **Done** button is enabled.

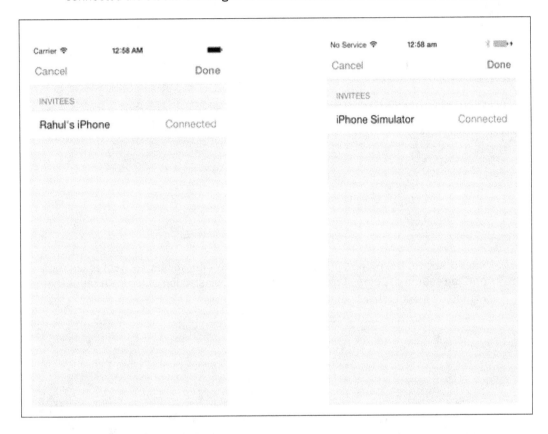

5. When the player selects **Done** or **Cancel**, we show them the appropriate text, **Devices Connected** on clicking on the **Done** button and **Tap to connect** on clicking the **Cancel** button. Now, the devices are logically connected to each other and are sharing the same session. This session will be used further in the multiplayer game by the user to play.

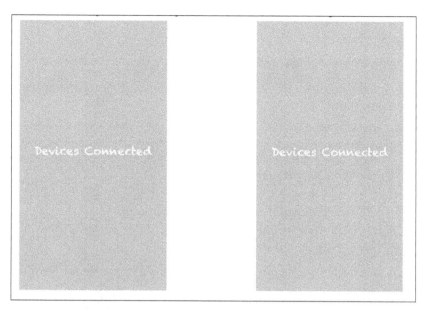

Here, in all this process, we will see some network lagging also, so if the devices are not connecting, try to reconnect by cancelling the controller and again clicking on the screen to refresh the controller again.

Assigning roles to players

In this recipe, we will take our game template to the next step by assigning the roles to our players. This means we will be logically dividing the users and assigning roles to them. This will provide an individual identity to the players.

Getting ready

Before starting with assigning or as we can also call it, an allotment of players identity (which is first player and second player), we should be familiar with the Multipeer Connectivity framework. We must also have a basic knowledge of network packet sending and receiving. In this section we will be assigning the first and second player identities to the players once they are connected using the `MCBrowserViewController` having just described it in the preceding recipe by pressing the **Done** button.

How to do it

To accomplish the assignment of players, following are the steps to be followed:

1. For a set up purpose for this add some enums, hash define constants and properties as shown below:

   ❑ Declare an `enum` called `NetworkPacketCode` in which we add only the `KNetworkPacketCodePlayerAllotment` packet code for now, and in the future more packet codes can be added for sending and receiving packets from the game.

   ```
   typedef enum {
       KNetworkPacketCodePlayerAllotment,
       // More to be added while creating the game
   } NetworkPacketCode;
   ```

   ❑ Add texts to be shown to players when the player roles are being decided.

   ```
   // Blue is the First and Red is the Second Player
   #define kFirstPlayerLabelText  @"You're First Player"
   #define kSecondPlayerLabelText @"You're Second Player"
   ```

   ❑ Add the max packet size constant and some properties like `gamePacketNumber`, `gameUniqueIdForPlayerAllocation` in `GameScene.m` to be used while sending packets.

   ```
   #define kMaxTankPacketSize 1024
   int gameUniqueIdForPlayerAllocation;
   @property (nonatomic, assign) int gamePacketNumber;
   ```

2. Now to send data from one device to another, we have an encapsulated data container, which is called a packet. Now this packet is sent over the network and the other player's device will update the view and position accordingly. For this, create a method to send the packet with a header `NetworkPacketCode` and data specifying `peerId` to which the data packet has to be sent and whether the packet should be sent with a reliable service or not.

   ```
   - (void) sendNetworkPacketToPeerId: (MCPeerID*) peerId
      forPacketCode: (NetworkPacketCode) packetCode
          withData: (void *) data
             ofLength: (NSInteger) length
                reliable: (BOOL) reliable
   {
       // the packet we'll send is resued
       static unsigned char networkPacket[kMaxTankPacketSize];
   ```

```objc
    const unsigned int packetHeaderSize = 2 * sizeof(int);
// we have two "ints" for our header
    if(length < (kMaxTankPacketSize - packetHeaderSize))
    {
// our networkPacket buffer size minus the size of the
  header info
        int *pIntData = (int *)&networkPacket[0];
        // header info
        pIntData[0] = self.gamePacketNumber++;
        pIntData[1] = packetCode;

        if (data)          {
          // copy data in after the header
            memcpy( &networkPacket[packetHeaderSize], data,
              length );
          }

        NSData *packet = [NSData dataWithBytes:
            networkPacket length: (length+8)];
            NSError* error;
        if(reliable == YES)
        {
            [self.gameSession sendData:packet
                toPeers:[NSArray arrayWithObject:peerId]
                    withMode:MCSessionSendDataReliable
                        error:&error];
        }
        else
        {
            [self.gameSession sendData:packet
                toPeers:[NSArray arrayWithObject:peerId]
                    withMode:MCSessionSendDataUnreliable
                        error:&error];
        }
        if (error)
        {
            NSLog(@"Error:%@",[error description]);
        }
    }
}
```

Here `networkPacket` is created with a header and data. A variable `pIntData` is declared, which is the header containing the `NetworkPacketCode` and a `gamePacketNumber` so that a unique number is assigned to a packet to serialize the network packets to be used to sync or update the game properly. Once the packet is created, a method called `sendData` of `MCSession` is called with the packet to be sent, `peerID` to which the packet has to be sent, the mode, which can be `MCSessionSendDataUnreliable` or `MCSessionSendDataReliable` and `error` to check whether an error has occurred while sending the packet.

This method will be reused everywhere in the game to send packets to peers of the same game.

3. Generate a random number and store it in the variable `gameUniqueIdForPlayerAllocation` declared above, which will help to decide which will be the first and second player. Add this line in the `didMoveToView` method of `GameScene`.

```
gameUniqueIdForPlayerAllocation = arc4random();
```

4. Add the following code to receiving data delegate method of `MCSession` for handling of received packets based on their `NetworkPacketCode` as shown in the following code:

```
- (void) session: (MCSession *) session didReceiveData: (NSData
    *) data fromPeer: (MCPeerID *) peerID {
    // Data has been received from a peer.
    // Do something with the received data, on the main
      thread
    [[NSOperationQueue mainQueue]  addOperationWithBlock:^{
    // Process the data
      unsigned char *incomingPacket = (unsigned char
        *) [data bytes];
      int *pIntData = (int *) &incomingPacket[0];
      NetworkPacketCode packetCode =
        (NetworkPacketCode) pIntData[1];

      switch( packetCode ) {
       case KNetworkPacketCodePlayerAllotment:
       {
        NSInteger gameUniqueId = pIntData[2];
        if (gameUniqueIdForPlayerAllocation > gameUniqueId)
         {
            self.gameInfoLabel.text =
              kFirstPlayerLabelText;
         }
        else
          {
```

```
                    self.gameInfoLabel.text =
                        kSecondPlayerLabelText;
                    }
                    break;
                }
                default:
                break;
            }
        }];
    }
```

While receiving the data, it should be processed on a `mainQueue` operation block. In this block, we will remove the header in the `pIntData` pointer variable and get the `NetworkPacketCode` sent in the packet. In this code, we will check the type of packet which is sent. Then we will parse the packet based on its type. In this, a player allotment packet type named `KNetworkPacketCodePlayerAllotment` is passed, hence the data retrieved is `gameUniqueId`. As discussed above, in `didMoveToView`, we assigned a random number to a variable named `gameUniqueIdForPlayerAllocation` for both the devices. Hence for both devices, different numbers are generated & while sending the allotment packet from both devices, this is passed as the data (the allotment packet to be sent would be discussed in next point). Finally to decide which is first and second player, the local value of `gameUniqueIdForPlayerAllocation` would be compared with the value sent in the packet, on this comparison one would be assigned as the first player and other as the second player, informing the users by changing appropriate text of `gameInfoLabel` as shown in the delegate method.

5. Remove the following written line from the public method `startGame` of `GameScene` as now, the `gameInfoLabel` will be set according to the packet received.

   `self.gameInfoLabel.text = kConnectedDevicesText;`

6. All these earlier processes start when the user clicks on the done button. This button is an indication that the players have been connected and a delegate method `didChangeState` of `MCSession` will be called with a `MCSessionState` called `MCSessionStateConnected`, and as a checking protocol is already in-built in this method of connected state, add the following code in the `if` statement:

```
- (void)session:(MCSession *)session peer:(MCPeerID
    *)peerID didChangeState:(MCSessionState)state {
    // A peer has changed state - it's now either
       connecting, connected, or disconnected.

    if (state == MCSessionStateConnected)
    {
        NSLog(@"state == MCSessionStateConnected");
```

```
            // Remember the current peer
            self.gamePeerID = peerID;
            // Make sure we have a reference to the game
              session and it is set up
            self.gameSession = session;
            self.gameSession.delegate = self;
            self.gameState = kGameStatePlayerAllotment;

            self.gameInfoLabel.text = kGameStartedText;

            [self sendNetworkPacketToPeerId:self.gamePeerID
              forPacketCode:KNetworkPacketCodePlayerAllotment
                withData:&gameUniqueIdForPlayerAllocation
                  ofLength:sizeof(int)
                    reliable:YES];
        }
        else if (state == MCSessionStateConnecting)
        {
            NSLog(@"state == MCSessionStateConnecting");
        }
        else if (state == MCSessionStateNotConnected)
        {
            NSLog(@"state == MCSessionStateNotConnected");
        }
    }
}
```

Here, in this method, set all properties that come from the method, as it is the remote player information, and set the game state to kGameStatePlayerAllotment locally. Then, we send the packet of the allotment of the player to peerID, for which the connection has been established with a NetworkPacketCode and a data part, which would be received at the remote end as discussed previously.

Finally, we are done with connecting two players for a multiplayer game and assigning them a unique identity for further identification to build the game. This recipe acts as the solution kit for this chapter.

How it works

The entire assignment of players depends on what action and data the packet is sent with, and how it is parsed at the receiver's end according to the convention set by the sender. To accomplish the allotment of the player's identity, we used a random number variable, which is locally generated and passed in the allotment packet. At the receiving end, the logic of allotment is written, checking the locally set and remotely passed random number. Based on this comparison, the first and second players are decided.

Some text is shown on both the devices, informing the players about their identity, as shown here:

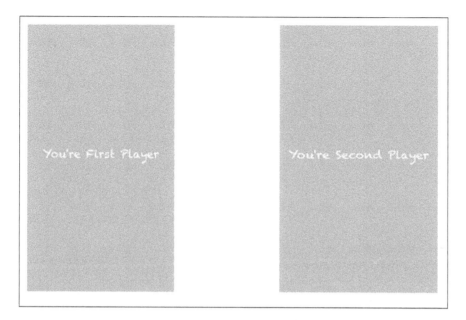

There's more

In the preceding section, we have used the Multipeer Connectivity framework. We can also use the GameKit framework. For more information on this take a look at https://developer.apple.com/library/ios/documentation/GameKit/Reference/GameKit_Collection/index.html.

See also

For better understanding and learning the Multipeer Connectivity framework, visit https://developer.apple.com/library/prerelease/ios/documentation/MultipeerConnectivity/Reference/MultipeerConnectivityFramework/index.html.

12
Implementing Multiplayer Games

In this chapter we will be focusing on the following topics:

- Creating our TankRace environment
- Movement of players
- Implementing game play

Introduction

In the previous chapter, we covered the handshaking of players like connection establishment and assigning a unique identification to the players. Now we shall move forward to exploring more about multiplayer games, and create a multiplayer game called TankRace. We will be implementing the following things while creating the game:

- Creating a visual game setup, like adding players, backgrounds, and other assets
- Implementing movement of players on touching of the screen and also syncing the players across devices
- Implementing gameplay, which is the game logic for winning and losing on players actions

Creating our TankRace environment

The name of the game itself suggests that it's a racing game, where there will be two players and tanks named the blue tank and the red tank. The tanks will be placed on either side of the screen in the portrait mode on the iPhone and there will be two finishing lines, a blue line and a red line, to be crossed by blue tank (let's say first player) and red tank (let's say second player) respectively. The movement of player will be a touch based behavior and the player whose tank crosses their finish line first will win and the other will lose. We will be creating the environment for the game, TankRace, which will include adding players, game background, and finishing lines.

Getting ready

In the previous chapters, you have learned all about adding sprites and backgrounds and updating their attributes like position, rotation, and so on. Now, we will be adding all the assets needed in the game to make it playable.

How to do it

The steps to add all the assets required to be added to the game are as follows:

1. Drag and add the resources provided with the with the code bundle for this chapter, which are: `BlueTank.png`, `RedTank.png`, and `Background.png` to the project, After adding the files, the project navigator will look like this:

2. Now, here, we will be using GameKit, which is a great framework to create social games. This framework provides various features such ass peer-to-peer connection, game center, and in-game voice chat. Import GameKit and declare some enums, structures, properties, and constants to be used in the coming code as shown:

   ❏ Import `GameKit` to use CGPoint for storing data structures:

   ```
   #import <GameKit/GameKit.h>
   ```

   ❏ Add two more `NetworkPacketCode` for players to move and a packet code for when game finishes, for example, a packet for losing a game:

   ```
   typedef enum {
       KNetworkPacketCodePlayerAllotment,
       KNetworkPacketCodePlayerMove,
       KNetworkPacketCodePlayerLost,
   } NetworkPacketCode;
   ```

   ❏ Declare a structure called `TankInfo`, which will be used as a data structure for sending the information on tanks; the same structure will be used to sync at the remote player's receiving end.

   ```
   typedef struct {
       CGPoint          tankPreviousPosition;
       CGPoint          tankPosition;
       CGPoint          tankDestination;
       CGFloat          tankRotation;
       CGFloat          tankDirection;
   } TankInfo;
   ```

   ❏ For the movement of Tanks, add `Speed` and `TurnSpeed` constants

   ```
   const float kTankSpeed = 1.0f;
   const float kTankTurnSpeed = 0.1f;
   ```

   ❏ Change the text of the first and the second player's labels to blue and red respectively

   ```
   // Blue is the First and Red is the Second Player
   #define kFirstPlayerLabelText  @"You're Blue"
   #define kSecondPlayerLabelText @"You're Red"
   ```

   ❏ Add text hash defines for when someone wins or loses.

   ```
   #define kGameWonText           @"You Won"
   #define kGameLostText          @"You Lost"
   ```

3. Add some properties to the private interface of `GameScene`, like a local data structure of the tank to be maintained and updated, so that it can be sent to the remote end as well. Also, declare all the `SKSpriteNodes` and `SKShapeNodes` to be used in the game.

```
TankInfo tankStatsForLocal;

@property (nonatomic, strong) SKSpriteNode* redTankSprite;
@property (nonatomic, strong) SKSpriteNode* blueTankSprite;
@property (nonatomic, strong) SKShapeNode* blueFinishLine;
@property (nonatomic, strong) SKShapeNode* redFinishLine;
@property (nonatomic, strong) SKSpriteNode* localTankSprite;
@property (nonatomic, strong) SKSpriteNode*
  remoteTankSprite;
```

4. Now, we shall add some nodes to the scene, hence the GameScene needs to be of the correct size. Click on `GameScene.sks` and open the right panel from the last icon on the right top bar of Xcode. From there, change the size of the GameScene to `320 x 568` which is the size of the iPhone 4 inch.

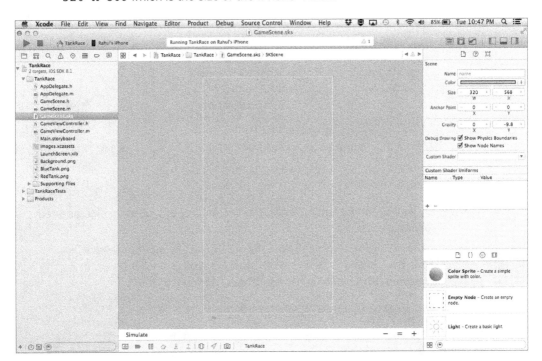

5. Add a method `addGameBackground` under the `adding assets` method's `pragma` mark in which a `SKSpriteNode` is created, with the image `Background.png` added previously in the project. Keep the *z* position of background as 0 as it will be below all other nodes of the game.

```
- (void)addGameBackground
{
    SKSpriteNode *gameBGNode =
    [SKSpriteNode spriteNodeWithImageNamed:@"Background.png"];
    {
        gameBGNode.position =
        CGPointMake(self.frame.size.width/2,self.frame.size.
height/
            2);
        gameBGNode.zPosition = 0;
        [self addChild:gameBGNode];
    }
}
```

6. Add two different methods under the `adding assets` methods `pragma` mark for players, namely, blue and red tank with `BlueTank.png` and `RedTank.png` images respectively as `SpriteNodes`.

```
- (void)addBlueTank
{
    self.blueTankSprite = [SKSpriteNode
      spriteNodeWithImageNamed:@"BlueTank.png"];
    self.blueTankSprite.position =
      CGPointMake(self.frame.size.width/2,self.frame.size.height
      * 0.95);
    self.blueTankSprite.zRotation = M_PI;
    self.blueTankSprite.zPosition = 2;

    [self addChild:self.blueTankSprite];
}

- (void)addRedTank
{
    self.redTankSprite = [SKSpriteNode
      spriteNodeWithImageNamed:@"RedTank.png"];
    self.redTankSprite.position =
      CGPointMake(self.frame.size.width/2,self.frame.size.height
        * 0.05);
    self.redTankSprite.zRotation = 0.0;
    self.redTankSprite.zPosition = 2;

    [self addChild:self.redTankSprite];
}
```

7. Also, create two methods under the `adding assets` methods `pragma` mark for the finishing lines, which both the players will have to reach to win.

```
- (void) addBLueFinishLine
{
    CGRect frame = CGRectMake(0, self.frame.size.height *
        0.15, self.frame.size.width, 1);

    self.blueFinishLine = [SKShapeNode
        shapeNodeWithRect:frame];
    {
        self.blueFinishLine.strokeColor = [UIColor
            blueColor];
        self.blueFinishLine.zPosition = 2;
        [self addChild:self.blueFinishLine];
    }
}

- (void) addRedFinishLine
{
    CGRect frame = CGRectMake(0, self.frame.size.height *
        0.85, self.frame.size.width, 1);

    self.redFinishLine = [SKShapeNode
        shapeNodeWithRect:frame];
    {
        self.redFinishLine.strokeColor = [UIColor
            redColor];
        self.redFinishLine.zPosition = 1;
        [self addChild:self.redFinishLine];
    }
}
```

8. Here we use the `SKNodeShape` class objects, which are used to draw any required shape on the screen using the core graphics path. We are thus adding the red and blue lines at either end of the game scene.

9. To set the tanks in the initial positions both in the data structure and in the `GameScene`, we will write a method, namely, `resetLocalTanksAndInfoToInitialState`.

```
#pragma mark - Game Updation Methods

- (void) resetLocalTanksAndInfoToInitialState
{
```

```
    if (self.localTankSprite == self.blueTankSprite &&
        self.remoteTankSprite == self.redTankSprite)
    {
        tankStatsForLocal.tankPosition =
          CGPointMake(self.frame.size.width/2,self.frame.size.
height
            * 0.95);
        tankStatsForLocal.tankRotation = M_PI;
        self.localTankSprite.position =
          tankStatsForLocal.tankPosition;
        self.localTankSprite.zRotation =
          tankStatsForLocal.tankRotation;

        self.remoteTankSprite.position =
          CGPointMake(self.frame.size.width/2,self.frame.size.
height
            * 0.05);
        self.remoteTankSprite.zRotation = 0.0;
    }
    else if (self.localTankSprite == self.redTankSprite &&
        self.remoteTankSprite == self.blueTankSprite)
    {
        tankStatsForLocal.tankPosition =
          CGPointMake(self.frame.size.width/2,self.frame.size.
height
            * 0.05);
        tankStatsForLocal.tankRotation = 0.0;
        self.localTankSprite.position =
          tankStatsForLocal.tankPosition;
        self.localTankSprite.zRotation =
          tankStatsForLocal.tankRotation;

        self.remoteTankSprite.position =
          CGPointMake(self.frame.size.width/2,self.frame.size.
height
            * 0.95);
        self.remoteTankSprite.zRotation = M_PI;
    }
}
```

10. In this method, the local data structure `tankStatsForLocal` and the local player's attributes position, `zRotation` using the only `tankStatsForLocal` are set to the initial state of the game. The remote player's position and `zRotation` are hardcoded in the initial state of the game. All this is set on the basis of who out of blue and red is the local and remote tank on the device.

11. To animate the players identity text, add a method
    `hideGameInfoLabelWithAnimation`.

```
- (void)hideGameInfoLabelWithAnimation
{
    SKAction* gameInfoLabelHoldAnimationCallBack =
      [SKAction customActionWithDuration:2.0
         actionBlock:^(SKNode *node,CGFloat elapsedTime)
      {
      }];

    SKAction* gameInfoLabelFadeOutAnimation =
      [SKAction fadeOutWithDuration:1.0];

    SKAction* gameInfoLabelRemoveAnimationCallBack =
    [SKAction customActionWithDuration:0.0
      actionBlock:^(SKNode *node,CGFloat elapsedTime)
      {
          [node removeFromParent];
          self.gameInfoLabel = nil;
      }];

    NSArray* gameLabelAnimationsSequence =
     [NSArray
       arrayWithObjects:gameInfoLabelHoldAnimationCallBack,
          gameInfoLabelFadeOutAnimation,
             gameInfoLabelRemoveAnimationCallBack, nil];
    SKAction* gameInfoSequenceAnimation =
     [SKAction sequence:gameLabelAnimationsSequence];
    [self.gameInfoLabel
       runAction:gameInfoSequenceAnimation];
}
```

12. Using sprite `SKAction` a sequence of animations is created, having a delay initially, fading the label and then using a callback to remove it at last. This is done when the users are connected. For fading in and out of the labels, we use the same animation code that we used earlier in *Chapter 3, Animations and Texture*.

13. Now, edit the `didChangeState` delegate method of `MCSession`, when the state changes to connected as shown in the following:

```
- (void)session:(MCSession *)session didReceiveData:(NSData
   *)data fromPeer:(MCPeerID *)peerID {
   // Data has been received from a peer.

   // Do something with the received data, on the main
     thread
```

```objc
[[NSOperationQueue mainQueue]  addOperationWithBlock:^{

   // Process the data
   unsigned char *incomingPacket = (unsigned char
     *)[data bytes];
   int *pIntData = (int *)&incomingPacket[0];
   NetworkPacketCode packetCode =
     (NetworkPacketCode)pIntData[1];

   switch( packetCode ) {
     case KNetworkPacketCodePlayerAllotment:
       {
             NSInteger gameUniqueId = pIntData[2];
           if (gameUniqueIdForPlayerAllocation >
             gameUniqueId)
             {
                self.gameInfoLabel.text =
                   kFirstPlayerLabelText;
                 self.localTankSprite =
                   self.blueTankSprite;
                 self.remoteTankSprite =
                     self.redTankSprite;
             }
           else
             {
                self.gameInfoLabel.text =
                   kSecondPlayerLabelText;
                 self.localTankSprite =
                   self.redTankSprite;
                 self.remoteTankSprite =
                   self.blueTankSprite;
             }
           [self
              resetLocalTanksAndInfoToInitialState];
           break;
       }
     case KNetworkPacketCodePlayerMove:
       {
           break;
       }
     case KNetworkPacketCodePlayerLost:
       {
           break;
       }
```

```
            default:
            break;
        }
    }];
}
```

14. In the receiving `MCSession` method, add all `NetworkPacketCode` in the `switch` case and make changes when the `KNetworkPacketCodePlayerAllotment` packet is received. When allocating the players, set the identity name accordingly and assign the local and remote sprite objects depending on the `gameUniqueIdForPlayerAllocation`. Finally, call a private method `resetLocalTanksAndInfoToInitialState`, in which initial states of both local and remote sprites with their local data structure are set. All these steps will be executed on both the connected devices in sessions, which will ensure that both the devices are in sync.

15. Now once the `gameInfoLabel` displaying player identity is set, then insert the code to change the state of the game and to animate `gameInfoLabel` by hiding it in the `startGame` method of `GameScene`, called by a delegate method of `MCBrowerViewController`.

```
-  (void) startGame
{
    if (self.gameState == kGameStatePlayerAllotment)
    {
        self.gameState = kGameStatePlaying;
        [self hideGameInfoLabelWithAnimation];
    }
}
```

16. When the method is called by the delegate method, it checks if the allotment of the player has been done, then changes the state to playing and animates the hiding of the label on which either **You're blue** or **You're red** is written.

After all these asset addition of games, its environment is setup and player's identities or we can say names, have been assigned as blue and red. All this comprises of the starter kit of this chapter.

How it works

The whole section was about using SpriteKit as a way to add game assets and as a part of multiplayer, the players were assigned as blue and red. The working part of the node addition on `GameScene` has already been explained in _Chapter 11, Getting Started with Multiplayer Games_, and as a result of the outcome of these additions, the game looks like this on both the devices:

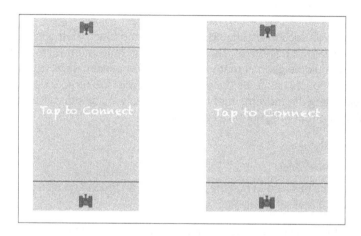

In the multiplayer part, when the user presses the **Done** button, the connection is established and both the players are connected. Also, when the user presses the **Done** button, names have been assigned to the players as blue and red as shown in the following image for both the devices. These labels are on two different devices and will animate on the allocation as well:

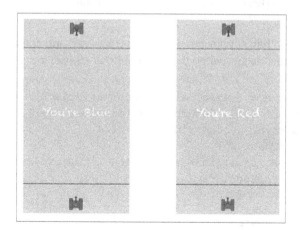

Movement of players

Once the environment for multiplayer is ready, it's time for the actual action: making the player move when a user touches or drags on screen. As it's a multiplayer game the movement is to be synced with the remote device, which a good challenge and a magical thing to experience.

Getting ready

Before starting with this section we should be aware of the touch methods of SKScene like touchBegan, touchMoved, and touchEnded as all the movement will be done on the basis on touch. Also we should be good at mathematics, as this movement of tanks with its head to be in the direction of touch, has to be done and synced with the remote device. In this section, we will be implementing the movement of tanks and also syncing the movement on other device by sending and receiving network packets.

How to do it

Following are the steps involved in making a tank move on touch and also sync on a remote device by sending and receiving packets:

1. On touching the screen, these methods of SKScene are called, which will be used to move the tank in the local device.

   ```
   - (void)touchesBegan:(NSSet *)touches withEvent:(UIEvent
       *)event
   - (void)touchesMoved:(NSSet *)touches withEvent:(UIEvent
       *)event
   - (void)touchesEnded:(NSSet *)touches withEvent:(UIEvent
       *)event
   ```

2. The first method has already been implemented. Let's add some updated lines of tank info on touch begins when the game state is kGameStatePlaying as shown in the following:

   ```
   UITouch *thumb = [[event allTouches] anyObject];
   CGPoint thumbPoint = [thumb locationInNode:self];
   // hold to move, second finger to fire
   if(thumb.tapCount==0) {
       tankStatsForLocal.tankDestination = thumbPoint;
       tankStatsForLocal.tankDirection =
         atan2( thumbPoint.y -
           tankStatsForLocal.tankPosition.y, thumbPoint.x -
             tankStatsForLocal.tankPosition.x ) - (M_PI/2.0);
       // keep us 0-359
   ```

```
    if(tankStatsForLocal.tankDirection < 0)
      tankStatsForLocal.tankDirection += (2.0*M_PI);
    else if(tankStatsForLocal.tankDirection > (2.0*M_PI))
      tankStatsForLocal.tankDirection -= (2.0*M_PI)

    [self updateLocalTank];
}
```

3. In this piece of code from the event received by the `touch` method, a `UITouch` object is fetched and, using that, the location of touch is determined with respect to the `GameScene`. Then if the touch `tapCount` is 0, that is, the user is dragging the code to move, the player is executed. In this code the `tankStatsForLocal` is updated on the basis of the position of the touch on screen. The destination is set as the touch location, the direction is calculated by using vector mathematics using the touch point and the current position of tank. To keep the direction angle of the tank between 0 to 359 degrees, extra checks should be put in place once the direction is calculated. After all this, to update the actual position and rotation of the tank, a method called `updateLocalTank`, which we will be discussing soon, will be implemented.

4. Implement the two other touch methods as well, `touchMoved` and `touchEnded`, in GameScene.

5. In `touchesMoved`, if the game state is `kGameStatePlaying` then execute the same code as in `touchesBegan` method, explained in the preceding point.

```
- (void)touchesMoved:(NSSet *)touches withEvent:(UIEvent
  *)event
{
    if (self.gameState == kGameStatePlaying)
    {
        if([touches count] == 1)
        {
            UITouch *thumb = [[event allTouches]
              anyObject];
            CGPoint thumbPoint = [thumb
              locationInNode:self];

            tankStatsForLocal.tankDestination = thumbPoint;
            tankStatsForLocal.tankDirection =
              atan2( thumbPoint.y -
                tankStatsForLocal.tankPosition.y,
                  thumbPoint.x -
                    tankStatsForLocal.tankPosition.x ) -
                      (M_PI/2.0);
```

```
                // keep us 0-359
                if(tankStatsForLocal.tankDirection < 0)
                    tankStatsForLocal.tankDirection +=
                        (2.0*M_PI);
                else if(tankStatsForLocal.tankDirection >
                    (2.0*M_PI))
                        tankStatsForLocal.tankDirection -=
                            (2.0*M_PI);

                [self updateLocalTank];
            }
        }
    }
```

6. In `touchesEnded` we must not do what we did in the other two touch methods; here we will only update the `tankDestination` and `tankDirection` with the local data structure and then call the same `updateLocalTank` method to update the final position and rotation.

```
- (void)touchesEnded:(NSSet *)touches withEvent:(UIEvent
    *)event
{
    if (self.gameState == kGameStatePlaying)
    {
        if([touches count] == [[event
            touchesForView:self.view] count])
        {
            tankStatsForLocal.tankDestination =
                tankStatsForLocal.tankPosition;
            tankStatsForLocal.tankDirection =
                tankStatsForLocal.tankRotation;

            [self updateLocalTank];
        }
    }
}
```

7. In all the touch methods, the `updateLocalTank` method is called to update the final position and rotation. After updating these attributes for the local tank a network packet is sent to sync with the remote tank player.

```
- (void)updateLocalTank
{

    if( (fabs(tankStatsForLocal.tankPosition.x -
        tankStatsForLocal.tankDestination.x)>kTankSpeed) ||
```

```
(fabs(tankStatsForLocal.tankPosition.y -
tankStatsForLocal.tankDestination.y)>kTankSpeed) ) {

// check facing
float ad = tankStatsForLocal.tankDirection -
    tankStatsForLocal.tankRotation;

if(fabs(ad) > kTankTurnSpeed) {

    // we need to turn, work out which way (find
        the closest 180)
    while(ad > M_PI) {
        ad -= (2.0 * M_PI);
    }
    while(ad < -M_PI) {
        ad += (2.0 * M_PI);
    }

    if(ad < 0) {
        tankStatsForLocal.tankRotation -=
          kTankTurnSpeed;
        if(tankStatsForLocal.tankRotation < 0)
            tankStatsForLocal.tankRotation +=
                (2.0*M_PI);
    } else if(ad > 0) {
        tankStatsForLocal.tankRotation +=
          kTankTurnSpeed;
        if(tankStatsForLocal.tankRotation >
          (2.0*M_PI))
            tankStatsForLocal.tankRotation -=
                (2.0*M_PI);
    }
} else {

    tankStatsForLocal.tankRotation =
      tankStatsForLocal.tankDirection;
    // if facing move along line towards
        destination
    float dx = tankStatsForLocal.tankPosition.x -
      tankStatsForLocal.tankDestination.x;
    float dy = tankStatsForLocal.tankPosition.y -
      tankStatsForLocal.tankDestination.y;
    float at = atan2( dy, dx );
    // 1.0 is the "speed"
```

```
                     tankStatsForLocal.tankPosition.x -= kTankSpeed
                        * cos(at);
                     tankStatsForLocal.tankPosition.y -= kTankSpeed
                        * sin(at);
        }
    } else {

        tankStatsForLocal.tankPosition.x =
            tankStatsForLocal.tankDestination.x;
        tankStatsForLocal.tankPosition.y =
            tankStatsForLocal.tankDestination.y;
    }

    tankStatsForLocal.tankPreviousPosition =
        self.localTankSprite.position;

    self.localTankSprite.position =
        tankStatsForLocal.tankPosition;
    self.localTankSprite.zRotation =
        tankStatsForLocal.tankRotation;

    // Send NetworkPacket for syncing the data at both the
        players

    [self sendNetworkPacketToPeerId:self.gamePeerID
    forPacketCode:KNetworkPacketCodePlayerMove
                        withData:&tankStatsForLocal
                        ofLength:sizeof(TankInfo)
                        reliable:YES];
}
```

Initially, check that the destination vector does not have a difference greater than the kTankSpeed. Then, update the position by the tankStatsForLocal destination and if the difference is greater, then write the code for turning around; that is, calculate the angle difference between the tank direction and tankRotation.

8. Check if the difference is greater than kTankTurnSpeed, then find the closest 180 degrees to be rotated, and according to that subtract or add the kTankTurnSpeed with the rotation. If the difference is not greater than the facing, move around the line towards the destination. Set the rotation as the direction and calculate the position of the tank using current position, destination, and kTankSpeed.

All these calculations should be assigned to the `tankStatsForLocal` data structure. After all this, set the `tankPreviousPosition` of the local data structure as the current position of the local player sprite. Update the position and rotation calculated in the `tankStatsForLocal` structure. To sync the player's movement produced in this method, we need to send a packet to the other player with `NetworkPacketCode` as `KNetworkPacketCodePlayerMove` data part will be in the structure of `tankStatsForLocal` and this packet should be sent unreliably because it is been sent very frequently.

9. In the delegate method of `MCSessiondidReceiveData`, the packet for the movement of the player with type `KNetworkPacketCodePlayerMove` is received.

```
case KNetworkPacketCodePlayerMove:
{
    // received move event from other player, update other
      player's position/destination info
    TankInfo *ts = (TankInfo *)&incomingPacket[8];
    self.remoteTankSprite.position = ts->tankPosition;
    self.remoteTankSprite.zRotation = ts->tankRotation;
    break;
}
```

10. Here, `TankInfo` is the structure that holds all the location and rotation related data of the user. The `TankInfo` structure is sent over the network to sync both the devices.

The data is parsed in a `TankInfo` variable `ts`, which contains the sent tank position and rotation. Hence it is the data of the remote tank, so update it with the attributes received. As a result, we will be able to see the tank moving in the remote device, the same as the user driving the tank in the other device

How it works

The movement of the tanks is done by vector mathematics using the point on which the user has touched, what direction the tank is facing at the time of the touch, and so on. We have finally achieved the multiplayer behavior in our game where a tank moves remotely as per the local tank moves in the device and this can be seen in the following snapshot. Synchronization of remote devices entirely depends on the network.

If the network is weak, then user may face some lag in sync between devices.

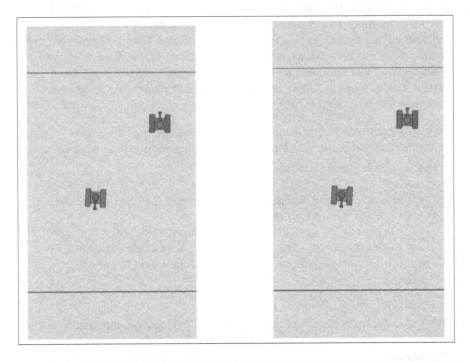

Implementing game play

It is now time to implement the game play in which, how the players (tanks) are going to win or lose in the game called TankRace will be determined. The game play is that, whichever player first reaches the finish line on their opposite side, of the same color as their own, wins the race and other loses.

Getting ready

Before we begin, we must know how to detect collision from sprites in the SpriteKit and a little about playing with the labels of SpriteKit. In this section, we will be implementing the game play and also show an alert when there is no connection between the devices.

How to do it

Following are the steps involved for implementing the game play and deciding who wins or loses:

1. We will be detecting the collision in the update method of the GameScene by using a method called CGRectIntersectsRect. In this, we can pass the two frames of nodes and it will check if the two frames intersect with each other or not. With this check, we will only check this for local player collision, and if collision happens update the game state to kGameStateComplete and show the local player **You Won** who has reached the finish line. Also, as the game has ended, to auto start the game, call a method called restartGameAfterSomeTime, which we will understand as we proceed.

2. After this, the local player is shown the correct result and the game is restarted, but as it is a multiplayer game, the reaction of this collision should also be reflected on the other device. So, pass a packet with a NetworkPacketCode named KNetworkPacketCodePlayerLost which will be sent to the other player who has lost the game. Following is the codes to achieve this:

```
#pragma mark - Update Loop Method

-(void)update:(CFTimeInterval)currentTime {
    /* Called before each frame is rendered */

    CGRect blueFinishLineFrame =
    CGRectMake(0, self.frame.size.height * 0.15,
      self.frame.size.width, 1);

    CGRect redFinishLineFrame =
      CGRectMake(0, self.frame.size.height * 0.85,
        self.frame.size.width, 1);

    if (self.localTankSprite == self.blueTankSprite &&
      CGRectIntersectsRect(self.localTankSprite.frame,
        blueFinishLineFrame))
    {
        self.gameState = kGameStateComplete;

        [self addGameInfoLabelWithText:kGameWonText];

        [self restartGameAfterSomeTime];

        [self sendNetworkPacketToPeerId:self.gamePeerID
```

```
                                    forPacketCode:KNetworkPacketCodePlayerLost
                                        withData:nil
                                        ofLength:0
                                        reliable:YES];
        }
        else if(self.localTankSprite == self.redTankSprite &&
            CGRectIntersectsRect(self.localTankSprite.frame,
                redFinishLineFrame))
        {
            self.gameState = kGameStateComplete;

            [self addGameInfoLabelWithText:kGameWonText];

            [self restartGameAfterSomeTime];

            [self sendNetworkPacketToPeerId:self.gamePeerID
                            forPacketCode:KNetworkPacketCodePlayerLo
st
                                withData:nil
                                ofLength:0
                                reliable:YES];
        }
    }
```

3. When the preceding game lost packet is sent to the other player, a delegate method of `MCSession` named `didReceiveData` is called, with a `NetworkPacketCode` in the header of the packet named `KNetworkPacketCodePlayerLost`. When this packet is received, the game state is changed to `kGameStateComplete` and the game information label is shown as **You Lose** to inform the other user of losing the game. Also, we call a method `restartGameAfterSomeTime`, which will reset the game to its initial state and the players can restart the game again.

```
case KNetworkPacketCodePlayerLost:
{
    self.gameState = kGameStateComplete;
    [self addGameInfoLabelWithText:kGameLostText];
    [self restartGameAfterSomeTime];
    break;
}
```

After using these two block of codes, about one player winning and the other player losing, the game looks like the following image for both devices:

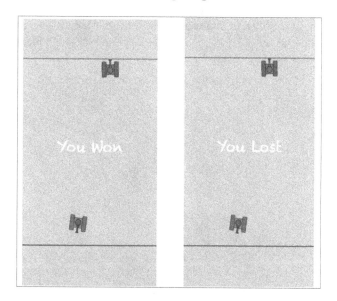

4. As `restartGameAfterSomeTime` is used at the time of sending and receiving the packet, let us write this method as shown in the following code:

```
- (void) restartGameAfterSomeTime
{
    [NSTimer scheduledTimerWithTimeInterval:2.0
                        target:self
                        selector:@selector(restartGame)
                        userInfo:nil
                        repeats:NO];
}

- (void) restartGame
{
    gameUniqueIdForPlayerAllocation = arc4random();

    self.gameState = kGameStatePlayerToConnect;
    self.gameInfoLabel.text = kConnectingDevicesText;
    [self resetLocalTanksAndInfoToInitialState];
}
```

5. In this method, a `NSTimer` of 2.0 seconds will be triggered, calling a function `restartGame` in which, again, the `gameUniqueIdFoPlayerAllocation` will be generated, the game state set to `kGameStatePlayerToConnect`, and the label text changed to **Tap to connect**. For visual initial state, we call the method `resetLocalTanksAndInfoToInitialState` in which the local data structure and the visual attributes of tanks are set.

6. Whenever the game completes the `restartGameAfterSomeTime` method is called, on both local and remote devices, to set the initial state of game and it looks like this:

7. Sometimes, due to a weak network, the connection can be lost and the screen gets stuck, thereby showing no message to the user. Thus, we will add an alert, saying that there is a network problem, and to play, restart your app on both the devices, as shown in the following method:

```objc
- (void)showNetworkDisconnectAlertView
{
    UIAlertView* alertView =
      [[UIAlertView alloc] initWithTitle:@"Network
        Disconnected"
            message:@"Sorry due some network problem
              devices are disconnected. To start game
                again kill apps in both devices and
                  restart the app!!"
            delegate:self
            cancelButtonTitle:@"OK"
            otherButtonTitles:nil, nil];

    [alertView show];
}

- (void)alertView:(UIAlertView *)alertView
  clickedButtonAtIndex:(NSInteger)buttonIndex
{
    // do nothing
}
```

8. To show the network has disconnected alert, call the showNetworkDisconnectAlertView when the delegate method of MCSession named didChangeState is called with a change of state as MCSessionStateNotConnected. It should be shown only when the current game state is kGameStatePlaying.

```objc
else if (state == MCSessionStateNotConnected)
    {
        NSLog(@"state == MCSessionStateNotConnected");

        if (self.gameState == kGameStatePlaying)
        {
            [self showNetworkDisconnectAlertView];
        }
    }
```

9. Whenever the game is disconnected, `showNetworkDisconnectAlertView` is called and an alert view is shown as depicted in the following snapshot:

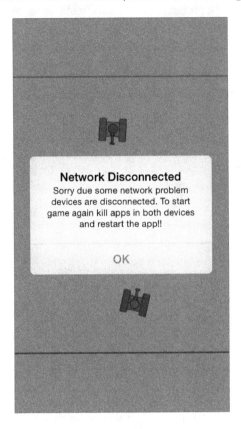

After all these implementations of game play logic, or we can say the game mechanics, we have accomplished making a multiplayer game and this is the solution kit for this chapter.

How it works

This section was all about the game play and the game mechanics; it had two parts, one detecting the collisions to decide the winner and second resetting the game to the initial state once the game ended.

To accomplish this, using the intersection of frame method, we detected the collision and declared the local player as winner and the other player as loser by sending a packet. As the game ended here, to help the user restart it again, at the same time as declaration of winner and loser takes place, we also reset the game to its initial state so that the players can restart the game again.

There's more

We have used the Multipeer Connectivity framework whereas we can also use the GameKit framework; you can use the following link for more on the same:

```
https://developer.apple.com/library/ios/documentation/GameKit/
Reference/GameKit_Collection/index.html
```

See also

For better understanding and learning of the Multipeer Connectivity framework you can visit the following link:

```
https://developer.apple.com/library/prerelease/ios/documentation/
MultipeerConnectivity/Reference/MultipeerConnectivityFramework/index.
html
```

Index

Thank you for buying
iOS Game Programming Cookbook

About Packt Publishing

Packt, pronounced 'packed', published its first book, *Mastering phpMyAdmin for Effective MySQL Management*, in April 2004, and subsequently continued to specialize in publishing highly focused books on specific technologies and solutions.

Our books and publications share the experiences of your fellow IT professionals in adapting and customizing today's systems, applications, and frameworks. Our solution-based books give you the knowledge and power to customize the software and technologies you're using to get the job done. Packt books are more specific and less general than the IT books you have seen in the past. Our unique business model allows us to bring you more focused information, giving you more of what you need to know, and less of what you don't.

Packt is a modern yet unique publishing company that focuses on producing quality, cutting-edge books for communities of developers, administrators, and newbies alike. For more information, please visit our website at www.packtpub.com.

About Packt Open Source

In 2010, Packt launched two new brands, Packt Open Source and Packt Enterprise, in order to continue its focus on specialization. This book is part of the Packt open source brand, home to books published on software built around open source licenses, and offering information to anybody from advanced developers to budding web designers. The Open Source brand also runs Packt's open source Royalty Scheme, by which Packt gives a royalty to each open source project about whose software a book is sold.

Writing for Packt

We welcome all inquiries from people who are interested in authoring. Book proposals should be sent to author@packtpub.com. If your book idea is still at an early stage and you would like to discuss it first before writing a formal book proposal, then please contact us; one of our commissioning editors will get in touch with you.

We're not just looking for published authors; if you have strong technical skills but no writing experience, our experienced editors can help you develop a writing career, or simply get some additional reward for your expertise.

iOS Development with Xamarin Cookbook

ISBN: 978-1-84969-892-4   Paperback: 386 pages

Over 100 exciting recipes to help you develop iOS applications with Xamarin

1. Explore the new features of Xamarin and learn how to use them.

2. Step-by-step recipes give you everything you need to get developing with Xamarin.

3. Full of useful tips and best practices on creating iOS applications.

iOS and OS X Network Programming Cookbook

ISBN: 978-1-84969-808-5   Paperback: 300 pages

Over 50 recipes to develop network applications in both the iOS and OS X environment

1. Use several Apple and third-party APIs to develop both server and client networked applications.

2. Shows you how to integrate all of the third-party libraries and APIs with your applications.

3. Includes sample projects for both iOS and OS X environments.

Please check **www.PacktPub.com** for information on our titles

Sparrow iOS Game Framework Beginner's Guide

ISBN: 978-1-78216-150-9   Paperback: 274 pages

Create mobile games for iOS devices with the Sparrow iOS game framework

1. Learn the principles of Game Mechanics and implement them with Sparrow's powerful framework.

2. Build an entire game throughout the course of the book.

3. This is a practical guide with step-by-step instructions to learn the art of mobile game development.

Core Data iOS Essentials

ISBN: 978-1-84969-094-2   Paperback: 340 pages

A fast-paced, example-driven guide to data-driven iPhone, iPad, and iPod Touch applications

1. Covers the essential skills you need for working with Core Data in your applications.

2. Particularly focused on developing fast, light weight data-driven iOS applications.

3. Builds a complete example application. Every technique is shown in context.

4. Completely practical with clear, step-by-step instructions.

Please check **www.PacktPub.com** for information on our titles

www.ingramcontent.com/pod-product-compliance
Lightning Source LLC
Chambersburg PA
CBHW060517060326
40690CB00017B/3307